Honoured in Places

Remembered Mounties Across Canada

William J. Hulgaard and John W. White

Heritage
House

National Library of Canada Cataloguing in Publication Data

Hulgaard, William J. (William Joseph), 1932-
Honoured in places

    Includes bibliographical references.
    ISBN 1-894384-39-3

    1. Royal Canadian Mounted Police—Biography. 2. Names, Geographical—Canada. I. White, John W. (John Wesley), 1931- II. Title.

FC3216.3.A1H84 2002   363.2'092'271   C2002-910311-8
HV8158.7.R69H84 2002

First edition 2002

    Heritage House acknowledges the financial support for our publishing program from the Government of Canada through the Book Publishing Industry Development Program (BPIDP), Canada Council for the Arts, and the British Columbia Arts Council.

Cover design by Darlene Nickull
Book design by Katherine Hale
Edited by Terri Elderton

HERITAGE HOUSE PUBLISHING COMPANY LTD.
Unit #108 - 17665 66 A Ave., Surrey, B.C. V3S 2A7

Printed in Canada

The Canada Council | Le Conseil des Arts
for the Arts | du Canada

Dedicated to all those members who lost their lives
in performance of their duty—many
not included and many lost to time—and
with special thanks to our respective wives,
Lana Hulgaard and
Helen White,
for their patience and time lost
to these endeavours.

Acknowledgements

The authors acknowledge the assistance they received from the following archives: City of Calgary; City of Edmonton; Fort Walsh Office, Maple Creek, Saskatchewan; Lacombe, Alberta; Lethbridge, Alberta; Maple Creek, Saskatchewan; Medicine Hat, Alberta; Prince Albert, Saskatchewan; Red Deer, Alberta; Saskatoon, Saskatchewan; Wetaskiwin, Alberta; and Yellowknife, Northwest Territories. In addition they accessed the following government agencies: Government of Alberta; Government of Canada, Natural Resources, Geographical Names: toponomist Andrew Geggie; Government of Canada, Public Archives; and the Government of Manitoba: toponomist Gerry Holm.

Introduction

Whether by chance or by intention, to honour them, more than a few members of the North West Mounted Police (NWMP), the Royal North West Mounted Police (RNWMP), and the Royal Canadian Mounted Police (RCMP) have had their names immortalized at places across western and northern Canada. Others, as pioneers, gave their choice of names to points of interest. Our intent is to remind the reader of these place names' origins before their historical contexts are forever lost to time. In consideration of the reader who may be taking a first glance at the "Force"[1] through the wanderings of these words, we will now give an overview of its history.

The North West Mounted Police was not by any means the first police force in Canada. Setting aside city departments, there were several police organizations predating the NWMP that affected its later development. The distinction for the earliest one must go to the Newfoundland Constabulary (now known as the Royal Newfoundland Constabulary).[2] The St. John's Constabulary began in 1807, when a few tavern keepers were given their annual licences on the condition that they agree to perform police duties as may be required. This group grew to become the Newfoundland Constabulary. They wore uniforms for the first time in 1856, and by 1871 their organization was patterned after the Royal Irish Constabulary. The colony of B.C. followed Newfoundland with its police in 1858, which evolved into the B.C. Provincial Police. In turn, they were followed in 1868 with the beginning of the Dominion Police, which was first organized to guard government buildings in Ottawa. In later years, its responsibilities broadened to include Canada's first fingerprint bureau and the enforcement of selected federal statutes. In 1871, before the NWMP was formed, the Manitoba Provincial Police had its beginnings. The remaining portion of Canada—from Manitoba west to B.C. and north to the Arctic Ocean—was known as the Northwest Territories, which had been under control of the Hudson's Bay Company until 1870. It had been left to the Indians and Métis, the occasional trapper or explorer, or to those who would take advantage of the Indians. In short, it had been ignored.

Events such as the advancement of the Canadian Pacific Railway across Canada, whites trading whiskey among the Indians, various skirmishes across the prairies, and Americans ignoring the recently established boundary along the 49th parallel each contributed pressure on the federal government for policing in the west. In April 1873, Prime Minister Sir John A. Macdonald formulated a plan to establish a police force for this undeveloped area of the northwest. By May a bill was before parliament for "the administration of justice and the establishment of a police force in the Northwest Territories."[3] If parliament needed any convincing, it arrived the very day the bill was signed with news of the butchery of a camp of innocent Assiniboines by a gang of marauding whites—from the American side of the border—in the Cypress Hills (in present-day southwest Saskatchewan).

Action was swift. The birth of the North West Mounted Police came on September 25, 1873, when the first nine officers were appointed, followed promptly with general recruiting. This new force began moving west that same fall—by boat to Port Arthur (present-day Thunder Bay) and then overland to winter at Lower Fort Garry some 32 kilometres south of present-day Winnipeg, Manitoba.

By June 1874 the first epic steps began when a second body of members with horses and provisions departed Toronto by train—via Detroit, Chicago, and St. Paul—to Fargo, Dakota Territory, arriving there June 12. Three days later the last of this contingent rode north to join the earlier group at Dufferin (present-day Emerson, Manitoba) for the real beginning of their overland western trek. They departed west on July 8, 1874, with a total of 295 personnel to begin policing several hundred thousand square miles of territory (see details in Appendix 3). By September 29, 1874, they had crossed the vast deserted prairies through present-day Manitoba, Saskatchewan, and Alberta to the junctions of the Oldman and St. Mary's rivers, where they began the construction of their first headquarters, called "Fort Macleod." Not including a major side trip by some troops to Fort Edmonton far to the north, they had travelled over 1,290 kilometres one-way by horseback—quite some step for a raw, untrained group. It was, in fact, the longest march in British military history of any column carrying its own supplies.

Those early years through to the beginning of the twentieth century included many indelible events—both in the history of western Canada and in the reputation of the Force—that we still, at least in part, feel proud of today. Some of the epic endurances had little to do with any present-day concept of police work. Force members' accounts were often downplayed in the historical records because of the seeming simplicity in the description of a task and the subsequent recording of its execution. For example, just one of many such basic instructions was given in the commissioner's letter of 1897 to Inspector Moodie, ordering that he take a small party from

Edmonton to the headwaters of the Pelly River, mapping the route and noting all work necessary to build a road, including bridges and corduroying. Moodie was also to note the available feed for horses, navigable waters, and depot points. This report would then be used to forewarn any party leaving Edmonton about exactly what to expect at all points en route to potential goldfields in the Yukon. The commissioner's instructions are straightforward; however, when consideration is given to the distances involved or to the large amount of the route that was unknown and was either muskeg or vertical rather than horizontal, then those instructions become quite complex. In fact, Inspector Moodie departed Edmonton with five men and several horses and in two months travelled about 563 kilometres in a direct line to present-day Fort St. John, B.C. Two months later they reached Fort Graham, where they wintered. The following summer they reached the Pelly River and from there rafted down to Fort Selkirk, having travelled more than 1,450 kilometres in a direct line over some of North America's most difficult terrain.

The overall recorded results of those first years might lead one to believe that either nothing ever happened or that only the best were chosen and that they were overly capable. Both statements are partly true and—just as surely—partly false. Most of us have earnestly endeavoured to keep the highest ideals and the oaths taken at enlistment, but the early recruiting was not so refined. The Force was fortunate to have had some experienced military men and many stalwart individualists who possessed what may be seen as key essentials: in good physical condition and able to ride a horse. As in any family, there can be a wayward child, and the Force's "family" was no exception. Some of the original recruits who marched west viewed this new Force as little more than a ticket to a new land and new opportunity, so there were more than a few deserters.

For the most part, those early years were a direct pioneering of new territory. Each first patrol meant the routine of cutting or mapping new trails, building their own detachment quarters, supplying rations to indigent Indians or settlers, and treating the sick. According to their annual reports, Force surgeons were kept busy treating both members and civilians. The usual disabilities seemed evenly shared between frostbite, fractures, syphilis, and typhoid, as well as a good number of cases categorized as "biliousness" or "bilious derangements." By such terms one is led to believe there was no real knowledge of the problem except that the individual was sick. Care is also necessary when reading the earlier reports to determine whether a reference is to a member or a horse, for both were referred to by regimental number and often the injuries were common to both (for example, being kicked by a horse). The treatment varied only to the extent that in serious cases the member was invalided while the horse was shot!

Movies and novels of that era often depict those days as a "shoot-em-up" affair, but this view stems more from the actions of the U.S. Cavalry and not the Mounties. They were involved in the battles of the North-West Rebellion of 1885, and other isolated murders of policemen, but taken in total, the Mounties injured themselves more often than they did others. Their history is well sprinkled with firearms accidents, whether from faulty ammunition or plain carelessness through inexperience. A firearm also led to one of the earliest incidents of a member being charged in criminal court. In 1893 Constable Charles Glave (NWMP #2458) was patrolling when his horse bolted into a herd of range cattle. Alarmed by the wild steers, Glave fired his revolver to scare them away, but in the melee of bucking horse and milling cattle he unfortunately killed a steer. The owner charged him with cattle theft!

Despite setbacks, the proof of the overall integrity of the Force is and always has been that the remaining members promptly expose and deal with the dishonest or disloyal despite any temporary embarrassment. This philosophy is pure common sense, as one man's actions could determine the reputation of the whole Force. There were also many incidents that could easily have become disasters but for the good fortune and singular achievement of resourceful and dedicated individuals (or "a squad of one," as they were often called). Written histories have focussed on those few while—for the most part—the Force went quietly about its daily duty, shunning publicity. It neither looked for plaudit nor responded to criticism. Canada achieved a rather remarkable result for nickels and dimes, and—just as surely—counted each and every one, as the quoted letter on the next page illustrates.

From the outset, the Force was organized on a paramilitary arrangement and began with uniforms—from available military stores—that had been both accepted and respected by the Indians. It also took the military pattern of discipline. During the following two decades or more, the Force's own code of ethics evolved, based in law and promulgated through orders and instructions of the commissioner who was authorized to issue regulations. The act of parliament even gave commissioned officers the authority to punish other ranks for specific offences in an internal service court (Orderly Room) without reference to any civil court. Many received such punishment.

The best of the hardworking were selected for promotion and leadership, but occasionally some were passed by who might have paused and wondered about the selection criteria. Consider Murray

---

North West Mounted Police
Office of the Comptroller
17 Feb 1886
Superintendent Perry
NWMPolice
Prince Albert
Sir
    From the paylist of "F" Division under your command
for the month of November last I observed that Reg.
#1110 Constable J.H. Doyle was paid at the rate of 55
cents per diem from the 4th of that month.
    Constable Doyle was engaged on the 8th of November
1885 and was not therefore entitled to the 5 cents good
conduct pay until the 8th of that month, he has therefore
been overpaid 20 cents which be good enough to have
stopped from his pay on a future pay list.
I have the honour to be
Sir
Your obedient servant
(F. White)
Comptroller

Henry Edward Hayne, NWMP #869, who joined in 1882. He may have been one of the finest—we really do not know. It is a fact that in 1906 he had been dead 104 days at an Arctic post when he was promoted to inspector! This is penned, of course, with tongue in cheek, for in 1906 the rural mail delivery of the north was less than daily service. We can't blame the post office either, for in the north, mail delivery was just one more duty of the local policeman to perform—by dog team.

As the new century dawned, the west had settled into routine. In 1904 King Edward VII granted the prefix "Royal" to the North West Mounted Police (RNWMP) in recognition of its contribution to the peaceful opening of the west. In 1905 Alberta and Saskatchewan became provinces and began their own provincial police forces within a few years. By the time of the First World War, familiar duties of the Force had dwindled remarkably. Its activity had shrunk so much that the government even questioned whether there was need any longer for such an organization.

The turnaround and real growth of the youthful Force began February 1, 1920, with the absorption of the Dominion Police, along with its duties, and a broadening of federal roles Canada-wide. At the same time, in keeping with the new role, the name was changed to the Royal Canadian Mounted Police (RCMP). In the following Depression years, several provinces looked to the federal government for policing assistance, and one by one they discontinued their provincial police in favour of contracting for policing by the RCMP. The Force absorbed and took over from the Saskatchewan Provincial Police in 1928, then did likewise with the provincial policing in Alberta, Manitoba, New Brunswick, Nova Scotia, and Prince Edward Island in 1932.

The most recent spurt of youthful growth and some of its fastest developing years followed the Second World War when Newfoundland entered Confederation in 1949. In quick succession, the RCMP took over the provincial policing of Newfoundland on August 1, 1950, absorbing the Newfoundland Rangers and some members of the Newfoundland Constabulary together with some of their detachments; then on August 15, 1950, the B.C. Provincial Police was absorbed, along with its duties. Adulthood had arrived.

Throughout these years, members of the northern detachments— and to some degree even those in the west—were often the first and only local government representatives. During long northern patrols, members provided reports to the Department of the Interior, correcting existing maps and creating new ones with discoveries of lakes, islands, streams, and such. Those items would be passed on to the Geographical Board of Canada for map corrections, so it should not be surprising that many such features were named after the members involved.

It is against this background that over the years individual members were remembered with a permanent record of their names attached to local sites. Clearly, in most cases they were being honoured, while in a few cases "honour" may be a more lofty idea than the actual reason for the choice.

This project may not be entirely complete, for there could be places named for members of the Force across this great land that we have not identified. If you know of a place name missed from this book, we would be most interested in hearing of it. If it is found to be authentic, we would be glad to add it to any subsequent edition, giving due credit to the person who has provided it. We may be contacted through our publisher: publisher@heritagehouse.ca.

Thank you for your interest.

Bill Hulgaard   *Jack White*

Bill Hulgaard   Jack White

Please refer to page 217 for helpful notes on reading the entries.

Abbott Creek, Saskatchewan (Lat: 50°02'00"N, Long: 109°58'00"W), near the town of Maple Creek, is named after Sergeant-Major William Richard Abbott, NWMP #314.

In 1871 Abbott joined the Battery Corps militia at Kingston, Ontario, and then served as artillery instructor at Fort Garry. He joined the NWMP and served from June 9, 1879, to June 8, 1884, mainly at Fort Walsh and at Maple Creek. For his minimum three years' good service he was awarded Land Warrant #0510.[4]

He then took up a homestead southwest of Maple Creek, Saskatchewan. With the eruption of the North-West Rebellion in 1885, he organized the Volunteer Home Guard at Maple Creek. Afterwards he went into business, freighting from the newly arrived railroad north to Battleford with ten Red River carts and starting a shoe and harness repair at Maple Creek.

He was elected mayor of Maple Creek from 1904 to 1907 and was the first secretary in the organization of the Agricultural Society. From 1902 to 1909 he was the first weighmaster at the local stockyards. In 1908 he sold his store and returned to his original homestead.

His son, Constable Harold W. Abbott (NWMP #3223), also served briefly—from 1898 to 1900—in the Yukon. Sergeant-Major Abbott died on June 1, 1934. Both he and his son are buried at Maple Creek, Saskatchewan.

Acland Creek, Yukon (Lat: 60°18'00"N, Long: 127°30'05"W), flows into the Coal River east of Watson Lake. In 1956 this creek was named after Sergeant Arthur Edward Acland, RNWMP #3234, who served in this area in 1910.

Acland was born in England in 1874 and immigrated to Canada with his family in 1886. He enlisted in the NWMP on March 18, 1898. Over the summer of 1910 he commanded a summer patrol from Dawson to Fort McPherson. He later served at Kluane from 1912 to 1914. During his seventeen years in the Yukon, Acland rose through the ranks from a constable at Dalton Post to officer commanding the Whitehorse Subdivision district (he had received a promotion to the commissioned ranks on April 1, 1912, as O.165).[5] He was transferred to Depot Division, Regina, in 1915, having been hospitalized for three months with typhoid. By then, the First World War was raging in Europe, so in 1918 he volunteered for the RNWMP "A" Squadron Cavalry to serve overseas in France. Upon return from the war as a lieutenant he continued with the Force as the commanding officer of Saskatchewan with the rank of assistant commissioner until his retirement on October 15, 1933. He died at Coquitlam, B.C., on May 28, 1952.

Adams Creek, Saskatchewan (Lat: 49°29'00"N, Long: 109°50'00"W), south of Maple Creek, is named after Constable George Alexander "Grizzly" Adams, NWMP #621.

Adams served from May 10, 1882, to September 3, 1891, mainly in Fort Walsh and Maple Creek. As a recruit, he came west via rail through Chicago to Bismarck at the end of the line, and then he travelled by the riverboat *Red Cloud* to Benton, Montana. The I.G. Baker bull teams took him north to Fort Assiniboia.

Adams ran afoul of the infamous Orderly Room (service court). At Maple Creek on November 12, 1889, he was charged for being absent from his barracks room and fined two dollars (almost four days' wages) by Inspector Sanders. After his service he ranched on Adams Creek, south of Maple Creek. He died December 10, 1945, at the age of 81 in a fire at the Maple Creek hospital in Maple Creek, Saskatchewan. Adams is buried at Banff, Alberta.

Agar Lane, Depot Division RCMP, Regina, Saskatchewan, is named

T.J. Agar, March 18, 1977

in honour of Constable Thomas James Agar, RCMP #33580, Honour Roll #166.[6]

Constable Agar was engaged with the Force on September 23, 1976, and served in "E" Division upon his graduation from Depot. In Vancouver, B.C., on September 18, 1980, a man named Steve LeClair, who had been drinking in the Palace Hotel and ejected, returned to the bar with a handgun, opened fire, and killed two people. He then commandeered a car and forced the driver to take him to nearby Richmond, saying he "had to kill a cop." Arriving at the Richmond detachment, he let the driver go and entered the office where Constable Agar was on desk duty. As Constable Agar approached the counter, LeClair suddenly pulled out his gun and shot Agar in the chest. In a nearby office Constable Wayne Hanniman (RCMP #35115) heard the noise and ran out. He was shot in the leg, but managed to draw his own revolver and wound LeClair. Corporal Peter J. Lucas (RCMP #22667) also ran when he heard the first gunshot. He drew his revolver, and LeClair surrendered. LeClair was convicted of murder and sentenced to life imprisonment. In 1984 his fellow inmates stabbed him to death.

Constable Agar was buried in Burnaby, B.C.

Aklavik, Northwest Territories (Lat: 68°13'10"N, Long: 135°00'20"W), on the delta of the Mackenzie River, is the name suggested by Superintendent George Leslie Jennings, OBE, RNWMP and RCMP O.147.

The Northwest Territories Language Bureau indicated the traditional Inuktitut name for the community is "Aklarvik," meaning "barren-ground grizzly place." Other suggestions of the Inuktitut translation are "that is the place where the Inuit saw brown bears for a time" and simply "meeting place."

See the following entry.

Aklavik Channel, Northwest Territories, is the westernmost channel of the multi- channelled Mackenzie River delta, and was named by Superintendent George Leslie Jennings.

Jennings served in the Canadian army, seeing action in the Boer War in 1900 and 1901 before being appointed to the commissioned ranks of the RNWMP on August 1, 1906. He served in "F" and "K" Divisions before being transferred north to "G" Division (Northwest Territories). While in the north, he found there was a need for a police post and a post office for that part of the territories where Aklavik lies, and suggested the "Aklavik" name, which was accepted.

In 1911 he was chosen to be part of the "coronation contingent" to

S/Sgt. W.J. Hulgaard at Albert Johnson's gravesite, Aklavik, NWT

England for the Coronation of King George V. When the Force was called upon to raise a cavalry squadron to serve in France during the First World War, Jennings led the "A" squadron. He was "mentioned in dispatches" and given the Order of the British Empire for his services. At war's end he returned to the Force and served in "K," "F," and "O" Divisions, and also at Headquarters, retiring as deputy commissioner on August 1, 1938.

He retired to the West Coast, died on December 26, 1958, at North Vancouver, B.C., and was buried in the Capilano View Cemetery.

Allison Creek, Alberta (Lat: 49°38'00"N, Long: 114°35'00"W), in the southwest corner of Alberta is named after Sub-Constable[7] Douglas Alison, NWMP #425 (Original Series).[8]

See the following entry.

Allison Peak (2,643 m), Alberta (Lat: 49°45'00"N, Long: 114°39'00"W), located in the southwest corner of the province, is also named after Sub-Constable Douglas Alison (see above).

Alison served from May 25, 1875, until May 25, 1878, mainly in the Macleod[9] area. In November 1876 he was charged in the Orderly Room for being "improperly dressed out of barracks" and was admonished. Such charges were commonplace in the face of early-day harsh military discipline. We don't know, but we suspect that his "improper" dress may have been as simple as not having his jacket correctly buttoned! Nevertheless, he received Land Warrant #0159 upon his discharge and settled near Waterton Park in southern Alberta.

Amey Street, Depot Division RCMP, Regina, Saskatchewan, is named in honour of Constable Robert Weston Amey, RCMP #22240, Honour Roll #127.

R.W. Amey

Constable Amey served in "B" Division from January 3, 1962, until his death on December 17, 1964. On that day, Amey and two other constables—David C. Keith (#21018) and Garry J. Cluley (#22164)—cornered four escaped prisoners from the St. John's Penitentiary in a stolen car near Whitbourne. Keith was watching the arrested foursome as Amey got into the police car to radio for assistance. The escapees took the opportunity to rush Constable Keith, and one named Young managed to wrest his service revolver loose. As the other members closed to assist, Young fired three shots, killing Amey. The escapees were then subdued. Young was sentenced to life imprisonment for murder and paroled eight years later. Constable Amey was buried at Arichat, Nova Scotia.

Anderton Channel, Northwest Territories (Lat: 68°47'15"N, Long: 135°59'15"W), is named after Sergeant Major Frederick Anderton, RNWMP and RCMP #5694.

Anderton first served in a constabulary in England from 1910 to 1912 before coming to Canada. On August 9, 1913, he joined the RNWMP, serving until August 8, 1937, in Alberta, Yukon, and the Northwest Territories ("K," "M," and "G" Divisions). In 1927 he was in charge of the Aklavik detachment, and he became the only member known to have travelled the channel ("Anderton") of the Mackenzie River delta to Shingle Point without a guide. He was in charge of the *St. Roch*[10] from 1928 to 1933. In 1934 he was awarded the Member of the British Empire (MBE) for his service in the Arctic.

In 1935 he was invited to Newfoundland to organize the new Newfoundland Ranger Force. He also served in the First World War as a corporal of "A" Squadron Cavalry with the Canadian Expeditionary Force as #2684153. He died on October 20, 1974, at Surrey, B.C. His brother, William Henry Anderton (RNWMP #5695), also served from 1913 to 1916.

Andreasen Head, Nunavut (Lat: 70°48'00"N, Long: 96°35'00"W), on the western shore of Boothia Peninsula, is named after Special Constable Ole Andreasen, RCMP #S8472.

Special Constable Andreasen served as mate on the RCMP schooner *St. Roch* during its second voyage through the Northwest Passage in 1944.

He died on December 8, 1947.

See also the **Larsen Sound** and **St. Roch Island** entries.

Anson, Douglas Bernard. See **Schrader–Anson Sport Field** entry.

Anstead Point, Nunavut (Lat: 76°28'00"N, Long: 81°31'00"W), on the eastern shore of Devon Island, is named after Constable Edward Anstead, RCMP #9663.

Anstead served from November 25, 1920, to August 31, 1947, retiring as sergeant-major. Through his years in the Force, he served in "N" Division, Headquarters, and "A" and "O" Divisions. In 1929 he was at the Bache detachment on the Bache Peninsula, Ellesmere Island. This is almost as far north as one can go without going south again! That year he performed a dog-team patrol from Bache across the island, exploring the northeast coast of Axel Heiberg Island and the Greely Fiord area of Ellesmere Island, which must have been a difficult trek in Arctic conditions.

He died on August 20, 1989, at Brockville, Ontario.

Anxiety Butte, Saskatchewan (Lat: 49°36'00"N, Long: 108°48'00"W), nine kilometres from Eastend, is named after Constable Daniel Houston Pollock, NWMP #1104.

Constable Pollock, known as "Old Anxiety," served in the NWMP from October 21, 1884, until June 9, 1896. He began his life's journey laying track for the Canadian Pacific Railway along the shores of Lake Superior in Ontario. In 1880 he was driving a four-horse team, hauling supplies from Winnipeg, Manitoba, to Medicine Hat, Northwest Territories (now Alberta), for a survey crew. He is credited with building the first log building at Eastend in 1888, which later became a post office. In 1896 he purchased[11] his discharge from the NWMP as the member in charge of the Eastend detachment. He then started the Z-X Ranch on the south fork of Swift Current Creek near Eastend, where he remained until his death in 1932.

See also **Pollock Coulee** entry.

Arden Avenue, Yellowknife, Northwest Territories, is named after Special Constable D'arcy Arden, RCMP #S1549.

From April 8, 1935, to March 10, 1937, Arden served as a special constable guide and interpreter at Cameron Bay in the Northwest Territories. The majority of his two years of service was in the Great Bear Lake area. He now lives in retirement at Yellowknife.

Arnold Mews, Depot Division RCMP, Regina, Saskatchewan, is named in honour of Constable George Pearce Arnold, NWMP #1065, Honour Roll #8.

Prior to coming to Canada and joining the NWMP on August 11, 1884, Arnold had been a scout with the U.S. cavalry and had been wounded three times in the Cheyenne Campaign. At the outbreak of the North-West Rebellion of 1885 he was stationed at Fort Carleton. He was in a group of 43 men of the Prince Albert volunteers and 53 members of the NWMP under Superintendent Crozier.[12] Arnold and two other men were killed in the first engagement of the Rebellion at Duck Lake; seven others were wounded. He was buried at Fort Carleton, but with the closure of the fort two years later, his body was re-interred in St. Mary's Cemetery at Prince Albert, Northwest Territories (now Saskatchewan).

Arrowsmith Coulee and Creek, Alberta (Lat: 49°56'00"N, Long: 112°30'00"W), flowing into Little Bow River approximately 30 kilometres east of Lethbridge, is named after Constable William George Arrowsmith, NWMP #1494.

"George," as he preferred, served in the Force from May 29, 1885, to May 28, 1890, mainly in the Lethbridge area.

He left the Force at the end of his contracted time to be the manager of the Cameron Ranch. He later homesteaded his own quarter section at Turin, Alberta. He was also the local postmaster until his death.

He died at Turin on December 24, 1935, and was buried in the Mountain View Cemetery, Lethbridge, Alberta.

Bailey Boulevard, Canadian Police College, Rockcliffe, Ontario, is named in honour of Corporal Maxwell George Bailey, RNWMP #4968, Honour Roll #39.

Corporal Bailey began his service on November 20, 1909. On April 23, 1913, he and Constables Reginald Tetley (#5288), Lambertus Stad (#5393), and Samuel Whitley (#5535) went to Grassy Lake with an insanity warrant to arrest Oscar Fonberg for shooting at his neighbours. Fonberg began shooting as the four members approached, killing Bailey and wounding both Stad and Whitley. Constable Tetley managed to remove the wounded and call for help. More members quickly arrived, but Fonberg had escaped into the surrounding bush. Sergeant Louis Holbrook (#4893) was riding to the scene when he met a farmer with horse and wagon in which the wounded Fonberg was riding. He arrested Fonberg, who was later sentenced to life imprisonment. Corporal Bailey was buried at Edmonton, Alberta.

See also **Grassy Lake** entry.

Barker Avenue, Depot Division RCMP, Regina, Saskatchewan, is named in honour of Sergeant Arthur Julian Barker, RNWMP #7606, Honour Roll #64.

Barker joined the RNWMP April 10, 1919, and served in Saskatchewan. He left the Force to join the Saskatchewan Provincial

Police and then returned to the Force when the latter was absorbed into the RCMP. He continued to serve in Saskatchewan. A former associate, retired sergeant Gardner Greenlay (#3805), had a troubled son, Victor. Barker befriended Victor, who called him on March 16, 1940, from a hotel at Shaunavon. Barker went there to see Victor, and after a brief visit, he left Victor's room. He was downstairs in the hotel lobby, pulling on his overshoes, when Victor suddenly appeared with a revolver and shot him three times. Victor Greenlay was tried for murder, found criminally insane, and was committed to a mental hospital. Sergeant Barker was buried in the Force Cemetery at Depot Division, Regina.

Barker's brother, Staff Sergeant Francis W.J. Barker (#6397), also served in the Force from 1915 to 1946. Victor Greenlay's brother, Corporal William S. Greenlay (#10714), was also a member, serving from 1929 to 1962. One of Barker's nephews, Staff Sergeant Bernard O. Barker (#13963), also served from 1941 to 1967.

Barnett Avenue, Lacombe, Alberta, is named after Constable Edward Barnett, NWMP #165.

See the following entries.

Barnett Lake, Alberta, (Lat: 52°16'00"N, Long: 112°35'00"W), ten kilometres southeast of Stettler, is named after brothers Jack Barnett and Edward Barnett, NWMP #165.

Barnett Lake, Lacombe, Alberta

Barnett Lake, Alberta, (Lat: 52°29'00"N, Long: 113°45'00"W), four kilometres from Lacombe, is where brothers Jack Barnett and Edward Barnett, NWMP #165, took up land.

Barnett Siding, Lacombe, Alberta, is named after Constable Edward Barnett, NWMP #165.

Constable Barnett served in the Force from August 17, 1878, until August 17, 1881. He received Land Warrant #0459; in 1883 he took up residence with his brother Jack where the present-day town of Lacombe is located. When the Canadian Pacific Railway (CPR)—which ran through the area—made a stop at this site, it became known as "Barnett Siding," because the brothers operated a rest stop service there for travellers going between Edmonton and Calgary. The president of the CPR, William Van Horne, renamed the siding "Lacombe" in honour of Father Albert Lacombe. Barnett died at Erskine, Alberta, in September 1939.

Barracks Square, Lethbridge, Alberta, is the site of a number of municipal buildings and sports facilities, as well as the current RCMP offices in Lethbridge. The Square is bounded by 4th Avenue South (on the north), 6th Avenue South (on the south), 9th Street South (on the west), and 11th Street South (on the east).

Basler Lake, Northwest Territories (Lat: 63°57'00"N, Long: 115°58'00"W), northwest of Yellowknife, is named after Corporal Lawrence Basler, RCMP #10362.

Corporal Basler served in the Force from November 4, 1927, until November 3, 1947, in "D" and "G" Divisions.

Beaulieu Bay, Nunavut (Lat: 62°47'00"N, Long: 70°17'00"W), on the south coast of Baffin Island near Lake Harbour, is named after Constable Joseph Oliver Leo Beaulieu, RCMP #10603.

Leo Beaulieu served from June 1929 to June 12, 1950, in "A" Division, mainly in the eastern Arctic at the Lake Harbour detachment. In the Second World War he served in the Number One Provost Corps as #C41976.

Following his retirement from the Force he was employed with the Canadian Fire Underwriters Investigation Bureau and was a life member of the RCMP Veterans' Association. He died at Ottawa, Ontario, in 1999.

Belcher Avenue, Fort Saskatchewan, Alberta, is named after Sergeant-Major Robert Belcher, NWMP #3, who was stationed at that detachment in the early days.

See the following entry.

Belcher (Colonel Belcher Hospital), Calgary, Alberta, is named after Officer Inspector Robert Belcher, CMG, NWMP #25 (Original Series) and #3 (New Series), O.101.[13]

Belcher began his service on November 3, 1873, and was on the March West of 1874. He left the Force after serving over three years, receiving Land Warrant #0003. He reengaged in 1885 as regimental number #1023, but was soon reverted to his previous #3. He was promoted to the commissioned ranks on February 1, 1893.

In 1897 he was selected for the contingent that went to England for Queen Victoria's Diamond Jubilee celebration. Belcher served in "D," "F," "K," and "M" Divisions. He served at the Chilkoot Pass and Dawson City during the Klondike gold rush. He also served in the Boer War as a volunteer with the Lord Strathcona's Horse regiment and was duly honoured with the Companion Most Distinguished Order of St. Michael and St. George medal.

He left the Force in 1908 to accept the command of the 19th Alberta Dragoons with the rank of lieutenant-colonel. He held this rank until 1912 when he was promoted to command the 5th Cavalry Brigade. He saw some service in Europe during the First World War and was in charge of a military information bureau when he died suddenly on February 10, 1919, at Calgary. His son, Percy Belcher, was killed in action at Passchendaele during the First World War.

Bell Street, Calgary, Alberta, is believed to be named after Constable Ralph Alexander Gascoigne Bell, NWMP #590, who resided in Calgary from 1882 until his death at age 92 on December 21, 1953.

Bell served in the NWMP from June 21, 1881, to June 21, 1886, and saw service in the North-West Rebellion. He was also the Force's ferryman in Calgary and greeted the pioneers coming to Calgary before the arrival of the railroad. He was buried in the Union Cemetery, Calgary, Alberta.

Beyak (Constable Della Beyak Road), Winnipegosis, Manitoba, was named in honour of Constable Della Sonya Beyak, RCMP #40153, Honour Roll #187.

Beyak joined the Force on June 30, 1988. She was serving in her first detachment at Assiniboia, Saskatchewan, when she was killed in a police car accident. While working voluntary overtime on March 15, 1989, she was called to assist at a fatal motor vehicle accident. Driving in a snowstorm, she attempted to pass a slow-moving vehicle and was tragically involved in a double fatal head-on collision. She was buried at Winnipegosis, Manitoba.

Beyts Cove, Nunavut (Lat: 63°59'00"N, Long: 94°18'00"W), south of Rankin Inlet on the west side of Hudson Bay, is named after Inspector Walter James Beyts, NWMP, RNWMP, and RCMP O.161. This name first appeared on an RNWMP chart prepared by Constable Alfred B. Kennedy, RNWMP #5626.[14]

Beyts joined the NWMP on February 15, 1893, as #2866 and first served in the north. He was granted leave of absence to serve in the Boer War in 1900, and on his return he served with the RNWMP in Alberta. He was promoted to the commissioned ranks on November 1, 1910, and returned north; he then went to "D" Division and then finally Sault Ste. Marie, where he died January 25, 1923, while still serving. He was buried in the Force Cemetery at Depot Division.

His brother, Stanley Beyts (#2867), joined at the same time and served to 1904, leaving as a sergeant. He then moved west to serve in the B.C. Provincial Police.

Big Point, Northwest Territories (Lat: 61°23'00"N, Long: 118°24'00"W), west of Hay River on Great Slave Lake, was named in 1979 from 1955 RCMP patrol maps showing "Teekeeahjuak," meaning "a big finger sticking out" in Inuktitut.

Bingham Crescent, Edmonton, Alberta, is named after Assistant Commissioner Lloyd Bingham, RCMP #12531, O.342.

Bingham served from November 26, 1934, until May 7, 1967, in "F" and "K" Divisions. On May 1, 1944, while in "K" Division, he received his promotion to the commissioned ranks. He then served in "F," Headquarters, "N," "J," "K," and then back to Headquarters, retiring as the director of Criminal Investigations. Following his retirement from the Force, he was appointed chief constable of the Edmonton City Police, where he served until his death on April 16, 1968.

Blackfoot Crossing, near Cluny, Alberta, is the site of the signing of Treaty Number Seven. The location was named by Jerry Potts, a scout and interpreter for the NWMP.

Blackfoot Crossing, near Cluny, Alberta, where Treaty Number Seven was signed

Jerry Potts served with the NWMP from 1874 until his death in 1896. Several of his direct descendants have served or are still serving—as of 2002—in the Force. See also **Potts (Jerry Potts Street)**.

Blanchard River, Yukon (Lat: 60°02'00"N, Long: 136°53'00"W), southeast of Whitehorse near the B.C. boundary and joining the Tatshenshini River near Dalton Post, was originally named Kleheela River by the NWMP in 1898. This name sounded like the name given by the local Indians.

Bonner Drive, Depot Division RCMP, Regina, Saskatchewan, was named in honour of Master (Lieutenant Commander) John Willard Bonner, RCMP #12130, Honour Roll #73, who was lost at sea September 11, 1942, in the sinking of the HMCS *Charlottetown*.

Bonner began his life at sea in 1907 with the Great White Fleet of the United Fruit Company and by the First World War was sailing with the Great Northern Line, transporting troops to Europe. He joined the Canadian Preventive Service in 1929 and was absorbed into the RCMP Marine Section on May 1, 1932. With the marine rank of master, he "skippered" several RCMP patrol vessels until the Second World War, when the RCMP marine services—with vessels and crews—were transferred to the Canadian military. In 1941 he was given command of the corvette HMCS *Charlottetown*, and by 1942 was promoted to lieutenant commander.

On the fateful day of September 11, 1942, German U-boat *U-517*, under command of Hartwig, was lurking at periscope level in the St. Lawrence River, having already sunk several ships in the river and near the approaches to the coastline of Newfoundland. After escorting a convoy, the *Charlottetown* and another vessel were moving down the St. Lawrence River about 402 kilometres below Quebec City when—without warning—two torpedoes struck the starboard side of *Charlottetown* and it began sinking very quickly. Bonner ordered all hands to abandon ship, organized the evacuation, and was the last to leave. As he swam away, there was a violent underwater explosion and he was killed. Members of the crew managed to pull his lifeless body onto a raft, but it soon became so overcrowded that they were forced to return his body to the water; it was never recovered. Eight others of the crew were also lost either directly or from injuries.

Bonnet Plume Road, Inuvik, Northwest Territories, is named after the Bonnet Plume family, which lived in the Fort McPherson and Arctic Red River areas since the 1890s.

One member of the family was Stephen Bonnet Plume, who was a member of the first RNWMP patrol between Dawson City and Fort McPherson in 1904–05. There is no record of such a person as a special constable guide, so it is presumed that he was contracted locally on a casual basis.

Botterley Lake, Cypress Hills, Saskatchewan, is named after Staff Sergeant Thomas Reginald Downes Botterley, NWMP #2208.

Botterley served from November 20, 1888, until December 5, 1899, when he purchased his discharge. He reengaged April 29, 1904, and served in "K" and "F" Divisions to July 15, 1918, when he left to the newly formed Alberta Provincial Police. He died on August 26, 1941, and was buried in the Queens Park Cemetery, Calgary, Alberta.

Boundary Commission–NWMP Trail, Manitoba. This historically important route west along the southern border of Manitoba begins at Emerson (Fort Dufferin) and generally follows present-day Highway #3 to Pierson, Manitoba, near the Saskatchewan border.

For the most part, this route followed an old Indian trail, and prior to the arrival of the Canadian Pacific Railway it was the common route west for early settlers and fur traders from Fort Dufferin. The International Boundary Commission surveyors, who from 1872 to 1876 fixed the position of the 49th parallel as the Canada–U.S.A. border, followed this trail. On their March West, the NWMP followed the known route as far as present-day Saskatchewan. While neither the NWMP nor the International Boundary Commission established the route, it is because of their use that it has become well-known. Today the trail is clearly identified with signs depicting two mounted riders facing each other. They are William Hallett, a renowned Métis scout who served as the chief guide for the International Boundary Commission, and Colonel French, the first commissioner of the NWMP.

Boundary Commission NWMP Route, now Highway #3 in Manitoba

Highway #3, which generally follows the route from Emerson west, takes the traveller through Gretna, Winkler, Morden, Manitou, Pilot Mound, Killarney, Boissevain, Deloraine, Melita, and to Pierson. In the original survey, the survey points used for fixing this portion of boundary were Lake of the Woods, Northwest Angle, Pine Ridge, Michal, East Pembina Mountain, Long River, Sleepy Hollow, Turtle Mountain East, Turtle Mountain West, First Souris, South Antler Creek, and Second Mouse River.

See also **French Crescent** and **French Lake** entries.

Boutilier Island (Caddy Lake), Manitoba (Lat: 49°48'59"N, Long: 95°12'54"W), southeast Manitoba, was named in 1985 after Constable David Ainslie Boutilier, RCMP #26428.

Constable Boutilier served in the Force from March 28, 1968, to April 30, 1978, in Manitoba. He then acquired ownership of Green Bay Resort on the eastern shore of Caddy Lake and built a campground, cabins, and marina. He died in 1985 at Whiteshell, Manitoba.

Box Lake, Northwest Territories (Lat: 63°56'00"N, Long: 109°24'00"W), midway between Lake Athabasca and Bathurst Inlet, is named after Constable Charles Frederick Box, RCMP #10706.

Box served from September 26, 1929, to November 30, 1954, retiring as sergeant. During his early years in the north in "G" Division he patrolled the area of this lake. In 1930 he participated in the RCMP Ride contingent at the International Horse Show in London, England. In his later years with the Force he was a riding instructor at Depot Division.

He died on March 26, 1974, at Calgary, Alberta.

Brackett River, Northwest Territories (Lat: 64°58'05"N, Long: 125°27'15"W), which flows into the Mackenzie River near Fort

Norman, is named after Corporal Redmond Brackett, RNWMP and RCMP #4847.

Brackett's service in the Force extended from April 24, 1909, to November 14, 1947, including service overseas with the Canadian Expeditionary Force in the First World War. While in the north, he served in both the Yukon and Northwest Territories, then later in "F" Division, Saskatchewan. He finished his service in "H" Division, Nova Scotia.

It is perhaps not surprising that in the isolation of the north he twice found himself standing rigidly at attention before a commissioned officer to answer to charges of being "intoxicated, however slightly" in 1915 and 1920. On both occasions he was fined ten dollars.

He died on October 18, 1955, at Halifax, Nova Scotia.

Braithwaite (Mount Braithwaite) (2,134 m), Alberta (Lat: 53°46'00"N, Long: 119°14'00"W), fifteen kilometres from Grande Cache, is named after Doctor Edward Ainslie Braithwaite.

See following entry.

Braithwaite Park, Edmonton, Alberta, is named after Doctor Edward Ainslie Braithwaite, NWMP #1025.

Braithwaite was born in Alne, Yorkshire, and studied medicine at Kings College Hospital in London, but left for Canada before graduating. He joined the NWMP as #1025 on May 7, 1884. With his medical background, he attained the rank of staff sergeant almost immediately and worked in the Force as a hospital orderly. During the North-West Rebellion he was attached to Colonel A.G. Irvine's column as a medical attendant and cared for the wounded from Duck Lake and Batoche. In 1890 he obtained his medical degree in Winnipeg. After leaving the NWMP on April 6, 1892, he began a medical practice in the Edmonton area, was named the city's coroner in 1896, and served as Edmonton's first western Canadian health officer. He was also appointed honorary surgeon to the Force. A monument erected in 1957 in Braithwaite Park, at the corner of University Avenue and 112 Street, displays an inscription that sums up his career:

> Dr. Edward Ainslie Braithwaite. Born Feb 16, 1862 – Died Dec 7, 1949. Pioneer physician and surgeon. First Commissioner of St. John's Ambulance in Alberta. Honorary surgeon to the RNWMP, Veteran of the Riel Rebellion. First medical Health Officer of Alberta. Chief Coroner of Alberta.

Erected in memory of his outstanding professional service
to the Indians, traders, early settlers and residents of Alberta.

Bray Crescent, Medicine Hat, Alberta, is named after Sergeant-
Major John Henry Gresham Bray, NWMP #92 (Original Series), #2
(New Series).

See following entry.

Bray Lake, Alberta (Lat: 53°19'00"N, Long: 112°58'00"W), 42
kilometres southeast of Edmonton, is named after Sergeant-Major
John Henry Gresham Bray, NWMP #92 (Original Series), #2 (New
Series).

From 1858 to 1868 Bray served with the 10th Hussars in India.
He then served in the NWMP from November 3, 1873, until
November 3, 1882. He was in the third party of new recruits to
leave Toronto for the west in the fall of 1873, sailing from
Collingwood to Prince Arthur's Landing and then to Fort Garry over
the Dawson Route. He was sergeant-major of "C" Troop on the
original March West in 1874. In the North-West Rebellion of 1885
he served in the Rocky Mountain Rangers.[15] In his last years of
service he was in charge of the NWMP horse farm at Pincher Creek.
After leaving the Force he ranched in the Pincher Creek area. He
sold his ranch in 1892 and moved to Medicine Hat where he became
a brand inspector and organized the Medicine Hat Stock Growers
Association. He died in Medicine Hat in 1923.

Brisebois Avenue, Calgary, Alberta, is named after Inspector
Ephrem A. Brisebois, NWMP O.8, who was also a co-founder of the
city of Calgary.

At the formation of the NWMP, nine commissioned officers were
appointed by the government to begin organizing this new force and
start recruiting members. Brisebois was the eighth officer appointed
on September 25, 1873 as O.8. His first task was to tour the Maritime
provinces on a recruiting campaign. On the 1874 March West he
was the officer in charge of "B" Troop. In 1875 he led "F" Troop to
establish the site of a new post and proposed the name "Fort Brisebois."
Commissioner Macleod decided instead to call it "Fort Calgary" after
his home area in Scotland. Inspector Brisebois resigned August 1,
1876, and moved to Manitoba. He died in 1890 at Minnedosa and is
buried in an unmarked grave at St. Boniface, a short distance from
Louis Riel, who led the North-West Rebellion of 1885.

His great-grandson, Inspector Jean Brisebois, served in the RCMP (#35253, O.1438) from 1967 to 1997.

Bruce (Constable Neil M. Bruce Memorial Park), Aberdeen Road, Westbank, B.C., is named in honour of Constable Neil McArthur Bruce, RCMP #20824, Honour Roll #130.

A stone cairn, engraved with the RCMP crest, reads as follows:

> At the bottom of this trail, on the morning of April 10, 1965, Constable Neil McArthur Bruce of the Royal Canadian Mounted Police was fatally wounded. He was attempting to rescue a young woman who was being sexually assaulted in a cabin adjacent to the creek.

Bruce died in hospital four days later. The park was dedicated on April 10, 1995.

Neil M. Bruce

See following entry.

Bruce (Constable Neil Bruce School), Westbank, B.C., was named May 1999 by the school trustees of the Central Okanagan School District to honour Constable Neil McArthur Bruce, RCMP #20824, Honour Roll #130.

Constable Bruce served from February 19, 1959, in "E" Division until his death on April 14, 1965. In early spring 1965, a young woman responded to a newspaper ad for a live-in babysitter and became the kidnapped victim of Russell Spears in a squalid shack adjacent to Westbank, B.C. Early on April 10, 1965, a newspaper boy passing by noticed her signalling from a window and reported to the police that something seemed wrong. Constables Bruce and Kenneth Jones (#23354) responded with little idea of what or whom they were dealing with. Constable Bruce removed his "Sam Browne"[16] and tucked his revolver into the rear waistband of his trousers to appear unarmed before approaching the shack, while Jones acted as cover just out of sight. Bruce called out to the shack and was promptly shot from within it. By the time backup support arrived and Bruce was removed to hospital, Spears had escaped to the surrounding bush. Four days later, while the manhunt continued throughout the area, Bruce succumbed to his wounds. On April 19, 1965, a search team cornered Spears some distance south near Peachland. Upon being ordered to surrender, Spears took his own life.

Spears' history of violence dated back to at least 1947, when he shot and wounded Constable Robert Mercer of the B.C. Provincial Police (BCPP). When the RCMP absorbed the BCPP in 1950, Mercer continued his service as RCMP #16497, retiring as staff sergeant.

When Constable Bruce died he left a widow and infant son. Years later, his widow remarried and the child was adopted by his stepfather. That child now also proudly serves as Corporal Donald I. Bruce-Fuoco, RCMP #40108 in "E" Division (as of 2001).

The canyon area above the site where Bruce was shot was

later developed into a regional park, and on the 30th anniversary of his death, a portion of the park—including the shooting site—was named after him, and a permanent cairn was put at the top of the road leading to the canyon.

In early 1999, Bill Lang, a schoolteacher and long-time resident of the area, proposed that a new middle school in Westbank be named after Constable Bruce. He collected an impressive list

Constable Neil Bruce Middle School, Westbank, B.C.

of supporters and asked Jack Hest[17] to serve on his committee for the presentation to the Board of Trustees. The Board voted unanimously in favour of the name. On June 2, 2000, the school was officially opened with dignitaries and members of both Bruce's training squad from 1959 and his family in attendance.

Bryant Lake, Alberta (Lat: 59°18'00"N, Long: 110°14'00"W), adjacent to Lake Athabasca, is named after Staff Sergeant William Hindle Bryant, RNWMP and RCMP #5677.

Bryant served in the Force from August 2, 1913, to August 31, 1945, beginning in Alberta. On October 4, 1915, he was awarded $25 from the Fine Fund[18] for a meritorious investigation of a lumber theft from a raft. On August 26, 1916, the Force quickly recouped a small portion of Bryant's award when he found himself in Orderly Room and fined 50 cents for negligence.

In 1918 he volunteered for service in the "B" Squadron cavalry draft of the Canadian Expeditionary Force (#2772549), which served in Siberia at the end of the First World War. On his return he was again transferred to "K" Division, Alberta, until his retirement.

Bryant then moved to Ladysmith, B.C., and was appointed provincial magistrate the same year. He died at Victoria, B.C., on August 27, 1963.

Bull Creek, Yukon (Lat: 61°32'00"N, Long: 140°22'00"W), a tributary of St. Claire Creek east of the Klutlan glacier, was named by Constable Thomas Alexander Dickson, NWMP #2101.

See also **Dickson Creek** entry.

Burke Creek, Alberta (Lat: 49°58'00"N, Long: 113°57'00"W), flowing into Trout Creek 85 kilometres northwest of Lethbridge, is named after Acting Corporal Denis Charles Burke, NWMP #3218.

Burke served from March 3, 1898, to April 8, 1902, at Depot Division and at Calgary. He then purchased his discharge to return to Ireland because his father had died.

On his return to Canada he took up ranching and worked as a forest ranger in southern Alberta. He died August 31, 1936, at High River, Alberta, and was buried in the Highwood Cemetery.

Burke Lake, Saskatchewan (Lat: 52°10'00"N, Long: 106°18'00"W), twenty kilometres east of Saskatoon, is named in honour of Constable Patrick Burke, NWMP #402, Honour Roll #11.

In searching for the location of this lake, we found a second "Burke Lake" a short distance south of Lac La Ronge (Lat: 55°58'00"N, Long: 105°41'00"W). The question remains whether this is also named after Constable Burke or for some other person.

"Paddy" Burke served in the NWMP from May 12, 1875, in present-day "K" Division, the NWMP band, and then in present-day "F" Division until his death on May 3, 1885. He had earlier been granted Land Warrant #0208. On May 2, 1885, during the North-West Rebellion, Superintendent William M. Herchmer (O.37) and Superintendent Percy Neale (O.34) led a force of 74 NWMP members in a total force of 319 men from Battleford to Cut Knife Hill about 61 kilometres from Battleford. In this engagement three members of the NWMP were killed: Burke, who died the following day, Corporal Ralph Sleigh (#565, Honour Roll #10), and Corporal

William H.T. Lowry (#907, Honour Roll #12). In addition, Sergeant John Ward (#36) was wounded.

Constable Burke was buried at Battleford. As was the practice of the day, Burke's worldly goods were auctioned among his barracks comrades and raised the princely sum of $7.25, which was passed to his widow. She was also granted a life pension of 37.5 cents per day!

Paddy Burke was from a family of members. He was father-in-law to Sergeant-Major Charles Parker (#742), and he had five sons who went on to serve: Constable Joseph Edward Burke (#2814), who served from 1891 to 1894; Sergeant William Henry "Tough" Burke (#3069), who served from 1891 until his death in 1917; Constable James Alexander Burke (#3101), who served from 1894 to 1904 and died after being gassed in the First World War; Constable Patrick Burke (#3124), who served from 1896 to 1900; and Constable Frederick George Burke (#3196), who served from 1897 to 1901.

See also **Lowry Place** and **Sleigh Square** entries.

Burstall Lake, Alberta (Lat: 59°20'00"N, Long: 110°11'00"W), 250 kilometres northeast of Fort McMurray, is named after Corporal Edward Brian Burstall, RCMP #10149.

See following entry.

Burstall Lake, Northwest Territories (Lat: 60°17'00"N, Long: 105°45'00"W), north of Dodge Lake, Saskatchewan, and west of Selwyn Lake, is named after Corporal Edward Brian Burstall, RCMP #10149.

Corporal Burstall served from December 30, 1925, until his death January 23, 1932. He had served in "G" Division before "F," and at the time of his death was posted at Stony Rapids.

Burstall had just inherited $70,000 from an estate—an astounding amount at that time—when in the early morning of what became a fateful day, flames were seen coming from his cabin. Another Force member, "Red" Gwyndwn Abraham (#10640), and guide H.G. Sinclair broke down the door and dragged Burstall's lifeless body outside, where they soon realized that he had died of a self-inflicted gunshot. His body was removed to Prince Albert for autopsy, but no logical reason for his suicide has ever been determined (as far as we have been able to learn). His burial place is unknown.

Calgary, Alberta, takes its name from an ancestral estate, Calgarry House, on the Isle of Mull, Scotland, of second permanent Commissioner Colonel James A. F. Macleod, NWMP O.4.

A.G. Irvine believed that "Calgarry" meant "clear running water" in Gaelic, but it is translated now as "bay pasture" or "bay farm."

In Gaelic, "Calgarry" means "clear running water." The original site and post was co-founded by Inspectors E.H. Brisebois (O.8) and Cecil Denny (#299 [Original Series], O.25). It was first known as "Fort Brisebois"; however, Colonel Macleod decided on the name "Calgarry" after both Calgarry House and a town called Calgarry on the Isle of Skye, near his grandfather's farm. In the course of time, one "r" was dropped.

Cameron Avenue, Depot Division RCMP, Regina, Saskatchewan, is named in honour of Constable Edison Alexander Cameron, RCMP #12856, Honour Roll #77.

Constable Cameron served from 1937 in Headquarters. At the outbreak of the Second World War he volunteered for the #1 Provost Corps that was being formed from members of the Force. His army number was C41983. He, Constable Terence G.N. Watts (#13064), and Constable David C.G. Moon (#13157) were all killed by enemy shellfire on December 28, 1943, at their post near Ortona, Italy. All were buried in the Moro River Cemetery. Constable Cameron had two brothers in the Canadian army, and his death closely followed his visit to the grave of his brother Gordon, who had been killed earlier in the war.

Carcoux Lake, Saskatchewan (Lat: 59°55'00"N, Long: 107°10'00"W), south of Fond du Lac in northern Saskatchewan, is named after Constable John Henry Carcoux, RCMP #9910.

See following entry.

Carcoux (Little Carcoux Lake), Saskatchewan (Lat: 59°53'00"N, Long: 107°18'00"W), in close proximity to Carcoux Lake, is also named after Constable John Henry Carcoux, RCMP #9910.

Carcoux served in the Force from June 30, 1923, to June 28, 1950, in "E," "M," "K," "F" Divisions and then in the #1 Provost Corps during the Second World War. On his return from the war he served in "A" Division until his retirement. Constable John Henry Carcoux died on June 27, 1993, at Edmonton, Alberta.

His father, Constable John Francis Carcoux (#9860), also served in the Force from 1921 to 1936.

Carlyle Coulee, Saskatchewan, (Lat: 49°03'00"N, Long: 104°51'00"W), in the Big Muddy area, is named after Constable Frank Carlyle, an ex-NWMP (#3578), who became an outlaw.

Carlyle served in the NWMP from April 7, 1900, until July 5, 1901, at which time he purchased his discharge. Almost as soon as he began his training he was a problem. On April 25, 1900, he was charged in the Orderly Room for the assault of a fellow recruit—Constable Findlay, NWMP #3568. Following his discharge, Carlyle fell in with the "Dutch Henry Gang,"[19] rustling in southern Saskatchewan and in Montana. We last find certain track of him in 1905 when he was in prison in Montana for attempting to pass a counterfeit coin. Confederates supposedly murdered him in southern Saskatchewan somewhere in the Big Muddy area, and his final resting place is unknown.

Carroll Court, Depot Division RCMP, Regina, is named in honour of Constable Thomas Percy Carroll, RCMP #20388, Honour Roll #131.

Constable Carroll was engaged by the Force on April 1, 1958, and posted to "D" Division. On February 11, 1966, he was a passenger with two others in a chartered de Havilland Beaver aircraft, flying to Ilford, Manitoba. The aircraft was running low on fuel, and the pilot radioed for a fuel delivery before landing on a frozen lake about 32 kilometres east of Ilford. The fuel was delivered by muskeg tractor, and as darkness began to fall and snow drifted down, the aircraft took off again. It rose about 45 metres, stalled, and crashed into the lake, breaking through the ice. The portion of the aircraft still above the ice burned fiercely and all men aboard were killed.

Constable Carroll was buried at Nelson, B.C.

Carter (Mount Carter) (1,448 m), Yukon (Lat: 65°40'00"N, Long: 137°03'00"W), located between the Blackstone and Hart Rivers, is named in honour of Special Constable Samuel Carter, NWMP and RNWMP #2127, Honour Roll #34.

Sam Carter served from April 28, 1888, to September 30, 1910, in "F" and "M" Divisions, and in 1897 was in the second contingent of members to the Yukon to police the Klondike gold rush. Following his retirement, he returned as a special constable guide and succumbed in the "Lost Patrol" in February 1911. He was buried at Fort McPherson.

See the **Fitzgerald Settlement** entry for details of the "Lost Patrol."

Cawsey Drive, Summer Village, Crystal Springs, Pigeon Lake, Alberta, is located off Highway 13, 45 kilometres west of

Wetaskiwin, and is named after Constable Robert Allan Cawsey, RCMP #13839.

Cawsey is from a proud family of service in the Force and to Canada. His great uncle, Staff Sergeant John Daniel Nicholson, NWMP #1709, also served with the Lord Strathcona's Horse regiment in the Boer War and was a superintendent in the Alberta Provincial Police Force.

Robert Cawsey's father, Sergeant John Nicholson Cawsey, RCMP #11462, first served in the Alberta Provincial Police. While stationed at Bassano, he purchased "Dale of Cawsalta"—a German shepherd that he trained as a tracking dog. When the Alberta Provincial Police were taken over by the RCMP on April 1, 1932, he became the first dog master in the Force. In 1935, pups of Dale, "Black Lux" and "Sultan," were the first additional dogs in the Police Dog Service. He served until February 13, 1944, and died in 1964 at Calgary.

Robert Cawsey's uncle, Staff Sergeant James Archibald Cawsey, RNWMP #6367, served in the Force from November 26, 1914, then in the Alberta Provincial Police, and then back with the RCMP in 1932 until November 30, 1951. He also served in the infantry in the First World War. He died in 1955 at Edmonton, Alberta.

Robert Cawsey's brother, Staff Sergeant Lorne Campbell Cawsey, RCMP #12807, served from September 1935 to May 28, 1964. He was also a dog master, and his dog called "Pilot" was a pup of his father's original dog, Dale. Pilot made a name for himself when he found a brooch valued at $10,000, which Princess Juliana of the Netherlands had lost while visiting in Ottawa. He died on December 5, 2001, at Gibsons, B.C.

Another brother, John N. Cawsey, served in the Royal Canadian Air Force in the Second World War and was killed in action February 1942.

Robert Cawsey served in the Force in "H" Division, Yarmouth, Nova Scotia, from January 1, 1941, until December 31, 1941, when he left to join the Canadian army and serve in the Second World War. He was soon transferred to officer training and was commissioned a lieutenant in July 1942. He then served in the Calgary Regiment (tanks) and landed in Sicily in July 1943. He was later wounded near Cassino and hospitalized for two months. He returned to his regiment and was wounded again near Florence, and this time he spent a year in hospital before being discharged.

On his return to Canada, he finished high school and then attended the University of Alberta, receiving his law degree in 1951. He practised law at Wetaskiwin, Alberta, until 1973 when he was appointed as an Alberta provincial court judge. In 1976 he was named the first Chief Judge of the Court. In 1979 he was appointed to the Court of Queen's Bench, Alberta. He retired in 1997.

See also the **Nicholson River** and **Shaw Street** entries.

Chabot Park, Fort Saskatchewan, Alberta, located between 100th Avenue and the North Saskatchewan River, is named after Constable Joseph Louis Chabot, NWMP #474.

Chabot joined the NWMP on September 22, 1880, and served first at Fort Walsh, then at Battleford, before becoming a bugler in Fort Saskatchewan on July 16, 1881. He was promoted to constable and remained there until completing his contracted term of engagement on September 21, 1885. In the North-West Rebellion of 1885 he served as a trumpeter in Steele's Scouts.[20]

He then took up farming near Fort Saskatchewan. From 1905 to 1907 he was a town constable for Fort Saskatchewan, renting the old fire hall for a dwelling at five dollars per month, which was convenient as part of his duties included being engineer of the fire hall's chemical engine. The position of town constable apparently also included duties such as bell ringer, sanitary inspector, weed inspector, and truant officer. In addition to farming, he was also the bailiff by 1911.

He died at Fort Saskatchewan on May 17, 1927, and was buried in the RCMP Cemetery at Fort Saskatchewan.

Chalmers Street, Red Deer, Alberta, is named after Superintendent Thomas Wellington Chalmers, NWMP O.74.

A graduate of the Royal Military College in Kingston, Ontario, and a surveyor by trade, Chalmers was appointed inspector in the NWMP on April 10, 1886. He served until April 30, 1893, when he resigned. Soon afterward he purchased—with other former members—a large tract of land within the new townsite of Fort Saskatchewan. Chalmers also surveyed the local cemetery site. With the outbreak of the Boer War, he volunteered for service. On November 2, 1900, Major Sanders (O.52) rode under heavy fire to retrieve a member who had lost his horse, and as the two were returning—riding double—the horse was killed and Sanders wounded. Chalmers rode out to attempt a second rescue and was killed. He was buried in South Africa.

Chandler Court, Depot Division RCMP, Regina, Saskatchewan, is named in honour of Constable Henry Charles Allington Chandler, RCMP #18656, Honour Roll #112.

Constable Chandler served from July 23, 1954, in "H" Division. On June 14, 1956, he was riding a police motorcycle on the Bedford–Halifax highway. Near Millview, a truck backed out onto the highway in front of him. He braked and skidded—glancing off the truck into a metal guardrail—and died of his injuries the following day. The inquest into his death recommended motorcycle helmets for all riders, and no charges were laid against the driver of the truck. Chandler was buried at St. Andrews, New Brunswick.

Chappuis Lake, Saskatchewan (Lat: 59°58'00"N, Long: 106°54'00"W), north of Scott Lake and adjacent to the Saskatchewan border, is named after Corporal Marcel Chappuis, RCMP #10418.

"Chappy," as he was fondly known, served in the Saskatchewan Provincial Police from January 14, 1918, until July 21, 1927, when he was discharged as part of a decision to have no single men in that Force. He then joined the RCMP on May 25, 1928, and served until October 22, 1945, in "F" Division, including some time at the Cumberland House detachment.

He made many long-distance dog team patrols of his area. The two patrols that stand out were the following: January 11, 1938, to April 27, 1938, from Cumberland House to the Lac du Brocket area, covering 3,653 kilometres; and January 16, 1939, to April 16, 1939, over a similar route, covering 3,280 kilometres.

He was medically invalided to pension and died at Sidney, B.C., on May 29, 1989.

Chartrand Lake, Nunavut (Lat: 70°04'00"N, Long: 94°20'00"W) on Boothia Peninsula, was named in 1959 after Constable Albert Joseph "Frenchie" Chartrand, RCMP #10155, Honour Roll #104.

See following entry.

Chartrand Star or Northern Star, Tania Borealis—part of the northern constellation Ursa Major ("Big Dipper")—is named after Constable Albert Joseph "Frenchie" Chartrand, RCMP #10155, Honour Roll #104.

A.J. Chartrand

Constable Chartrand served from January 22, 1926, until his death of an apparent heart attack February 13, 1942, while on duty near the Boothia Peninsula, Northwest Territories. He was a crewmember on the *St. Roch* while it was on the historic voyage through the Northwest Passage. He was buried at Pasley Bay, Northwest Territories.

Chataway Ranch, Ashcroft, B.C., bears the name of founder Constable George H. Chataway, NWMP #2807.

Chataway served in the Force from May 23, 1892, until May 22, 1897, in "K" Division. After his service in the Force he moved to Ashcroft, B.C., where he established the Chataway Ranch. He died in 1945 at Ashcroft and is buried there. The ranch has since been sold, but it still remains the "Chataway Ranch"; the main entrance is off the road from Ashcroft to the Highland Valley Copper Mine, about one kilometre from Ashcroft.

Clarke Stadium, Edmonton, Alberta, is named after Constable Joseph Andrew Clarke, NWMP #2786.

Clarke had a less than distinguished career in the Force! He served from March 25, 1892, until April 19, 1893, when he deserted with two other members from Calgary. The three men took NWMP horses and rode to Kalispell, Montana, where they arranged return of the horses with an Indian. Clarke later returned to his home; he was arrested and charged with desertion. In court, he had the good fortune of having a judge who was his uncle, so he was only fined $100. He was in the Yukon during the Klondike gold rush of 1898 before he finally moved to Edmonton, where he served as mayor for five terms. He died in Edmonton on July 27, 1941.

Claustre Avenue, Maple Creek, Saskatchewan, is named after Sub-Constable Jean Claustre, NWMP #83 (Original Series).

Claustre served in the French army in the Franco-Prussian War of 1870–71 before immigrating to Canada. He joined the NWMP when it was first being organized on September 26, 1873. He made the 1874 March West in "B" Division and then served at Fort Walsh[21] until he completed his three-year term on September 25, 1876. For his minimum three years' good service, he was awarded Land Warrant #0024.

He then opened a general store at Fort Walsh, catering to the Force and those attracted to the area. When the fort closed in 1883, he moved to the town of Maple Creek and opened the first store there. He also homesteaded a quarter section of land[22] on nearby Piapot Creek.

In 1909 he discovered coal nineteen kilometres east of Maple Creek. The following year he returned home to visit in France. In 1912 he rode in Calgary's Pioneer Parade in his original NWMP uniform.

He died in 1914 at Maple Creek, Saskatchewan.

Clay Point, Nunavut (Lat: 69°05'00"N, Long: 78°33'00"W), on the west side of Baffin Island and west of Barnes Ice Cap, is named after Staff Sergeant Sidney Gaisford Clay, RNWMP and RCMP #4279.

Clay served in the Force from October 22, 1904, to February 4, 1926, under arduous and heartbreaking circumstances. His service began in Alberta from 1905 to 1907 with the Peace–Yukon Trail party, building a wagon road to the Yukon. He then went north. In 1914 he received 25 cents extra pay per day for 43 days while building barracks at Fort McPherson. He also established and opened the Tree River detachment. During September 1919, all his personal effects, which were in a cache, were lost to fire while he was on patrol with Corporal Eric Cornelius (#5369).

Worse was to come. While he was away on patrol on September 20, 1924, his wife was attacked and mauled by sled dogs at Chesterfield Inlet, Nunavut. Constable Henry Stallworthy (#6316) and a local priest did an excellent job of amputating her leg, but they could not overcome the shock to her system and she died.

Staff Sergeant Clay spent his last years of service in Alberta and retired to Grimsby, Ontario, where he died November 1, 1947.

See also **Constantine (Mount Constantine)** and **Stallworthy (Cape Stallworthy)** entries.

Colebrook Place, Depot Division RCMP, Regina, Saskatchewan, is named in honour of Sergeant Colin Campbell Colebrook, NWMP #605, Honour Roll #19.

Until his untimely death, Sergeant Colebrook led the typically rigorous, disciplined life of the early member. He was engaged with the NWMP on October 16, 1881. On February 2, 1882, at Qu'Appelle he appeared in Orderly Room before Inspector Sam Steele, charged with "being away without leave." He luckily got away with only an admonishment. He saw service in the North-West Rebellion of 1885, but he was back in Orderly Room in 1890. This time he was charged for feeding horses chopped corn without authority and demoted from sergeant to corporal. By 1895 he had earned his sergeant stripes back and was posted at Prince Albert.

In October a young Cree named Almighty Voice from the One Arrow Reserve, who had been arrested for killing cattle, escaped from the guardroom at the Duck Lake detachment. On October 29, 1895, Sergeant Colebrook, with Métis Scout Francois Dumont, found the escapee and called on him to stop. As Sergeant Colebrook approached, Almighty Voice suddenly whirled and shot Colebrook at close range with a shotgun. This set off a wide-ranging manhunt that led to further deaths before the escapee was finally dealt with. Sergeant Colebrook was buried in St Mary's Cemetery, Prince Albert.

Constable Robert Dickson (#3048) had the misfortune of being in charge of the guard at Duck Lake when Almighty Voice escaped, so he soon found himself in the guardroom charged for carelessness in allowing the escape. He was sentenced to two months imprisonment with hard labour, and while serving this sentence he was made to dig the grave for the dead sergeant.

See also **Hockin Avenue** entry.

Coleman Road, Calgary. This street is believed to have been named after Sub-Constable John Coleman, former NWMP member #146 (Original Series).

Coleman served from January 3, 1874, until January 3, 1876, and took part in the March West of 1874. For his good service he received Land Warrant #0143. He then went on to serve as a land inspector at Edmonton and then as a forest ranger. He also hauled freight between Calgary and Edmonton in the early years. In later years he homesteaded at Ile La Crosse, Saskatchewan, and died there on March 31, 1934. His was the first burial in Jourdain's Point Cemetery.

Compton Lake, Northwest Territories[23] (Lat: 62°32'00"N, Long: 109°47'00"W), on the east end of Great Slave Lake near Reliance, is named after Constable Donald Frazer Compton, RCMP #15063.

Constable Compton served from May 9, 1947, to May 27, 1953, when he was medically invalided from service. He had served in "C," "K," "G," and "E" Divisions and from 1948 to 1951 was at the Reliance detachment in the Northwest Territories.

He died at Vancouver, B.C., on June 30, 1958.

Constantine (Fort Constantine), Yukon (Lat: 64°26'00"N, Long: 140°32'00"W), is named after founding Officer Superintendent Charles Constantine, NWMP O.79.

Fort Constantine was built in 1895 as the first NWMP post in the Yukon. It was placed on the north side of the Forty Mile River at its junction with the Yukon River, several kilometres from the Alaskan border. As the first established NWMP post in the Yukon Territory, it also served as the government seat from 1885 to 1887. In August 1896 two prospectors, Tagish Charlie and George Carmack, checked through the post as the first on a great rush to the gold fields. The Fort was abandoned in 1901.

See following entry.

Constantine (Mount Constantine) (3,138 m), Yukon (Lat: 61°25'00"N, Long: 140°34'00"W), near Klutan Glacier in the St. Elias Range, is named after Officer Superintendent Charles Constantine, NWMP O.79.

Superintendent Constantine had a pioneering and varied experience. In 1870 he took part in the Red River Expedition, serving in the Canadian militia. Next, he was commissioner of the Manitoba Provincial Police. In the North-West Rebellion of 1885 he served in the Winnipeg Light Infantry. He was then appointed inspector in the NWMP on October 20, 1886.

In 1894 there was government concern about the influx of prospectors to the Yukon and the lack of any official representation of government there, so Constantine was detailed to rectify the situation. On June 6, 1894, he departed for the Yukon with Staff Sergeant Charles Brown (#1694). They left Broadview (Saskatchewan) on the Canadian Pacific Railway, arriving in Victoria on June 17; they then travelled by the steamer *Queen* to Juneau, Alaska, arriving on June 26. On July 1 they departed for Fort Cudahy, Yukon. After an examination of needs, Constantine returned to Regina at the end of the summer, leaving Brown as the first NWMP member posted in the Yukon.

On May 5, 1895, Constantine departed Depot Division to lead the first permanent contingent to police the Yukon and the growing "gold fever." In this group were Inspector D'Arcy Strickland (O.99),[24] Assistant Surgeon Alfred Wills (O.102), and seventeen Force members. They journeyed to the West Coast by rail and then took the steamer to Juneau and on to the Yukon. They arrived at their destination July 26, 1895. By November they had established Fort Constantine by erecting nine buildings, including one 22 metres in length. Inspector Constantine was now commander of the Mounted Police, chief magistrate, and also home and foreign secretary. He used three separate tables to differentiate the work requirements of each role.

When Alberta and Saskatchewan became provinces in 1905 the anticipated influx of settlers and additional travellers to the Yukon led to new policing districts. Constantine was placed in command of northern Alberta with his headquarters at Lesser Slave Lake. He then received instructions to open a trail from Fort St. John, B.C., to Teslin Lake in the Yukon, which became known as the "Peace-Yukon Trail." His instructions, paraphrased, were as follows: "The trail should be built and you should bear in mind the fact that at some future time it may be made into a wagon trail. You should select your grades and ground with this in view. Through timber, the trail should be eight feet wide. All boggy and soft places should be brushed, and small streams should be bridged. The trail should be clearly marked, so that it can be followed without a guide. It should be posted every two miles with distances in miles from Fort St. John. Trees are to be blazed at frequent intervals through the timbered sections. Shelters are to be built every 30 miles, or at distances as are most convenient for camping—where wood and water is easily obtainable. The shelters should be simple in construction, ten or twelve feet square, and with mud roofs."

Constantine built that trail, along with two officers and 30 men, between 1905 and 1908. In 1905 they completed 94 miles (151 kilometres) northwest of Fort Grahame; in 1906 they built another 208 miles (335 kilometres), and in 1907 another 104 miles (167 kilometres) of trail were finished. The trail was completed in 1908.

By 1911, after his long years of rigour and harsh living conditions, Constantine was in failing health. In 1912 he was granted a medical leave of absence. While on his leave he died at Long Beach, California, on May 5, 1912.

Conway Point, Nunavut (Lat: 63°48'00"N, Long: 92°27'30"W), located on the west shore of Hudson Bay midway between Whale Cove and Rankin Inlet, is named after Constable (later Sergeant) Patrick Roger Conway, RNWMP and RCMP #4217.

Conway served from June 10, 1904, to June 9, 1924, in "K," "M," "D," "F," and "D" Divisions, retiring from Winnipeg. Between 1905 and 1907 he took part in the Peace-Yukon Trail project.

In 1908 he accompanied Inspector Ephrem A. Pelletier (O.122) and two other members for the task of establishing a link between eastern and western Arctic. From Fort Saskatchewan, Alberta, they travelled to Athabasca Landing, then via the Hudson's Bay boat they went across Athabasca Lake and down the Slave River to Fort Smith on the Alberta–Northwest Territories border. They then used canoes to cross the Great Slave Lake, paddle down the Hanbury and

Thelon Rivers to Baker Lake, and finally on to Chesterfield Inlet on the western shore of Hudson Bay. Here they were met by a whaleboat. That winter they returned south by dog team to Churchill, Norway House, and finally Gimli, Manitoba—over 4,830 kilometres in total. It was for this feat that Conway Point was named after him.

On April 1, 1919, he was promoted to sergeant in recognition of his excellent performance in a patrol to Coronation Gulf, Northwest Territories, following up on the reported murder of an Inuit woman. He died on May 24, 1964, at Toronto, Ontario.

See also the **Constantine (Mount Constantine)** and **Pelletier Point** entries.

Cormier Place, Depot Division RCMP, Regina, Saskatchewan, is named in honour of Special Constable Aircraft Engineer Joseph E.R. Cormier, RCMP #S10410, Honour Roll #99.

Joseph Cormier served in the Royal Canadian Air Force during the Second World War, from 1943 to 1945. He then joined the RCMP as an aircraft technician. On August 4, 1958, the body of a young woman was found in a fruit picker's shack in the south Okanagan Valley of B.C. Suspicion fell on a transient picker with several names but believed to be John Morrison, a prison escapee from the U.S. The next day, Corporal G. Ralph Browne (#14827) of nearby Summerland attempted to check a suspicious-looking individual who promptly pulled a revolver and shot Browne three times, fortunately only wounding him.

A massive manhunt now spread throughout the Okanagan. On August 6 a report came in concerning the sighting of the suspect on the sparsely treed hillside above the eastern shores of Skaha Lake. The police aircraft, a CF-FHW de Havilland Beaver on floats, was called for and attended by Staff Sergeant Stanley Rothwell (#10880) as pilot and Cormier as engineer. On August 6, 1958, a Penticton detachment Force member, Constable Richard W. Green (#14740), boarded the airplane to be a spotter with local knowledge. It was a very hot day, and with the aircraft flying low along the hillside, the conditions caused the plane to have a wing stall; it crashed and burned, killing the three members aboard. Rothwell is #97 on the Honour Roll and Green is #98.

A few days later the suspect was spotted at Tonasket, Washington, and after a considerable tussle was successfully arrested by Constable Stu Langdon (#16889). Compounding the tragedy of the plane crash was the later admission of the witness who said that he had made a false report of the sighting near Skaha Lake "just to see some excitement."

Coughlin Bay, Regina, Saskatchewan, is named after Sergeant James Campbell Coughlin, RCMP #12511.

Royal tour leaving RCMP Chapel, 1939; Constable Coughlin second from right

"Jimmy" served in the Force from November 27, 1934, to September 14, 1962, at Depot Division. He was a man of many talents. He was the Canadian welterweight boxing champion of 1934, and he put these talents to good use in his many years as a boxing instructor at Depot. It was probably due to his physical abilities that he was chosen as one of the four personal orderlies (body-guards) to King George VI and Queen Elizabeth on their 1939 Royal Tour of Canada.

He was also an artisan. He designed the wrought-iron gates that for many years welcomed all to Depot, at both the north and south entrances to the training facility. He also collaborated in the design of the steeple on the Force chapel at Depot, and in 1962 he painted a mural that adorns the sergeants' mess at Depot.

He died at Regina on August 24, 1964, and was buried in the Force Cemetery at Depot Division.

Counsell Street, Depot Division RCMP, Regina, Saskatchewan, is named in honour of Constable Frederick Gordon Frank Counsell, RCMP #11298, Honour Roll #65.

Constable Counsell served from March 21, 1932, in "K" Division until his death on May 22, 1940. On that day, police at Lethbridge, Alberta, heard that a resident of nearby Parkland, Charles Hansen, had reportedly shot his son and fled. Constable Counsell attended the address with Corporal William H. Wilson (#11331). When they arrived, Hansen began shooting at them from the house. Corporal Wilson called for backup; Staff Sergeant George Harvey (#8054) soon arrived. Eventually they enveloped the house with tear gas. After a long wait with no action, they cautiously entered. Constable Counsell began climbing a stairway to the attic. Hansen suddenly appeared and shot him. Soon afterward Corporal Wilson observed Hansen through a window; Wilson promptly shot at him. Hansen disappeared from view, and then a second shot was heard. When they entered again they found Hansen—wounded in the chest—had shot himself. It was later learned that Hansen had earlier served a prison term in Minnesota for killing his mother. Constable Counsell was buried at Lethbridge, Alberta.

Craigie Bay, Whitmore Park subdivision, Regina, Saskatchewan, is named after Constable Thomas Campbell Craigie, NWMP #611.

Craigie served in the Force from October 16, 1881, to October 30, 1886, at several posts through that part of the Northwest Territories that became the provinces of Saskatchewan and Alberta. At the outbreak of the North-West Rebellion in 1885, he was stationed at Fort Carlton and took part in the opening battle at Duck Lake[25] on March 26, 1885. His final posting was to Depot Division. When he left the Force he took up farming near Regina. He died at Regina on February 28, 1951.

As the years passed and Regina grew, his farmland was swallowed up by the city's expansion and became the present-day Whitmore Park subdivision.

Cripple Camp, Saskatchewan, near the present town of Gravelbourg, was named by Commissioner French, NWMP O.1.

This camp was established during the March West of 1874, becoming a camp where sick men and horses were left to recuperate. Commissioner French later picked them up on his return trip to Fort Ellice.

Crockett Way, Medicine Hat, Alberta, is named after Special Constable James "Barney" Crockett, RCMP.

Crockett was born in Galloway Hills of south Scotland and was 21 when he came to Canada. In 1931 he joined the Alberta Provincial Police and the following year was absorbed into the RCMP with the rank of special constable. He stayed with the Force until 1951. His main duties were working on livestock rustling and with the Cattlemen's Association of Alberta.

He died on November 23, 1959.

Cronkhite (Mount Cronkhite), Yukon (Lat: 65°32'00"N, Long: 137°37'15"W), west of the Blackstone River, was named in 1973 after Superintendent Howard Hooper Cronkhite, RCMP O.322.

During the First World War, from 1915 to 1919, Howard Cronkhite served with the 82nd Battalion 1st Canadian Machine

Gun Corps. On February 5, 1920, he joined the RCMP as #9024 and served in "N," "M," "E," and "K" Divisions before he received a promotion to commissioned ranks on November 1, 1940. He then served in both "F" and "M" Divisions and was the commanding officer of "G" Division with Headquarters in Ottawa at the time of his death December 28, 1949. While serving in "E" Division in 1935 he was one of the background riders in the Metro-Goldwyn-Mayer movie *Rose Marie*, which was partially filmed in the Lynn Canyon area of North Vancouver, B.C.

Crozier Bay, Saskatchewan (Lat: 56°42'00"N, Long: 108°12'00"W), in the northeast corner of Churchill Lake northeast of Buffalo Narrows, is believed—but as yet is not confirmed—to be named after Assistant Commissioner Lief Newry Fitzroy Crozier, NWMP O.10.

Two other landmarks are also believed to be named after Lief Crozier. See the next two entries.

Crozier Island, Saskatchewan (Lat: 58°32'00"N, Long: 103°11'00"W), in Wollaston Lake, northeast Saskatchewan, is also believed to be named after Lief Crozier.

See the previous and following entries.

Crozier Lake, Saskatchewan (Lat: 56°56'00"N, Long: 102°55'00"W), south of Reindeer Lake and adjacent to Kamatsi Lake near the Manitoba border, is also believed—but as yet not confirmed—to be named after Assistant Commissioner Lief Newry Fitzroy Crozier, NWMP O.10.

Crozier had served as major in the 15th Argyll Light Infantry prior to being appointed as the tenth officer of the NWMP on November 4, 1873. He took part in the March West of 1874 and was then posted to Fort Macleod.

In late 1874 he led a small party of members north of Fort Macleod some 80 kilometres to arrest five men who had been supplying liquor to the Indians. They were fined $200 and had their wagons and supplies confiscated,[26] an act that successfully ended the first official investigation of the newly arrived Force. In August 1876 he led a detachment of men from Fort Calgary to Fort Carlton as one contingent of the small force at the signing of Treaty Number Seven. More than 2,000 Indians had gathered for the occasion.

By 1879, as a superintendent, he took over from Major Walsh in the Cypress Hills, reporting to headquarters at Fort Walsh. He did not have the patience or sympathies for the Sioux that Walsh did. He soon warned them that he would no longer provide their provisions and strongly suggested they return to the U.S. Most did, although Sitting Bull held out through a very tough winter. In hindsight, it is fortunate there were no serious incidents.

In 1882 he drove another wedge into the good relations between the Force and the Indians. At Blackfoot Crossing a dispute arose between the Indian Agency and Bull Elk, who, in turn, shot at the buildings. Inspector Dickens and three men arrested Bull Elk, but a group of Indians took over their post, forcing Bull Elk's release. Chief Crowfoot arrived and calmed the situation, promising to have the offender appear for trial. Crozier did not accept the chief's word and, arriving with a show of strength, made an arrest that only served to negate the efforts the Force had made for good relations.

Lief Newroy F. Crozier

In 1884, with Indian and Métis unrest spreading, Crozier led Inspector William Antrobus (O.36), Surgeon Robert Miller (O.35), and 27 men to an incident that is often viewed as a precursor to the North-West Rebellion. This event has been referred to as the "Craig Incident" or the "Poundmaker Racket." Craig, an employee on Poundmaker's Reserve, was assaulted. Again, when Crozier strode in—with a show of force—to make the arrest, his approach did little to complement the Force.

In March 1885 he had moved a body of men from Prince Albert to Fort Carlton and acted as he always had in the face of threat and rising unrest among Indians and Métis by boldly going out in force. Crozier was well aware of the growing threat of insurrection. On March 26 he sent a party of eighteen members with eight sleighs under the command of Sergeant Alfred "Bull" Stewart (#400) and Mr. McKay to secure provisions and ammunition in a store at Duck Lake. En route they met four NWMP scouts riding toward them, pursued by a large number of Métis and Indians. They turned their sleighs and readied themselves. Despite being goaded and threatened there was no shooting, possibly because they were on flat ground with no cover for the challengers. They beat a hasty retreat to the fort to report the incident.

Crozier next led a force of 56 members and 43 civilian volunteers to both obtain and secure the provisions. Near the site of the earlier incident they met approximately 350 of the hostile Métis and Indians. Bravado was not sufficient to win this day for they faced a much greater and determined force. Shooting broke out, and Crozier's group was soon under murderous fire. The order was given to retire and they ran a moving battle back some 21 kilometres to Fort Carlton, during which twelve of his detachment were killed, including three Force members. Eleven were wounded, including eight members, with Crozier himself in this group. The North-West Rebellion had begun.[27]

There was considerable second-guessing of Crozier's decisions of that day, partly due to Commissioner Irvine's arrival with reinforcements soon after Crozier's return to the fort. In response to government and outside criticism, the commissioner later responded that he was "led to believe that Crozier's better judgement was overruled by the impetuosity displayed by both the police and the volunteers."

Crozier resigned June 30, 1886, as assistant commissioner. He died in 1901 at Battleford and was buried at Belleville, Ontario.

See also **Dickens Lake Recreation Site**.

Cruickshanks Lake, Northwest Territories (Lat: 65°55'00"N, Long: 117°26'00"W), south of Great Bear Lake near Hottah Lake, is named after ex-Constable Andrew David Cruickshank, RCMP #9959.

"Andy" Cruickshank served in the Force from August 13, 1923, until April 4, 1927, first in B.C. and then in the Yukon. During his time in Dawson City he played saxophone in a local band that included Claude Tidd (#6290).[28]

Cruickshank purchased his discharge from the Mayo detachment to begin his own business as a bush pilot, having arranged to purchase a new Ryan monoplane. Charles Lindbergh was next in line for a similar aircraft, and when he explained his urgency to be first across the Atlantic, Cruickshank allowed him to take first delivery of the aircraft that became famous as the "Spirit of St Louis."

Cruickshank took delivery of the next aircraft off the production line and named it "Queen of the Yukon." It bore the Canadian registration G-CAHR. He flew from the factory in the U.S. to Vancouver, B.C., and then shipped the aircraft north, where he operated a charter service with Wop May, the famed bush pilot of the north. The airplane crashed in 1929.

He then began flying for Canadian Airways. On July 1, 1932, he was flying a Fokker (registration G-CASL), taking two Canadian

"Queen of the Yukon" at the Whitehorse Museum

Airways engineers, Horace Tory and Harry King, from Great Bear Lake to Fort Rae. A piston blew and parts came through the windshield, killing Cruickshank in the pilot's seat. The aircraft crashed into a hillside at Mazenod Lake, and both passengers were killed. Ex-Constable Cruickshank was buried at Edmonton, Alberta. His friend and a former member of the Force, ex-Constable John M. Comyn-Ching (#3202), who had since become an Anglican minister, conducted the funeral service.

Andy Cruickshank was also paid tribute by West Coast folk singer/songwriter John McLachlan on his 1993 album *Wandrin' Boy*, which included his song "Chief Thunderbird" and the following dedication:

> A song about Andy Cruickshank who brought the first commercial air service to the Yukon with his plane "Queen of the Yukon." The early bush pilots and their aircraft were referred to as Chief Thunderbird by the native peoples.

Cunning Bay, Saskatchewan (Lat: 58°25'00"N, Long: 103°35'00"W), in northeast Saskatchewan between Wollaston and Reindeer Lakes, is named after Inspector William Angus Cunning, NWMP, RNWMP, and RCMP #2006, O.220.

See following entry.

Cunning Crescent, Regina, Saskatchewan, is named after Inspector William Angus Cunning, NWMP, RNWMP, and RCMP #2006, O.220.

Cunning joined the Force June 14, 1887, and first served on the Boundary Commission Patrol. He then served at Depot and in "F" Divisions (Saskatchewan) before being promoted to the commissioned ranks as an inspector on January 1, 1927. He continued to serve in Saskatchewan until his retirement April 15, 1932. In 1918 he won the annual Connaught Cup competition as best shot in the Force. He died on December 7, 1964, at Regina, Saskatchewan, and was buried in the Force Cemetery, Depot Division.

His son and grandson also served: Constable Cecil A. Cunning (#9897) served from 1923 to 1925, and Sergeant Arthur G. Cunning (#13842) served from 1941 to 1962.

d'Albenas Walk, Depot Division RCMP, Regina, Saskatchewan, is named in honour of Constable Kenneth Laurence d'Albenas, RCMP #13678, Honour Roll #80.

Constable d'Albenas joined the Force in September 1940 and served a short time in "F" Division before volunteering for the #1 Provost Corps (#C33523) in the Second World War. He was soon transferred overseas and then to Italy. On May 14, 1944, while driving a jeep in a reconnaissance party on the west side of the Liri River, he lost his life when a teller mine destroyed his jeep. He was buried in the Cassino War Cemetery.

Damour District, Saskatchewan (Lat: 53°04'00"N, Long: 107°00'00"W), eighteen kilometres west of Leask, is named after Constable Gustave Philippe D'Amour, NWMP and RNWMP #3190.

D'Amour served in spurts in the Force, from August 24, 1897, to 1900, 1901 to 1907, and 1912 to March 31, 1913, when he was dismissed. He served in the Yukon and at Edmonton. In his first absence from the Force, he served in the Boer War with the Lord Strathcona's Horse regiment. On his second absence in 1910, he filed on a homestead west of Leask, Saskatchewan, beside the lake that took his name. Later, the name was given to the local district. He clearly did not farm for long as he was back in the Force two years later. On March 3, 1913, he appeared in Orderly Room charged with "disobeying an order" and was demoted from corporal to constable. He was back in Orderly Room March 26, 1913, charged with being "intoxicated however slightly" and was fined ten dollars, confined to barracks for ten days, and ordered to be dismissed. It is not known if he returned to the homestead after leaving the Force in 1913.

From 1923 to 1965 there was also a Damour post office that took its name from the district.

Dawson Street, Red Deer, Alberta, is named after Constable John James Dawson, NWMP #658.

Dawson saw three separate engagements in the NWMP. He first served from April 19, 1882, to 1887 at Fort Walsh and Regina in "F" Division. He saw service in the North-West Rebellion of 1885 and on May 2, 1885, was in the Battle of Cut Knife Hill. He rejoined in 1888 and served to 1895 in "K" Division, then left for a year, rejoined, and continued service in "K" until his final discharge April 3, 1899. In 1889 Constable Dawson had served at Fort Normandeau (Red Deer). When he left the Force he returned to the Red Deer area and farmed west of the town. Dawson died on February 22, 1937, and was buried in the Red Deer Cemetery.

Dead Horse Coulee, Alberta, is in southern Alberta near the Milk River and crosses into the U.S.

Near the end of the 1874 March West, "B," "C," and "F" Divisions, along with some of "A" Division, were temporarily placed under the command of Inspector William Winder. Many horses had died on the long and arduous trek to this point, so when Winder established a camp in this particular coulee, his men dubbed the location "Dead Horse Coulee."

See also the **Winder Ranch** entry.

Deane House, near Fort Calgary, Alberta, now known as Deane House Historic Site and Tea Room, was built in 1906 for Superintendent Richard Burton Deane, NWMP and RNWMP O.49. It was designated a registered historic resource in 1978 and was restored and opened to the public in 1985.

Deane was born in India in 1848 and from 1866 to 1881 was a lieutenant in the Royal Marines. He came to Canada in 1882, and on July

Deane House near Fort Calgary

1, 1883, was appointed Inspector O.49 in the NWMP. He quickly became the recruiting officer in Toronto, then was transferred to Depot Division and promoted to superintendent in 1884. He was the officer directly responsible for Louis Riel while he was imprisoned at Regina.

Deane wrote the first rules, regulations, and orders for the Force and authored two books: *Pioneer Policing in Southern Alberta* and *Mounted Police Life in Canada.* By all accounts, he was a crusty individual and had a particular distaste for officers who outranked him—in particular, Commissioner Herchmer. When the commissioner would visit Calgary, Deane would go off duty, saying he was sick, and used an orderly to pass notes back and forth as required. He did little to hide his dislike for instructions or corrections. The following exchange of letters serves to illustrate:

Assistant Commissioner Z.T. Wood to Superintendent Deane, October 26, 1910, in response to a reported theft of horses (paraphrased): "Referring to your letter of 21 October, the Commissioner is of the opinion that a special party of police from Calgary should have been sent in pursuit of the horse thieves."

Superintendent Deane to Assistant Commissioner Wood, November 1, 1910 (paraphrased): "I attach hereto a list of Officers, NCOs, Constables and horses available for duty on the 14th October after receipt of message of stolen horses. I am curious to know what sort of patrol the Commissioner would have selected therefrom to be sent to Gleichen to pick up the three-day-old trail, which was already lost. Even if it had been possible, as it was not, to dispatch a patrol, it would have been in my view an act of eye-service as useless as this correspondence is unnecessary."

There was more to this exchange, such as the assistant commissioner demanding a retraction from Deane and a compliance with his order; one can easily see Deane's contempt for guidance from a higher authority.

Superintendent Deane retired on March 31, 1915, and died while holidaying at Diano, Marina, Italy.

DeBeaujeu (Saveuse DeBeaujeu Crescent), Depot Division RCMP, Regina, Saskatchewan, is named in honour of Constable George Quiqueran René Saveuse DeBeaujeu, NWMP #2439, Honour Roll #15.

René, as he preferred, joined the NWMP on April 29, 1890. Soon afterward he was assigned with Corporal Harry O. Morphy (#2162, Honour Roll #16) to the boat *Keewatin,* which was captained by civilian Matthew Watts. Their assigned duty was to control illegal liquor movement on Lake Winnipeg. They patrolled the area through the summer, but then they failed to report after several violent storms. Local Indians reported finding wreckage after a storm on September 8, 1890, and a search was launched. Searchers found the captain lashed across the wrecked hull at Rabbit Point. He told them that they had taken refuge at Swampy Island in the storm and that their anchor chain had broken, setting them adrift. Both members had to bail constantly to keep the vessel afloat, but at daylight on September 8 they struck a reef and breached. Over the next two days the members became overly exhausted and slipped away. The captain Watts died soon after his ordeal.

DeBeaujeu's body was found two months later and returned to his family for burial at Montreal. Despite rumours that Morphy was never found, a memo dated March 21, 1891, states that his body was found by Indians and buried on Tamarac Island. Another memo dated September 16, 1891, advised that the body was recovered and buried in the family plot at Toronto.

Dempster Highway, Yukon, is named after Inspector William John Dempster, NWMP, RNWMP, and RCMP #3193, O.233.

The route of the Dempster Highway follows roughly the track of the NWMP patrols from Dawson City to Fort McPherson, and until 1963 was known as the Eagle Plain Road.

See details in the following entry.

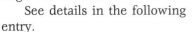

End of the Dempster Highway, Inuvik, NWT

Dempster (Mount Dempster), Yukon (Lat: 65°08'00"N, Long: 136°04'50"W), north of Little Wind River, was named in 1973 after Inspector William John Dempster, NWMP, RNWMP, and RCMP #3193, O.233.

Inspector Dempster joined the NWMP on September 7, 1897, and served in the Yukon until his promotion to commissioned ranks on March 1, 1931. He then served briefly in "K" Division before returning to the Yukon. He retired August 31, 1934, and moved to the West Coast where he died in 1964. He was buried in Forest Lawn Cemetery, Burnaby, B.C.

In his varied service, Dempster is best remembered for his actions as a corporal in the 1911 search for the "Lost Patrol."[29] When this

W.J.D. Dempster

RNWMP patrol was unduly overdue, Dempster was detailed with Constable Jerry Fyfe (#4937) and a former member, ex-Constable Frederick Turner (#4889), to make a search from Dawson City to Fort McPherson, Yukon. On March 21, 1911, they found the frozen bodies of Constable George F. Kinney (#4582, Honour Roll #36) and Constable Richard O. Taylor (#4346, Honour Roll #37) on the Peel River about 56 kilometres from Fort McPherson. The following day they found the bodies of Inspector Francis J. Fitzgerald (O.156, Honour Roll #35) and Special Constable Samuel Carter (ex-RNWMP #2127, Honour Roll #34) about 40 kilometres from Fort McPherson.

See also **Fyfe (Mount Fyfe)** and **Turner (Mount Turner)** entries.

Denison Court, Yellowknife, Northwest Territories, is named after Constable John Burton Denison, RCMP #13246.

Denison began his service in the Force on July 1, 1937, as a reserve constable; he became a regular member on November 10, 1939, and served to 1944, mainly in "E" Division. He then entered the armed forces to serve in the Second World War, returning to the RCMP in 1946. He was posted to "G" Division before purchasing his discharge May 22, 1947.

Denison then became associated with Byer's Transport in Edmonton, Alberta. When they received a contract in 1962 to haul equipment from the old mine site at Port Radium on Great Bear Lake to the south, the Denison Ice Road was born. Afterward, Denison decided to go into business for himself, opening ice roads from Yellowknife north to Great Bear Lake and beyond, supplying mines and drilling sites. This tundra area consists of countless bogs, ponds, and small lakes with a surface unsuitable for summer travel and environmentally sensitive to traffic. In the winter freeze-up, his maintained roads on the ice were the only means to get supplies to the many camps, even in weather often 50° below zero Fahrenheit.

His first ice road joined Great Slave and Great Bear Lakes. It began at Mile 150 of the Northwest Territories' Highway #3— approximately 113 kilometres from Yellowknife—and travelled 603 kilometres northeast to Echo Bay on Great Bear Lake. The operation switched to Echo Bay in 1965 when 762,000 kilograms of ore concentrate were transported over the road. Since 1965 the tonnage hauled has doubled annually, with the 1967 estimate being 2,500 tons (2,540,125 kilograms).

Denison was a life member of the RCMP Veterans' Association, and in 1998 he was awarded the Order of Canada for his opening of the far north with his ice roads. He died at Kelowna, B.C., on January 6, 2001.

Dersch Point, Nunavut (Lat: 62°45'00"N, Long: 69°38'00"W), on the south coast of Baffin Island at Lake Harbour, is named after Constable Paul Henry William Dersch, RCMP #10044.

Dersch served in the Force from December 1923 to December 4, 1948, in "K," Headquarters, "G," "F," and "M" Divisions. While in the north, he was stationed at Lake Harbour, Baffin Island, when that detachment was first opened.

He died January 24, 1988, at Fort Macleod,[30] Alberta, and is buried in the Union Cemetery there.

Diamond Street, Red Deer, Alberta, is named after Constable William Egerton Diamond, NWMP #457.

Formerly of Belleville, Ontario, Diamond served in the NWMP from August 21, 1880, to September 20, 1895, in "F" and "K" Divisions. At the outbreak of the North-West Rebellion in 1885 he was at Fort Carleton. He served at Fort Normandeau in 1890. By 1894 he had been promoted to staff sergeant but fell afoul of the Orderly Room. On February 14, 1894, he appeared before Superintendent Griesbach, commanding officer of the Fort Saskatchewan district, charged for being "absent from duty and intoxicated." He was demoted to constable. Only one month later he was again rigidly at attention before Griesbach, charged with "intoxication in barracks." This time he was fined ten dollars and one month imprisonment with hard labour. Upon his discharge he was an early settler in the Red Deer, Alberta, area.

Dickens Lake, Saskatchewan (Lat: 55°44'00"N, Long: 104°37'00"W), 80 kilometres northeast of Lac La Ronge, is named after Inspector Francis Jeffrey Dickens, NWMP O.29.

See following entry.

Dickens Lake Recreation Site, Saskatchewan (Lat: 55°44'55"N, Long: 104°40'10"W), at Dickens Lake, is named after Inspector Francis Jeffrey Dickens, NWMP O.29, son of noted English author Charles Dickens.

NWMP officers and NCO's at Fort Macleod in 1874— standing second from right is Inspector Francis Dickens, son of the novelist Charles Dickens

Inspector Dickens served from November 4, 1874, until he died in service on March 1, 1886. He had earlier been superintendent of the Bengal Police until his commission in the NWMP. On July 1, 1881, Inspector Dickens made a name for himself when he, Sergeant Frank Spicer (#155), and Constable G. Callaghan (#323) together made a daring recovery of fourteen stolen horses before a large hostile force of Indians on the Blackfoot Reserve.

He had less satisfactory results with his arrest of Bull Elk in 1882. Bull Elk was a minor chief of the Blackfoot, and it had been alleged that he shot at an Indian Agency representative on the reserve. Dickens, with a sergeant and two constables, went to arrest him. Bull Elk was cornered, captured, and marched to the police detachment at Blackfoot Crossing, where a group of angry Indians had gathered. Dickens' group had difficulty getting through the mob; they had to cross the frozen Bow River, and the defiant group—growing in size—tripped the member holding Bull Elk. One of the Indians snatched away Bull Elk's gun, which the member had been carrying. While Dickens was holding a part of the group back with his revolver, the downed member fired three shots to attract the attention of other members at their post, who soon came running. The police managed to get the prisoner, Bull Elk, to their quarters, but now a large number of protesting Indians arrived and took over the post. Dickens gave up the prisoner when Chief Crowfoot, after calming the angry crowd, promised to have the prisoner appear for trial. On hearing of the incident, Superintendent Crozier[31] responded with force. He made the arrest and—in his capacity as magistrate—tried the case, which only served to negate the efforts the Force had made for good relations.

Inspector Dickens was in charge of Fort Pitt at the outset of the North-West Rebellion. With 22 other men, he withdrew in what some suggested was cowardice; however, it was not quite that simple. The Indians wanted what Fort Pitt contained: ample supplies and ammunition. Little Pine and a large group of Indians faced the fort, and shortly Big Bear and an even greater number of Indians supported them. They demanded surrender. The Hudson's Bay Company factor was sent out to negotiate, but was taken prisoner. He returned a note to the fort, suggesting all civilians surrender, which they did, leaving Dickens and his small garrison. On April 15, 1885, Constables David L. Cowan (#635) and Clarence Loasby (#925), along with Special Constable Henry Quinn, were sent out to scout and were attacked a short distance away. Quinn was taken prisoner, Cowan was shot and killed by Métis Louison Mongrain,[32] and Loasby was shot in the leg, then in the side by Lone Man, who, in turn, shot and killed Loasby's horse. Loasby feigned death, and Lone Man alighted from his horse, cut off Loasby's gun belt, and departed. Loasby was able to drag himself back to the fort.

Dickens realized their position was grave and that they had only one chance out—by a very leaky scow on the river. During a snowstorm they destroyed what stores they could not carry and departed in the scow on the river. It promptly began to sink, but valiant bailing efforts organized by Constable Richard Routledge (#762) kept them afloat, and they reached Battleford safely.

In 1886 Dickens was in poor health and suffering from deafness. While in Ottawa, awaiting a decision on being invalided, he took a speaking engagement in Moline, Illinois, where he died of a heart attack. He was buried in the Rock Island Cemetery, Moline, Illinois.

Dickson Creek, Yukon (Lat: 61°07'00"N, Long: 138°56'00"W), a tributary of the Duke River, is named after Corporal Thomas Alexander Dickson, NWMP #2101.

Dickson served from April 9, 1888, until November 20, 1900, in "K" and "M" Divisions. On January 7, 1900, he arrested the infamous George O'Brien, who was wanted for the murders of three prospectors. O'Brien was hung at Dawson City, Yukon, on August 23, 1901. Dickson left the Force to become a bodyguard for Skookum Jim, who was an uncle of Dickson's Indian wife. He later ran a fish camp with two brothers[33] who had also served in the Force. Dickson then became a game warden at Kluane Lake. He died at Whitehorse on March 1, 1952.

Doak Court, Depot Division RCMP, Regina, Saskatchewan, is named in honour of Corporal William Andrew Doak, RNWMP #4396, Honour Roll #45.

See following entries.

Doak Crescent, Canadian Police College, Rockcliffe, Ontario, is named in honour of Corporal William Andrew Doak, RNWMP #4396, Honour Roll #45.

See following entry.

Doak Island, Nunavut (Lat: 68°23'00"N, Long: 111°27'00"W), in Coronation Gulf south of Victoria Island, was named in 1962 after Corporal William Andrew Doak, RNWMP #4396, Honour Roll #45.

Doak served from June 2, 1905, in "G" Division until his death on April 1, 1922, at the Tree River detachment, Northwest Territories. For 34 days in 1914 he had received extra pay of 50 cents per day while building barracks at Fort McPherson. On July 22, 1918, he barely survived a boat wreck in the Arctic with two other members.[34] In February 1922 he was holding two Cogmollock Inuit prisoners, Alikomiak and Tatamagama, in cells for the murders of five fellow Inuits involved in a feud. Alikomiak managed to escape. He retrieved the detachment rifle and shot and killed Corporal Doak, who was asleep in bed; he then shot and killed the Hudson's Bay Company factor, Otto Binder, as he walked past the detachment. Constable Daniel H. Woolams (#7802) was awakened by the shots and ran to the scene. He managed to subdue the escaping prisoner. Both prisoners were hanged for murder on February 1, 1924, at Herschel Island. Corporal Doak and Otto Binder were buried together at Tree River, Northwest Territories.

Donaldson Street, Prince Albert, Saskatchewan is named after Constable Samuel J. Donaldson, NWMP #288.

Donaldson served from July 15, 1876, until July 15, 1882, in what is now Saskatchewan and Alberta. When the Indian Department sent breeding cows to establish ranching stock for the band at the Duck Lake reserve, Chief Beardy had the cattle butchered to show his authority. On July 29, 1880, Superintendent William Herchmer (O.37) and six members went to the reserve to arrest the chief, but he refused to stand. Sub-Constable William Ramsay (#294) and Constable Harry Nash (#399) yanked him to his feet and arrested him. Other Indians began shooting over their heads. Constables Donaldson and John Carruthers (#174) arrested one of them, One Arrow. Constables Harold Ross (#383) and Alfred "Bull" Stewart (#400) arrested Cut Nose. They were then followed by about 200 shouting, threatening Indians back to the post.

After he left the Force, Donaldson ran a livery stable in Prince Albert. He then served for seventeen years as alderman and mayor of Prince Albert before being elected as a Member of the Legislative

Assembly. He also served in the First World War with the rank of lieutenant-colonel. He was buried in the South Hill Cemetery in Prince Albert.

Dubuc Crescent, Depot Division RCMP, Regina, Saskatchewan, is named in honour of Sergeant Louis Romeo Dubuc, RCMP #10982, Honour Roll #69.

Sergeant Dubuc served in the RCMP from August 19, 1931, until his death at Dundalk, Ireland, on September 27, 1941. He served in "D," "K," "C," and "G" Divisions and was a pilot in the Air Section. On November 20, 1939, with the recent outbreak of the Second World War, he was temporarily transferred to the ferry command of the Royal Canadian Air Force to move aircraft across the Atlantic to Great Britain. On September 27, 1941, he left Canada, flying a new Hudson bomber, with two other crew. They fought storms all the way across the Atlantic and then—low on fuel over Ireland—faced dense fog. When attempting to land at Dundalk, the aircraft struck some obstruction and crashed, killing the three crewmembers. Sergeant Dubuc was buried at Newry, North Ireland.

Dunne Road, Notch Hill, B.C., between Chase and Salmon Arm, is named after Staff Sergeant Timothy Herbert Dunne, NWMP #506 (Original Series), #9 (New Series).

Dunne served in the NWMP from July 21, 1876, until 1882, then reengaged in 1887 and served until January 16, 1890. For his first term of good service he was granted Land Warrant #0274. In 1886 he was one of a group of 23 former members to organize the NWMP Veterans' Association. In his later years he resided at Notch Hill off Blind Bay Road on Dunne Road, which was named after him. He died at the age of 68 on September 16, 1918, at Vancouver, B.C. He is buried in Ocean View Cemetery, Vancouver, B.C.

Dunning Crescent, Saskatoon, Saskatchewan, is named after Constable Robert Edward Dunning, NWMP and RNWMP #3936.

Dunning served from October 9, 1902, until 1905 in "F" Division. In 1905 he was hired as Saskatoon's constable, fire inspector, and engineer for the new steam pump that the fire department had just purchased. In 1906 these functions were split and he became the chief of police. In 1915 a judicial inquiry found Dunning guilty of condoning the fabrication of evidence, of protecting certain thieves and prostitutes, of not investigating some crimes, and of "undue" oppression of those prostitutes who refused to pay off the police. Chief Dunning resigned his office. Some local constables were fired as a result of this inquiry, and one was sentenced to jail. Dunning died January 3, 1958, at Prince Albert and is buried in the South Hill Cemetery, Prince Albert, Saskatchewan.

Dunning Street, Red Deer, Alberta, is named after Staff Sergeant Sydney James Dunning, NWMP #1228, an early resident of Red Deer.

He served from April 21, 1885, to April 20, 1902, with the NWMP. He briefly held the rank of sergeant-major but reverted to staff sergeant in 1900. By an order-in-council on November 13, 1902, he was granted a pension of $185.15 *per year* for injuries sustained in service.

Eastend, Saskatchewan

Eastend, Saskatchewan, takes its name from the old NWMP post that was established here in 1877. It was named Eastend because it was at the easterly extremity of the Cypress Hills.

Edgar Street, Fort Macleod, Alberta, is named after Constable John Charles Edgar, RNWMP #7329.

Edgar served in the Force from May 5, 1918, until January 13, 1919, at Depot and Fort Macleod, breaking horses. He was dismissed from the Force after being convicted in criminal court for theft.

He later worked for the Canadian Pacific Railway and in 1924 had a role in a silent film about the NWMP. Edgar took up farming and then worked for the Fort Macleod waterworks department. In December 1991, on his 90th birthday, "Charlie Edgar Street" in Fort Macleod was named after him. He died on April 14, 1997, and is buried in the Union Cemetery at Fort Macleod.

Edgar (J.C. Edgar Building), Fort Macleod, is also named after the foregoing member.

Elliott Avenue, Depot Division RCMP, Regina, Saskatchewan, is named in honour of Constable Frank Orlando Elliott, NWMP #973, Honour Roll #13.

Elliott was an American with seven years' experience in the U.S. cavalry in Montana before coming to Canada and joining the NWMP on November 17, 1883. He saw his first action north of the border in the North-West Rebellion with the battle of Cut Knife Hill on May 2, 1885. On May 14, 1885, he, Sergeant John Gordon (#670), and Constables Thomas McAllister (#544), Charles Allen (#619), Harry Storer (#776), Brenton Robertson (#865), Edmund Racey (#969), and William Spencer (#983) were on patrol south of Battleford when they were surprised by an Indian war party. Because of the shots being fired during the running battle back toward Battleford, Elliott's horse began bucking frantically. He either dismounted or fell off, and although he was surrounded he continued to fight, despite being wounded many times. He finally ran out of ammunition and was killed. The only other casualty of the remaining party was Constable Spencer, who was wounded. Constable Elliott was buried in North Battleford.

On May 26, 1885, his father, Reverend D.T. Elliott, wrote the Force from Lansingburgh, New York, enquiring of his son, as he had not had contact with him for eleven years.

Ellis Street, Red Deer, Alberta, is named after Constable Thomas Frederick Ellis, NWMP #1038.

Ellis served in the Force from June 9, 1884, to June 8, 1892, both at Fort Saskatchewan and Fort Normandeau. He saw action during the North-West Rebellion in the battle of Cut Knife Hill on May 2, 1885. After his discharge he became an early pioneer in the Red Deer area. He died July 15, 1909, and is buried in the Red Deer Cemetery.

Ellis Street, Red Deer, Alberta

Etuksit Point, Nunavut (Lat: 63°51'00"N, Long: 93°27'00"W), at Rankin Inlet on the western shore of Hudson Bay, is a name authorized in 1955 from information supplied by the RCMP, which named the point locally as "Etookshee," Inuktitut for "stone stretcher."

Fairman Point, Nunavut (Lat: 76°30'00"N, Long: 81°17'00"W), southeast Ellesmere Island, is named after Corporal Charles George Fairman, RCMP #9520.

Fairman served from October 9, 1920, to October 27, 1938, in "G" Division, then at Depot Division as an assistant riding instructor, and then finally in "E" Division.

While in the north, he was one of the original members at the Craig Harbour detachment (1922–1923). As the assistant riding instructor, he toured Argentina with the RCMP Musical Ride in 1931. While stationed in Vancouver in 1935, he was one of the "background Mounties" in the Metro-Goldwyn-Mayer movie production of *Rose Marie*.

He died of Bright's disease on October 30, 1942, at Hamilton, Ontario.

Farrar (Cape Farrar), Nunavut (Lat: 69°19'15"N, Long: 94°16'00"W), on the east side of Boothia Peninsula, is named after Sergeant Frederick Sleigh Farrar, Pm, RCMP#10607.

Farrar served from June 18, 1929, until his death February 8, 1955. During his 26 years in the Force he served in "F," "E," and "K" Divisions before spending many years as first mate on the RCMP schooner *St. Roch*.[35] He was among the first to circumnavigate the North American continent—through the Northwest Passage with Inspector Henry Larsen (O.347) as skipper, and later through the Panama Canal with Inspector (later Chief Superintendent) Kenneth W.N. Hall (O.372) as skipper. For his epic voyage through the Northwest Passage he was awarded the Polar Medal.

He authored a book about his experiences in the north entitled *Arctic Assignment*, published in 1955, shortly after his death. His latter service was at Headquarters, Ottawa, where he died while still in service. He was buried in the Force Cemetery, Depot Division.

Ferguson Lake, Nunavut (Lat: 69°25'00"N, Long: 105°15'00"W), on the south shore of Victoria Island, is named in honour of Constable Douglas Earl Ferguson, RCMP #15802, Honour Roll #109.

Constable Ferguson served in the RCMP from June 8, 1949, in "H" Division and then "G" Division until his early death on

September 17, 1954. He spent two years on Boothia Peninsula, Nunavut, and patrolled—perhaps twice—to the area of the lake named after him, before being transferred to the Cambridge Bay detachment in 1953.

On September 16, 1954, five men, including Constable Ferguson, left Cambridge Bay, Northwest Territories, on the Hudson's Bay Company boat *Kingalik*. Ferguson was using the advantage of this trip to complete some investigations at Bathurst Inlet. They anchored the first night at Cape Alexander, had dinner, and then most retired about 9:30 p.m. in the engine room.

Lorne Woodward, the director of the Royal Canadian Air Force Survival School at Cambridge Bay, was along for the ride. Sometime later he passed the hatchway to the engine room and upon glancing down at one of the sleeping men, was concerned about his appearance. He dropped down, shook the man, received no response, and realized something was wrong—most likely carbon monoxide poisoning. He called to the remaining member on deck and together they dragged the three unconscious men to a safe area where they began giving artificial respiration. Two regained consciousness, but Constable Ferguson had succumbed.

Later investigation found the exhaust pipe was defective, allowing leakage into the confined area of the warm engine room. Constable Ferguson was buried at Brockville, Ontario.

Ferguson Manor, 152nd Street, Surrey, B.C., is named in memory of Constable Amos Gordon Ferguson, MM, RNWMP and RCMP #5905.

Ferguson moved to B.C. from Ontario in 1909 and worked in logging camps. On August 22, 1914, he joined the Force, but left a year later to join the Lord Strathcona's Horse, Canadian Expeditionary Force, for service in the First World War. He was wounded twice and awarded the Military Medal. On his

Amos Ferguson Manor, Surrey, B.C.

return from overseas in April 1919, he rejoined the Force and served in "K" Division, and by 1922 he had attained the rank of sergeant. His career effectively ended on March 8, 1922, when he was charged in Orderly Room with "rendering false and misleading reports" to his officer commanding respecting an investigation. He was fined $30, demoted to constable, and ordered dismissed. He was dismissed from the Force on August 7, 1922.

He then moved to Vancouver and joined the Harbour Police. In 1932 he moved to the Provincial Gaol Service and worked at Oakalla Prison Farm, Burnaby, B.C., until his retirement in 1955. He was a life member of the Royal Canadian Legion, Branch 6, Cloverdale, B.C.

In 1951 he and his wife, Martha, purchased a substantial piece of property just above the present-day Guildford Golf Course at 152nd Street and 82nd Avenue in Surrey. It became a gathering place for their many friends, and their motto was soon "come early and stay late." At one of these gatherings it was decided to hold an annual reunion for members of the Lord Strathcona's Horse and to plant a memorial tree on the property to provide a final resting place for the ashes of former cavalry members and their wives. The Royal Canadian Legion traditionally carries out an annual memorial service to this day. Ferguson donated the land to the Royal Canadian Legion with the request that it be used for senior-citizen low-rental housing. The Zone 7 contingent of the Pacific Command, Royal Canadian Legion, pooled its assets and—with the help of Canadian Mortgage and Housing—erected a 51-suite manor. Legionnaires have first chance at 75 percent of the suites; the remaining 25 percent are for low-income seniors in exchange for 33 percent of their pension income.

The original memorial tree had to be moved to accommodate the Manor, so it was transplanted to the west side at the south end of a mini-parade ground. Amos Ferguson died in 1982, and his ashes were placed at the base of that tree.

Field Lake, Yukon (Lat: 62°40'00"N, Long: 131°03'00"W), one of four lakes at the junction of Ross and Prevost Rivers, was named in 1907 after Constable Poole Field, NWMP #3328, by Joseph Keele of the Geological Survey of Canada.

Field was born at Fort Garry, Manitoba, where his father was a Hudson's Bay Company trader. He worked his way west across the territories and eventually was caught up in the stampede of the Klondike gold rush, joining the NWMP August 1, 1898. He served in the Yukon until November 20, 1900, and under the terms then in place received a free discharge for serving two years in the Yukon. Later he became a trapper and fur trader with a trading post at nearby Ross River. He died at Vancouver, B.C., on April 22, 1948.

Fielder Point, Nunavut (Lat: 76°31'00"N, Long: 82°08'00"W), on the southeast coast of Ellesmere Island, is named after Corporal Leonard Frank Fielder, RCMP #9521.

Fielder was born in England. He served briefly with the London Metropolitan Police and then with the British Expeditionary Force in the First World War before coming to Canada.

He served in the Force from October 9, 1920, to August 31, 1947. During his career he served in Headquarters, "N," "G" (Aklavik, Baillie Island, and Craig Harbour), "K" (Edmonton), "M" (Herschel Island and Mayo), and "E" (Vancouver, Hazelton, and Vanderhoof) Divisions. In 1922 he was one of the original members to serve at the Craig Harbour detachment on Ellesmere Island.

He died March 30, 1970, at Toronto, Ontario.

Fitzgerald, Alberta (Lat: 59°52'00"N, Long: 111°36'00"W), a hamlet southeast of Fort Smith, is named after Inspector Francis Joseph Fitzgerald, NWMP and RNWMP O.156, Honour Roll #35.

See following entries.

Fitzgerald Lane, Depot Division, Regina, Saskatchewan, is named in honour of Inspector Francis Joseph Fitzgerald, NWMP and RNWMP O.156, Honour Roll #35.

Fitzgerald Settlement, Alberta (Lat: 59°51'00"N, Long: 111°36'00"W), is 339 kilometres north of Fort McMurray and adjacent to the hamlet of Fitzgerald, whose name changed from "Smith Landing" in 1915, honouring Inspector Francis Joseph Fitzgerald, NWMP and RNWMP O.156, Honour Roll #35.

Fitzgerald engaged with the NWMP as regimental #2218 on November 19, 1888, and saw service in what are now "F" and "K" Divisions. In 1902 he was selected for the contingent that travelled to England for the Coronation of King Edward VII.

Fitzgerald, Taylor, Kinney, and Carter gravesite—Fort McPherson, N.W.T.

He was promoted to commissioned ranks December 1, 1909, in the RNWMP as O.156 and soon after was transferred north to "G" Division.

On December 21, 1910, Fitzgerald, together with Special Constable (ex-Constable) Samuel Carter (#2127, Honour Roll #34), Constable George Francis Kinney (#4582, Honour Roll #36), and Constable Richard O'Hara Taylor (#4346, Honour Roll #37), left Fort

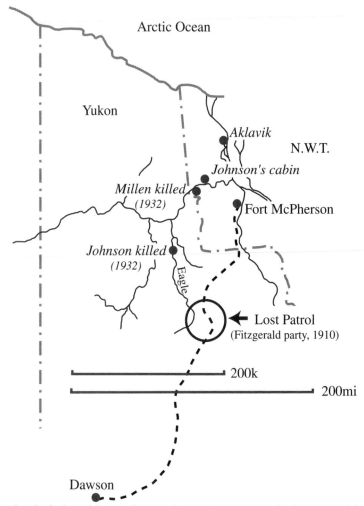

The dark dotted line indicates the mail route on which Fitzgerald and others became lost in 1910, an event that became known as the "Lost Patrol". See Millen Street *entry for the story of "The Mad Trapper", as is also depicted on this map*

McPherson, Northwest Territories, for Dawson City, Yukon, on the normal winter mail patrol of about 800 kilometres. By February 1911, word had spread of their now overdue patrol.

Corporal Dempster (#3193) was ordered to lead a search party from Dawson to find the missing members. With three dog teams of five dogs each, they headed for the Hart River Divide, which they knew the Fitzgerald party had to cross. Temperatures were very cold, and by March 12 they found one of the party's camps. The next day they found three more camps that were so close together it seemed apparent that the Fitzgerald party had turned to retrace its route to Fort McPherson. On March 16 they found a small cabin with abandoned equipment and cooked dog bones. Tracking was now easier for they were in forested terrain. On March 20 they found an abandoned cabin containing Fitzgerald's dispatch bag that held mail and money. More abandoned equipment was located the next day, followed by the discovery of two bodies—those of Constables Kinney and Taylor. Both lay emaciated in their eiderdown sleeping bags. In addition, Taylor had shot himself with his rifle. From all evidence, they had been starving and struggling to survive. At this camp they also found Fitzgerald's diary.

The next day, continuing toward Fort McPherson, the search party found the bodies of Fitzgerald and Carter by the remains of a fire. In Fitzgerald's pocket was a paper with a message written with char from their fire: "All money in despatch bag and bank, clothes, etc. I leave to my dearly beloved mother, Mrs. John Fitzgerald, Halifax. God bless all. F.J. Fitzgerald, RNWMP."

The bodies were carried back to Fort McPherson where they were buried. The resultant investigation concluded they met with severe conditions, became lost, had insufficient provisions, and used valuable time searching for the correct route once they realized they had missed the trail. Through the years since this misadventure occurred, it has been chronicled many times as the "Lost Patrol."

See also **Carter (Mount Carter)**, **Kinney (Mount Kinney)**, and **Dempster (Mount Dempster)** entries.

Fletcher Lake, Northwest Territories (Lat: 63°35'00"N, Long: 108°45'00"W), northeast of Great Slave Lake, was named in 1941 after Inspector George Frederick Fletcher, RNWMP and RCMP O.199.

Fletcher joined the Force November 20, 1903, as #4125 and first served in "K" Division. In the First World War he was accepted into the RNWMP "A" Squadron cavalry draft for service in France as Canadian Expeditionary Force #2684037. Following the war he returned to "K" Division; he was promoted to commissioned ranks on February 1, 1920, as O.199. He then went north, and as of 1925 was stationed at Fort Smith. On June 28 that year he lost all his effects in a fire at the detachment building.

He later served in "E," "O," "H," and "C" Divisions until his retirement November 21, 1938, when he moved to England where he was employed with the Bank of Montreal in London. He died on May 29, 1955, at Norfolk, England.

Fordham Lake, Saskatchewan (Lat: 57°39'00"N, Long: 103°13'00"W), adjacent to Nokomis Lake, is named after Constable Leonard Basil "Baz" Fordham, RCMP #12618.

"Baz" served in "F" and "K" Divisions from June 24, 1935, to August 31, 1939, when he purchased his discharge. With the outbreak of the Second World War, he shipped to England—at his own expense—to join the Royal Air Force.

He became a fighter pilot, and by 1940 he was flying Spitfires in the Battle of Britain. On July 17, 1941, his Spitfire was shot down by flak over the coast of France; he was killed when his aircraft crashed into the English Channel.

Forrest Creek, Yukon[36] (Lat: 65°04'30"N, Long: 135°57'00"W), a tributary to the Little Wind River, was named in 1905 after Constable Aubrey Ernest Forrest, RNWMP #3847.

Constable Forrest served from March 31, 1902, to March 2, 1907, in the Yukon. During those years he made numerous patrols by dog team between Dawson and Fort McPherson. On one occasion he carried the mail over this route—a distance of 800 kilometres— in nineteen days. He also saw service overseas in the First World War, but nothing is known of his later life.

Fort Constantine—See **Constantine**

Fort Herchmer—See **Herchmer**

Fort Macleod—See **Macleod**

Fort Saskatchewan—See **Saskatchewan**

Fort Sifton—See **Sifton**

Fort Steele—See **Steele**

Fort Walsh—See **Walsh**

Fraser Creek, Yukon (Lat: 60°18'30"N, Long: 137°19'48"W), a tributary to Alder Creek and Mush Lake, was named by a prospector to honour Surgeon[37] Samuel Martin Fraser, NWMP O.94.

In the summer of 1902 Mr. J.W. Smith discovered gold in this creek. He named the creek after Fraser, who, in addition to his primary duties as a doctor, was the mining recorder and customs officer at Dalton Post from 1901 to 1903.

Doctor Fraser was appointed assistant surgeon in the Force May 1, 1889, serving in "K" Division. He was promoted to surgeon and then served in both "M" Division (Yukon) and Headquarters, retiring on February 1, 1925. He died August 1, 1935, in London, Ontario.

French Crescent, Regina, Saskatchewan, is named after first permanent commissioner George Arthur French, NWMP O.1.[38]

See following entry.

French Lake, Saskatchewan (Lat: 55°38'00"N, Long: 104°37'00"W), ten kilometres from the hamlet of Missinipe, is named after first permanent commissioner of the Force, Commissioner George French, NWMP O.1, and after his nephew Inspector Francis Henry French, RNWMP and RCMP O.163.

French family members played a large part in the early years of the Force and were involved in several of its early historical events. They are introduced here to simplify the following narrative:

(a) Commissioner George Arthur French (O.1) was the first permanent commissioner from 1873 to 1876.

(b) Inspector John French (O.19), brother of (a), served from 1874 to 1883.

(c) Corporal John Poyntz French (#3031), son of (b), served from 1894 to 1901.

(d) Inspector Francis Henry French (#4355, O.163), son of (b), served from 1905 to 1924.

(e) Sergeant Dominick James French (#19345), great-grandson of (a), served from 1956 to 1960 and 1966 to 1979.

Commissioner French was born in Ireland and came to Canada to serve with the British army in the Royal Artillery from 1862 to 1864. When the British army units were withdrawn, he transferred to the Canadian militia, and by 1873 was an inspector of artillery. He was in this post when on October 16, 1873, he was appointed the commissioner of the newly formed NWMP. He led the March West in 1874 and began the opening of necessary posts across western

George French

Canada. All was not well, however, for in 1876 the Privy Council found that "conditions of the Force are unsatisfactory and reform required in command; services no longer required." French appealed, and the order-in-council was amended to "resigned." He left the Force July 22, 1876, and received a commission in the British army. He was in Queensland by 1883, in India in 1895, and in New South Wales in 1899. In 1900 he was promoted to major-general and retired in 1902. He died July 7, 1921, in London, England.

In 1874, at Commissioner French's request, his younger brother Inspector John French (O.19) came to Canada from Ireland, where he had been a captain in the Irish militia. Commissioner French also requested that John be appointed a sub-inspector in the Force. John left the Force in 1883 to farm in the Qu'Appelle Valley, but then promptly volunteered again with the outbreak of the North-West Rebellion in 1885. He was appointed in the militia as captain and raised a mounted troop known as "French's Scouts." He was killed in action on May 12, 1885, at Batoche.

Constable John Poyntz French, DSO, joined the NWMP (#3031) in 1894 to serve at Calgary, Gleichen, High River, and Banff. In 1898 he was transferred to the Yukon, where men were needed for the great Klondike gold rush, and served under Superintendent Sam Steele.[39] In 1899 he was transferred to Depot Division and promoted to corporal. He was granted a free discharge in 1901 to join the newly formed South African Constabulary, once again under the command of Steele. He returned to Canada in 1906. In the First World War he served with the Princess Patricia's Canadian Light Infantry as lieutenant and was awarded the Distinguished Service Order for his part in the battle of Vimy Ridge. Subsequently, he suffered considerably from being gassed in a later battle.

Francis Henry French, ISO, a nephew of Commissioner French, joined the RNWMP on April 6, 1905, as #4355. He was promoted to commissioned ranks on November 1, 1910, as an inspector (O.163), and in 1912 he was transferred from Depot Division to The Pas, Manitoba. He served until December 23, 1924, when he was invalided to pension. In 1918 his investigation into a murder case involved what became the longest dog team patrol in the history of the Force.

In 1909 an American, Harry Radford, journeyed to Fort Smith, Northwest Territories, after having obtained official permission to kill a wood buffalo for scientific purposes. A Canadian, Tom Street, joined him. They left Fort Smith in 1911 and were next heard of in 1912 when they reached Bathurst Inlet. Later, rumours were heard that Inuit "out on the ice" had murdered "two whites." The Force launched an investigation; Inspector Walter Beyts (O.161)[40] was sent north in 1914 to Chesterfield Inlet, Hudson Bay. His party experienced extreme weather conditions, so it was not until 1915 that this patrol established a base camp on Baker Lake. Difficult weather conditions and a scarcity of caribou prevented them from making further patrols.

In 1916 Inspector French came to relieve Inspector Beyts, who was ill. Sergeant-Major (later Assistant Commissioner) Thomas Caulkin (#4557) and four Inuit with twenty dogs joined French. They left Baker Lake on March 21, 1917, encountering extreme cold. On arriving at Bathurst, they were able to confirm that Radford and Street had been murdered. They were now required to continue northwest to Bernard Harbour to continue their investigation. Subsequently satisfying themselves that the killings had been committed in self-defence, French, Caulkin, and the patrol party returned to Baker Lake, arriving on January 29, 1918, after ten months and 8,292 kilometres by dog team. For this trek, French was awarded the Imperial Service Order and Caulkin was awarded the King's Police Medal.

During the First World War, in 1918, French served as a lieutenant in "B" Squadron cavalry draft of the Canadian Expeditionary Force in Siberia. By the time they reached Siberia, the war had ended, so after a few months—in May 1919—this Force returned to Canada. Following his retirement in 1924, French sold life insurance in Melville, Saskatchewan. He died March 30, 1961, at Regina, Saskatchewan, and was buried in the Force Cemetery at Depot Division.

The great-grandson of Commissioner French, Constable James French (#19345), served from 1956 to 1960—first in Nova Scotia and then in the Northwest Territories. Near the end of this northern posting in 1960, he and Corporal (later Staff Sergeant) Robert Milmine (#15293) arrested the murderer of Constable Colin Lelliott (#19731, Honour Roll #100).[41] He reengaged with the Force in 1966 and served to 1979 in Manitoba, retiring as a sergeant.

Fyfe (Mount Fyfe) (1,461 m), Yukon (Lat: 65°17'00"N, Long: 136°52'00"W), on the east side of the Hart River near the route of the Dawson–McPherson patrol, was named in 1973 after Constable Jerry F. Fyfe, RNWMP #4937.

Fyfe served from July 1909 to December 12, 1912, when he purchased his discharge in the Yukon. In 1911 he accompanied Corporal Dempster in the search for the "Lost Patrol."

See also **Dempster (Mount Dempster)** and **Fitzgerald Settlement** entries.

Gagnon Lake, Northwest Territories (Lat: 61°58'00"N, Long: 110°23'00"W), just north of the Alberta–Saskatchewan border, is named after Deputy Commissioner Henry Albert Royal Gagnon, RCMP O.213.

Henry Albert Royal Gagnon

During the First World War, Gagnon served as a major in the 12th Battalion, Canadian Expeditionary Force. He was serving in the Dominion Police when it was amalgamated with the RNWMP, and then the name was changed to the RCMP on February 1, 1920. He was taken into the Force at the commissioned rank of inspector.

He first served at Depot Division and "E," then in "G," "F," and "C" as a commanding officer, and finally at Headquarters in Ottawa as a deputy commissioner. He died while still serving on November 19, 1947.

In 1943, during the Second World War, he was second in charge of security under Assistant Commissioner Vernon A.M. Kemp (O.207) at the first Quebec conference between British Prime Minister Winston Churchill and U.S. President Franklin Roosevelt.

His father, Superintendent Severe Gagnon (O.20), also served in the NWMP from 1874 to 1901. He took part in the 1874 March West and in the construction of Fort Saskatchewan[42] in 1875. Father and son are buried side by side in Notre Dame des Neiges Cemetery, Montreal, Quebec.

Gamman Drive, Canadian Police College, Rockcliffe, Ontario, is named in honour of Constable Alexander Gamman, RNWMP and RCMP #5816, Honour Roll #86.

Constable Gamman served from June 1, 1914, in "F," "K," and "C" Divisions until his death May 26, 1950. On May 25, 1950,

Constable Gammon, unarmed but in uniform, was walking to lunch on Dorchester Street in Montreal, Quebec. Suddenly the manager of a bank ran onto the street and shouted "Hold-up!" before firing a shot with his bank revolver at a running man. Gamman chased and tackled the individual, who then shot him, broke free, and escaped. Gamman died of his wound the following day. The suspect, Thomas Rossler, was tracked across Canada until June 17, 1950, when he was arrested near Scobey, Montana. He had a wound in his thigh and carried a loaded .32 semi-automatic pistol. He was promptly deported. Rossler was identified in twelve robberies in the Montreal area and also in Gamman's murder. He was found guilty of murder and hanged December 15, 1950. Constable Gamman was buried in the Union Cemetery, Calgary, Alberta.

Garde Lake, Northwest Territories (Lat: 62°50'00"N, Long: 106°15'00"W), between Reliance and Boyd Lake, was named in 1947 from an RCMP sketch map of a patrol made between Reliance and Boyd Lake in 1935. The significance of the name is unknown as no member can be matched to a similar name.

Garrett Avenue, Depot Division RCMP, Regina, Saskatchewan, is named in honour of Constable George Knox Garrett, NWMP #852, Honour Roll #7.

Constable Garrett seems like an average young member of the era in which he served. He joined the Force July 4, 1882, and soon found himself in the dreaded Orderly Room. On August 9, 1882, he appeared before Inspector Griesbach at Qu'Appelle, charged with neglect of duty, but was let off with an admonishment. On March 27, 1885, he was among the 53 men under Superintendent Crozier involved in the first skirmish of the North-West Rebellion. Three members were killed: Constable Thomas J. Gibson (#1003, Honour Roll #6), Constable George P. Arnold (#1065, Honour Roll #8), and Constable Garrett. Eight members were wounded. Garrett was buried at Prince Albert, Saskatchewan, in St Mary's Cemetery.

See also **Griesbach Street** and **Crozier Lake** entries.

George (Doctor George House), Innisfail, Alberta, is named after Doctor Henry George, a former NWMP physician. In 1977 his home was registered as a provincial historic resource known as the "Doctor George House."

See following entry.

Doctor George House, Innisfail

George Crescent, Red Deer, Alberta, is named after Doctor Henry George, a former NWMP physician (as above).

While never a member of the NWMP, Doctor George worked on contract for the Force and carried the title of Acting Assistant Surgeon, which equated him to officer status within the Force.

Gladys Lake, B.C. (Lat: 59°54'00"N, Long: 132°52'00"W), near the B.C.-Yukon border, is named after the youngest daughter of Commissioner Aylesworth Bowen Perry, NWMP, RNWMP, and RCMP O.44. He chose the name for the lake in the 1880s, when he was stationed in this district.

See also **Perry River** entry.

Gleadow Road, Canadian Police College, Rockcliffe, Ontario, is named in honour of Constable Norman Alfred Gleadow, RCMP #11046, Honour Roll #63.

See following entry.

Gleadow Road, Depot Division RCMP, Regina, Saskatchewan, is named in honour of Constable Norman Alfred Gleadow, RCMP #11046, Honour Roll #63.

Gleadow served from September 11, 1931, until his death October 11, 1939. At Esterhazy, Saskatchewan, on October 10, 1939, Constable Gleadow arrested Ernest Flook for a series of burglaries. The following day he returned Flook to his home to search for evidence. While Gleadow was looking in a suitcase, Flook first struck him over the head with a hammer, then shot him twice with a .22

rifle before fleeing in the police car. Flook's sister called the police. The car was tracked for some 27 kilometres until it stopped. When the police approached it, Flook took his own life. Constable Gleadow was given a military funeral and was buried in the Regina Cemetery.

Goodwin House, Saskatchewan Landing Provincial Park, is named after Constable Frank Goodwin, NWMP #958.

From 1880 to 1881 Goodwin was employed with the Union Steamship Company in South Africa. He then served in the Force from September 6, 1883, until December 17, 1885, in "F" Division, seeing action in the North-West Rebellion of 1885 at the battle of Cut Knife Hill on May 2 of that year.

From 1885 to 1893 he worked for the Canadian Pacific Railway, and then—from 1893 to 1924—he ranched near Swift Current, Saskatchewan. Goodwin completed an impressive two-storey stone house in 1900, and it serves today as the Saskatchewan Landing Provincial Park's Visitor's Centre, which displays early area history. It is a prominent landmark on the southern edge of the valley just north of Swift Current. Constable Goodwin died in Victoria, B.C., on October 11, 1934.

Graburn Campsite, Alberta, in the Cypress Hills Provincial Park at Elkwater (southeast corner of Alberta), is named after Constable Marmaduke Graburn, NWMP #335, Honour Roll #3.

See following entries.

Graburn Coulee or Gap, Alberta (Lat: 49°38'00"N, Long: 110°01'00"W), 20 kilometres east of Elkwater, is named after Constable Marmaduke Graburn, NWMP #335, Honour Roll #3.

Graburn Creek, Alberta (Lat: 49°38'00"N, Long: 110°01'00"W), in the southeast corner of Alberta, is named after Constable Marmaduke Graburn, NWMP #335, Honour Roll #3.

Graburn Road, Cypress Hills Provincial Park at Elkwater (southeast corner of Alberta), is named after Constable Marmaduke Graburn, NWMP #335, Honour Roll #3.

Graburn Walk, Depot Division RCMP, Regina, Saskatchewan, is named in honour of Constable Marmaduke Graburn, NWMP #335, Honour Roll #3.

Constable Graburn served from June 9, 1879, until his death November 17, 1879. On that day, Graburn was on patrol a short distance from Fort Walsh, and when he did not return as expected, a search was launched. Sergeant Robert McCutcheon (#458, Original Series) located Graburn's body, finding that he had been shot in the back of the head. He was the first member of the NWMP to be murdered and was buried at Fort Walsh.

Suspicion immediately fell on a local Indian, Star Child, since Graburn had exchanged words earlier with him over his continual begging at Sick Horse Camp near Fort Walsh. In addition, Star Child was absent from the Indian camp on the morning Graburn was shot. Finally, Star Child was arrested in 1881 near Fort Macleod and was charged with the murder, but he was acquitted for lack of evidence. He was arrested later for horse theft, sentenced to five years in Stony Mountain Penitentiary, and died there. On July 29, 1882, the federal government awarded $500 and Graburn's Land Warrant #0484 to his mother.

See also the **Walsh Trail** and **Macleod Island** entries.

Grassy Lake, Alberta, between Taber and Bow Island, came to be known as such in 1874. As Jerry Potts led the first contingent of NWMP across the area, a member pestered him with countless questions. When asked if water could be obtained in a slough that was covered with reeds, Potts replied, "The only thing you can get off a slough in August is grass."

See also **Potts (Jerry Potts Street)**.

Grier Avenue, Calgary, Alberta, is believed to be named after Constable David Johnson Grier, NWMP #226.

Grier was in the second contingent to Fort Macleod, serving from June 5, 1877, until June 5, 1880. For his three years' good service he received Land Warrant #0367. He began farming and was one of the first to raise wheat in Alberta. He served as mayor of Macleod and, in the partnership of Swinarton and Grier, held ownership of three hotels. He died on February 1, 1935, and is buried in the Union Cemetery, Fort Macleod.

His nephew, Constable J.H. Grier (#9822), also served in the Force from 1921 to 1927.

Griesbach Armories, Edmonton, Alberta, is named after Major-General William Antrobus Griesbach, son of Superintendent Arthur Henry Griesbach, NWMP O.32.

See the following entries.

Griesbach Island, Alberta (Lat: 53°40'25"N, Long: 112°50'30"W), fourteen kilometres from Bruderheim, is named after Superintendent Arthur Henry Griesbach, NWMP O.32.

Griesbach (Mount Griesbach) (2,682 m), Alberta (Lat: 53°03'00"N, Long: 118°24'00"W), eighteen kilometres from Yellowhead Pass, is named after Major-General William Antrobus Griesbach, the son of Superintendent Arthur Henry Griesbach, NWMP O.32.

Griesbach Siding, Alberta, eight kilometres southeast of Fort Saskatchewan, is named after Major-General William Antrobus Griesbach, son of Superintendent Arthur Henry Griesbach, NWMP O.32.

William chose an army career and received many honours. He was promoted to major-general and in 1940 was inspector general for western Canada. He was buried beside his father in the family plot at the Edmonton Cemetery.

Griesbach Street, Edmonton, Alberta, is named after Superintendent Arthur Henry Griesbach, NWMP #1 (Original Series), O.32.

In 1913, Edmonton's streets changed from being named to being numbered, so Griesbach Street became 105A Avenue.

Griesbach Street, Fort Saskatchewan, Alberta, is named after Superintendent Arthur Henry Griesbach, NWMP #1 (Original Series), O.32.

Superintendent Griesbach served from the inception of the NWMP on September 29, 1873 until his retirement November 30, 1903, when—by order-in-council—he was granted a life pension of $1,200 per annum.

He had previously served in the 15th Hussars and the Cape Mounted Rifles in South Africa. In 1870 he took part in the Red River Expedition. On May 20, 1875, he became the fifth member in the Force to be promoted to the commissioned ranks. From 1883 to 1901 he was the officer commanding Fort Saskatchewan District. On retirement, he moved to Chemainus, B.C., where he died November 21, 1916. He was buried in the family plot at Edmonton Cemetery.

Griffin Bay, Regina, Saskatchewan, is named after Corps Sergeant Major George Frederick "Tim" Griffin, RNWMP and RCMP #5426.

Tim served for twelve years in the 18th Hussars before joining the Force on August 12, 1912. Due to his previous experience he was posted to Depot Division as a riding instructor. He spent his service at Depot, then "N" Division, and then back to Depot until his retirement on August 11, 1941.

In the First World War he served in the "A" Squadron cavalry draft to France as Canadian Expeditionary Force #2684291. As a riding instructor he made several tours with the Musical Ride, including the International Horse Show in London, England, in 1930 and the tour to St. Louis, Missouri, in 1936. In his last year of service he was given leave of absence to go to Hollywood, California, as a "technical advisor" on the movie *North West Mounted Police*. The movie held its premiere at Regina.

Tim retired to the West Coast and died at Surrey, B.C., on April 8, 1977. He was buried in the Force Cemetery at Depot Division.

Gunns Creek, Alberta (Lat: 55°26'00"N, Long: 117°01'00"W), which flows west into the Little Smoky River 42 kilometres southeast of Valleyview, is named after Constable Charles Thomas Gunn, RNWMP #6064.

Gunn served briefly in the Force from September 3, 1914, to September 2, 1915, at Battleford, Saskatchewan. He then lived at Sounding Lake, and in 1931 he moved to the area of the creek that bears his name.

Guyader Lake, Saskatchewan (Lat: 54°38'00"N, Long: 102°54'00"W), north of Cumberland Lake, is named after Constable Michael Joseph Guyader, RCMP #14652.

Guyader served from March 15, 1946, until January 15, 1968, in "B," "H," "HQ.," and "D" Divisions. He died on June 14, 1986, at Winnipeg, Manitoba. His son, Corporal M.O. Guyader (#34668), also served in the RCMP from 1978 to 1999.

Half Way House, Saskatchewan, is located about halfway along the trail that ran north from Swift Current to Battleford.

The NWMP built a station here, including a stable and log house. The police also had a special name for their station, 60 Mile Bush, because it was centred in the bush that actually spread for 60 miles (96 kilometres).

Hamilton (Paddy Hamilton Peninsula), Nunavut, located in Glacier Strait near King Edward Point, was named on July 29, 1975, by the Canadian Permanent Committee on geographical names to commemorate the service of Sergeant Robert Warren "Paddy" Hamilton, RCMP #10196.

Paddy, as he was known, served in the Royal Ulster Constabulary from 1921 to 1926 before he came to Canada and joined the RCMP on May 19, 1926. He served until November 30, 1952, spending 17 of his 26 years in the north.

During 1931 to 1932, along with Sergeant Stallworthy (#6316), he completed a 65-day dog team patrol of about 2,253 kilometres, searching for the Dr. Krueger Expedition. From the Bache detachment, they crossed Ellesmere Island, circled Exel Heiberg Island, and then returned. They found a record left at Peary's Cairn on the cape. At that time, this was the most northerly patrol completed by the Force.

On September 9, 1940, when stationed at Pangnirtung, Paddy married Dorothy Boehmer. The ceremony was performed by the Reverend Fleming on the supply ship *Nascopie* while at sea near Thule, Greenland—another first, as the most northerly marriage ceremony in Canada.

On July 21, 1947, he was on transfer with Inspector Albert Parsons (O.341), Corporal William Stewart (#10416), Constable Arthur Bates (#13272), and Constable Murray Cottell (#14554) aboard the *Nascopie*. They lost all their personal belongings when the ship was wrecked on a reef.

Paddy died at Ottawa, Ontario, on December 26, 1974, and was buried in the Force Cemetery at Depot Division.

Harbottle (Mount Harbottle), Yukon (Lat: 65°48'00"N, Long: 138°20'00"W), south of the Whitestone River, is named after Constable Francis Edmond Harbottle, NWMP #3788.

Harbottle served in the Yukon from May 15, 1901, to July 13, 1905, before leaving to join the Canadian Customs Service. The only information found regarding his service was his appearance before Superintendent Snyder in Orderly Room in November 1901, when he was fined five dollars for "being asleep on sentry duty," and his final posting being at White Pass Summit. He died on October 19, 1943, at Whitehorse, Yukon.

Heacock Road, Edmonton, Alberta, is named after Sergeant Kenneth Ernest Heacock, RCMP #11703.

He joined the Alberta Provincial Police in 1917 and served until the absorption of that Force by the RCMP on April 1, 1932. He continued to serve in Alberta until being medically invalided August 11, 1945. He died at Edmonton, Alberta, on January 31, 1964.

Helmsing Street, Regina, Saskatchewan, is named after Constable Walter Hewitt Helmsing, RCMP #12776.

Helmsing served in the Force from July 16, 1935, to July 31, 1946, in "F" Division, Depot, and "N" Division. During the Second World War he took time out from the Force to serve in the Royal Canadian Air Force from 1939 to 1943.

Following his service in the Force, he was employed as a salesman with Canadian Motors, Regina, and then in 1958 with the Sheriff's Service in Regina.

He died on February 12, 1984, at Regina.

Herchmer, Manitoba (Lat: 57°22'13"N, Long: 94°10'10"W), a Canadian National Railway–Hudson's Bay Railway route station between Silcox and O'Day on the Owl River, was established in 1928 and named after Commissioner Laurence William Herchmer, NWMP O.72.

See following entries.

Herchmer Elementary School, 1132 McTavish Street, Regina, Saskatchewan, is named after Commissioner Laurence William Herchmer, NWMP O.72.

Herchmer (Fort Herchmer), Dawson City, Yukon, is a restored fort named after Commissioner Laurence William Herchmer, NWMP O.72.

Herchmer Pass, B.C. (Lat: 56°35'00"N, Long: 124°09'00"W), west of Fort St. John, was named—by the Peace-Yukon Trail Party (1905-07)—after Commissioner Laurence William Herchmer, NWMP O.72.

Fort Herchmer, Dawson City, Yukon

Herchmer Street, Regina, Saskatchewan, is named after Commissioner Laurence William Herchmer, NWMP O.72.

Herchmer grew up in Kingston, Ontario, where his father was a childhood friend of John A. Macdonald, who later became prime minister of Canada. He attended the Royal Military College in England, and in 1858 was commissioned with Her Majesty's 46th

Regiment, in which he served for four years in India and Ireland. He then returned to Canada and was appointed commissary for the Boundary Commission, surveying the 49th parallel boundary between Canada and the U.S. Later, he was appointed inspector of Indian Agencies. It is not surprising that he was appointed on April 1, 1886, to be the fifth permanent commissioner of the NWMP.

In 1888 he established a school for NWMP dependants in a vacant area of the Regina Barracks. Later, a building was acquired in downtown Regina. In 1930 the Regina School Board opened a new Herchmer School that has continued to the present day (2002).

In 1892 Herchmer faced the first Commission of Inquiry into the operations of the Force, brought on by numerous complaints about him from among his officers. Some of these complaints were undoubtedly spurred on by his appointment of his brother William Macauley Herchmer (O.37)—over several officers senior to him— to the rank of assistant commissioner. Another brother, Staff Sergeant George Herchmer (#359 Original Series, #14 New Series) had also served earlier. The Commission of Inquiry concluded that "the commissioner was ill-tempered and over-zealous, but that was no cause to dismiss him."

Herchmer served to August 1, 1900, and was then appointed as commanding officer of the Canadian Mounted Rifles in the Boer War. Following his retirement he moved to Vancouver, B.C., where in 1913 he became a charter member of the "A" Division, RNWMP Veterans' Association. He died February 17, 1915, at Vancouver, B.C., and was buried in Mountain View Cemetery, Vancouver.

Herring-Cooper Way, Edmonton, Alberta, is named after Staff Sergeant William "Barney" Herring-Cooper, NWMP #593.

Herring-Cooper joined the NWMP on July 4, 1881, and served until July 3, 1893. He took part in the North-West Rebellion of 1885. He served at both Fort Macleod and Fort Saskatchewan, and after his service in the Force, became a provincial licence inspector. In 1897, at a special ceremony given in his honour by Indian bands from Stony Plain, Hobbema, and Onion Lake, he was made chief of the Crees and given the title of "Mekupuckiwan." He died on January 28, 1930, at Fort McMurray and is buried at Edmonton, Alberta.

Herronton, Alberta (Lat: 50°38'00"N, Long: 113°25'00"W), a hamlet 56 kilometres southeast of Calgary, is named after Sub-Constable John Herron, NWMP #378 (Original Series).

Herron served in the Force from November 27, 1874, to May 7, 1878, mainly as a blacksmith in present-day southern Alberta. He attended the signing of Treaty Number Seven on September 22, 1877. For his three years of good service, he was awarded Land Warrant #0139.

To explain his next adventures we must digress. In 1878 Prime Minister Macdonald selected Captain John Stewart as organizer of the Princess Louise Dragoon Guards to escort visiting dignitaries in western Canada. Herron became his sergeant-major. With the threat of the North-West Rebellion looming in 1885, and with only a scattered few NWMP in the west, Stewart sought to form the Rocky Mountain Rangers[43] as a volunteer militia to supplement the NWMP at Fort Macleod. Approval was given for three troops, and when the rebellion broke out, they were ordered to report to General Strange. Several former members of the NWMP promptly joined, including James Christie (#118), William Reid (#102), James Schofield (#154), John Bray (#2), Charles Kettles (#184), Edward Larkin (#281), Alfred Lynch-Staunton (#241), Samuel Sharpe (#206), and, of course, John Herron. As the NWMP left the Macleod area for the rebellion, the Rocky Mountain Rangers assumed many of their patrol duties. With the end of the rebellion, the Rocky Mountain Rangers were disbanded, and all 113 members received the Northwest Medal in addition to the rebellion scrip, which was redeemable for either $80 or 320 acres of land.

From 1904 to 1911, Herron served as a Conservative Member of Parliament for the Macleod area and continued to ranch at Pincher Creek. In his later years he composed the poem "A Veteran Mountie's Soliloquy," which was published in the RCMP Veterans' Association magazine *Scarlet and Gold*. He died at Pincher Creek, Alberta, on August 20, 1936, and was buried there.

See also the **Bray Lake** and **Kettles Creek** entries.

High River, Alberta, was originally known as "Spitze," a Blackfoot word meaning "tall" or "high timber."

Jerry Potts, scout and interpreter for the NWMP, shortened the name to High River.

See also **Potts (Jerry Potts Street)**.

Hobbs Lake, Saskatchewan (Lat: 54°32'00"N, Long: 102°50'00"W), north of Cumberland Lake, is named after Sergeant Leonard John Hobbs, RCMP #10363.

Hobbs served from November 12, 1927, until January 12, 1949, in "F," "D," "G," and Depot Divisions. During his service he authored *Police Manual on Arrests and Searches*. He died at Nanaimo, B.C., on January 11, 1987.

Hockin, Manitoba (Lat: 55°16'35"N, Long: 97°49'50"W), a Canadian National Railway–Hudson's Bay Railway route station at mile 179 from The Pas and ten kilometres from La Perouse, is named in honour of Corporal Charles Home Sterling Hockin, NWMP #3106, Honour Roll #23.

See following entry.

Hockin Avenue, Depot Division RCMP, Regina, Saskatchewan, is named in honour of Corporal Charles Home Sterling Hockin, NWMP #3106, Honour Roll #23.

Hockin had previously served for twelve years in the British army and left as a captain in the 44th Essex Regiment. He was the eldest son of Admiral Charles Hockin. He served in the NWMP from October 12, 1894, until his death on May 29, 1897.

In October 1895 a young Cree Indian known as Almighty Voice killed a cow, which set off a violent chain reaction. He was arrested on One Arrow Reserve near Batoche, Northwest Territories (now Saskatchewan), and then taken to the Duck Lake detachment to appear before the Indian agent, who was also Justice of the Peace. He was sentenced to one month's imprisonment but escaped that very same night. A few days later, Sergeant Colebrook (#605) tracked him down. As Colebrook advanced to arrest him, Almighty Voice shot and killed him.

By chance, Constable Charles Tennant (#1880) was the first on the scene; he attempted to trail the assailant, but was unsuccessful. For several months, despite many search patrols and a reward of $100, no trace was found of the fugitive. Almighty Voice simply broke all contact with the Indian community. Then in May 1897, while chasing a horse thief, a Métis scout blundered upon Almighty Voice with two other Indians. Whirling to flee on his horse, the scout was wounded by a quick shot. He rode as hard as he could to spread the word to the Duck Lake detachment. Advice was promptly passed to the district headquarters at Prince Albert.

In response, Inspector "Bronco Jack" Allan (O.55) set out from Prince Albert with ten members and one volunteer civilian, Mr. Grundy. They rode through the night some 125 kilometres to the Minnichinas Hills, where the fugitives had been seen. Early the next morning they spotted the three moving behind a heavily treed bluff and believed they had them trapped. Allan rode toward the bluff, but he had not gone far before a shot wounded him in his right arm, knocking him from his horse. He drew his revolver, shot back, and wounded his attacker in the ankle. Allan tried to crawl away, but was suddenly confronted—at gunpoint—by an Indian demanding that he throw his cartridge belt to him. Allan sensed they were low on ammunition or he would have been shot again, so he loudly refused. Just then, Constable William Hume (#2259) fired some well-aimed shots, and the Indian withdrew. By this time, Sergeant Charles Raven (#1128) had also been wounded.

The wounded were attended as best as possible while others renewed the attack. A fire was started around the bluff, but the fresh spring foliage would not easily ignite and refused to spread. Now the remaining members, under command of Corporal Hockin, attempted to crawl into the dense undergrowth. The fugitives were well concealed in a dug-out pit, however, and in a hail of gunfire, Mr. Grundy was killed. Hockin and Constable John Randolph Kerr (#3040, Honour Roll #22) were also mortally wounded. Constable Andrew O'Kelly (#3052) managed to drag Hockin to a place of cover. He shot one of the assailants at close quarters while having his own spur shot off.

At sundown, eight additional members arrived. The decision was made to withdraw to a safe distance and maintain a close watch to prevent escape. In the meantime, they waited for reinforcements, as they had managed to keep headquarters reasonably up-to-date by telegraph.

A special train from Regina brought Superintendent John McIllree (O.13) with 26 men and a nine-pound field gun. They arrived about the same time as another contingent from Prince Albert with a seven-pound gun. By now, a small crowd of Indians and settlers had gathered on the nearby hills to watch. Almighty Voice's mother arrived and began a death chant for her son.

Members began blasting the bluff with the field guns until return rifle fire ceased. They then moved in and found the three fugitives dead. The Indian men were buried on One Arrow Reserve. Both Hockin and Kerr were buried in St. Mary's Cemetery at Prince Albert.

See also **Colebrook Place** and **Kerr Road** entries.

Hoey Road, Canadian Police College, Rockcliffe, Ontario, is named in honour of Third Class Constable John Terrance Hoey, RCMP #20307, Honour Roll #81.

Hoey joined the Force in January 1958 and was only three weeks out of training when he met his death on November 6, 1958. A waitress at the Harbourview Café in Botwood, Newfoundland, reported that the café was unexpectedly closed when she reported for work. Constables Hoey and A.A. Bowen (#19393) drove to the scene. They could get no response from within, yet they knew that the owner, Tom Ling, lived in the building.

They returned to the detachment office and discussed the matter with Constable L. Robert Healey (#18846), and then all three returned to the café. Again, there was no answer to their knocks. Fearing some tragedy, they skillfully opened a side window without damaging it, entered, and went to the living area. The door was barricaded, but they could hear incoherent talk from within. Without warning there was a shot through the door, and Constable Hoey was killed. A second shot was heard—Ling had committed suicide.

Constable Hoey's body was returned home and buried in St. Peter's Cemetery, Peterborough, Ontario.

J.J. Hoey

Hogans Trail, Hawke's Bay, Newfoundland (Lat: 50°36'00"N, Long: 57°10'00"W), inland from Daniel's Harbour on the west coast of Newfoundland, is named after Newfoundland Ranger and later RCMP #16167, John Hogan.

Hogan joined the Newfoundland Rangers on February 10, 1941. On May 8, 1943, he hitched a ride on a Royal Canadian Air Force flight from Goose Bay, Labrador, to Gander, Newfoundland. Along the way the plane filled with smoke, and the pilot instructed that the passengers bail out. Hogan parachuted down safely. The following day he came upon Corporal Butt of the Royal Air Force, who had also been on the flight but was now too badly injured to travel (both were presumed dead at that time). Hogan remained with Butt, and they managed to survive on berries and the rabbits Hogan was able to snare with his shoelaces. After 52 days they were found at West Lake. In 1944 Hogan was awarded the King's Police Medal for his actions.

In 1949 Newfoundland joined Confederation to become the tenth Canadian province, and on August 1, 1950, the RCMP took over the provincial policing of the majority of Newfoundland. When the Force absorbed the Newfoundland Rangers, Hogan became a member. He remained with the RCMP in Newfoundland until his retirement March 19, 1967, as the St. John's Sub-Division non-commissioned officer, with the rank of staff sergeant. He died on April 19, 1977, at St. John's, Newfoundland.

Hollies Coulee, Beaver Creek–Spring Point district (Lat: 50°20'00"N, Long: 114°20'00"W) in southwest Alberta, is named after Sub-Constable John Hollies, NWMP #463 (Original Series).

Hollies served in the Force from May 24, 1875, until May 24, 1878. For his three years' good service he received Land Warrant #0172. In 1878 he had a small ranch at Hollies Coulee in southwest Alberta. Later on he managed the Queen's Hotel in Fort Macleod. From there he went on to have a trading post at Olson Creek in the Porcupine Hills, and then he became a clerk for the Indian Department at the Peigan Reserve. He died in 1912.

Hooper Crescent, Edmonton, Alberta, is named after Constable Stanley George Hooper, RCMP #10174.

Hooper served from March 18, 1926, until March 17, 1929, in the Northwest Territories. In 1928, along with Constables Ray Williams (#9582) and W. Racicot (#9965), he erected the detachment buildings at Reliance.

He joined the Edmonton City Police in 1929, and after serving in the Second World War, returned to that Force until 1971. Constable Hooper died at Edmonton, Alberta, on March 7, 1988.

Huget Place, Regina, Saskatchewan, is named after Assistant Commissioner Albert Huget, RCMP #13016, O.469, and chief constable of the Regina City Police.

"Al" Huget served in the Force all across Canada from April 25, 1938, to April 24, 1973. He saw service in "J" and "E" Divisions before being promoted to the commissioned ranks on February 1, 1956. He then went on to serve in Depot, "G," "E," "G," "HQ," "J," "G," and finally "HQ" again.

As his retirement leave commenced in late 1972, he was appointed chief of the Regina City Police and served in that capacity until 1982. He died on July 6, 1983, at Regina and was buried in the Force Cemetery at Depot Division.

His brother, Werner Huget (RCMP #14184, O.513), also served from 1941 to 1973, retiring as chief superintendent.

Inglewood Bird Sanctuary, Calgary, Alberta, was named in honour of Superintendent (Colonel) James Walker, NWMP O.18, by his son, Selby Walker. This place of tribute to Walker is on the site of his original home and sawmill. After leaving the Force, Walker ran a sawmill that from 1882 on supplied much of the lumber for the fast-growing town of Calgary as well as the Canadian Pacific Railway.

See the **Walker (Mount Walker)** entry.

Irvine, Alberta, 24 kilometres from the Saskatchewan border on Highway #1, is named after third permanent Commissioner (Colonel) Acheson Gosford Irvine, ISO, NWMP O.30.

See following entries.

Irvine Lake, Saskatchewan (Lat: 56°59'00"N, Long: 102°41'00"W), north of Island Falls near the Manitoba border, is named after Colonel and third permanent Commissioner Acheson Gosford Irvine, ISO, NWMP O.30.

Irvine (Colonel Irvine Junior High School), Calgary, Alberta, is also named in honour of Colonel Irvine, ISO, NWMP O.30.

Irvine took part in the 1870 Red River Expedition and then— from 1871 to 1875—had command of the Provisional Battalion of Rifles, Manitoba.

Irvine received his commission as superintendent in the NWMP on May 7, 1875. In 1877, as assistant commissioner, on behalf of Canada, he signed Treaty Number Seven with the Blackfoot confederation. In 1885 he was posted to Headquarters at Depot Division, and at the threat of rebellion to the north, led a forced march from Regina to Fort Carlton—a distance of 485 kilometres. By the time his contingent arrived, the North-West Rebellion had begun.

In 1880 Irvine was named the third commissioner of the NWMP, a position he held until he resigned March 31, 1886. He became the warden of the Stony Mountain Penitentiary in Manitoba in 1892. Colonel Irvine died January 19, 1916 at Quebec City, Quebec.

Jarvis In the early days of the Force there were no less than ten members named Jarvis who served. Those having places named after them were the following: Inspector Arthur Murray Jarvis (NWMP and RNWMP #418, O.104), who served from 1880 to 1911; Inspector William Drummer Jarvis (NWMP O.2), who served from 1873 to 1881; and Constable William Morley Puncheon Jarvis (NWMP #2083), who served from 1888 to 1893.

It has been a struggle to feel confident that credit is given where it was originally intended because some references have clearly erred by crediting the wrong member.

Jarvis Bay Provincial Park, Sylvan Lake, Alberta, is named after Constable William Morley Puncheon Jarvis, NWMP #2083.

Summer village of Jarvis Bay, Sylvan Lake, Alberta

Jarvis Bay Village, Sylvan Lake, Alberta (near Jarvis Bay Provincial Park), is named after Constable William Morley Puncheon Jarvis, NWMP #2083.

Jarvis served in the NWMP from 1888 until 1893 at Regina, Maple Creek, Medicine Hat, Fort Macleod, and Lethbridge. He moved to the Red Deer area in 1899 and opened a lumberyard. In 1905 his family established a cottage at Sylvan Lake to which they gave their name. Mr. Jarvis died on Octobert 6, 1929, and is buried in the Red Deer Cemetery.

He was a nephew of Inspector William Drummer Jarvis, NWMP O.2. (See next entry.)

Jarvis Crescent, Edmonton, Alberta, is named after Inspector William Drummer Jarvis, NWMP O.2.

Inspector Jarvis had previous military service with the British army in the South African "Kaffir War." When he came to Canada he became the second officer appointed (O.2) with the establishment of the NWMP on September 25, 1873. During the March West of 1874, he was dispatched—upon arriving at Roche Percée—to Fort Edmonton with the sick men and sick horses. They spent the winter recovering at the Hudson's Bay post.

The task of the following spring was to find a suitable site for establishing a new post. Soon, Fort Saskatchewan was erected near the mouth of the Sturgeon River, about 32 kilometres northeast of Edmonton. Inspector Jarvis served until June 15, 1881, and died August 4, 1914, at Nelson, B.C.

Jarvis Glacier, B.C. (Lat: 59°27'00"N, Long: 136°32'00"W), on the northwestern tip of B.C. and west of Bennett, is named after Inspector Arthur Murray Jarvis, NWMP and RNWMP O.104.

See following entries.

Jarvis Park, Fort Saskatchewan, Alberta, at the corner of 101st Street and 100th Avenue, is named after Inspector Arthur Murray Jarvis, NWMP and RNWMP O.104.

Jarvis River, Yukon (Lat: 60°46'00"N, Long: 138°08'00"W), a tributary to the Kaskawulsh River, was named about 1889 by the first prospectors in the area to honour Inspector Arthur Murray

Jarvis, CMG, NWMP and RNWMP O.104. He established the Police Post and Customs House on the Dalton Trail in the early days of the Yukon gold rush.

Arthur joined the NWMP on June 25, 1880, as regimental #418, and then served in that part of the Northwest Territories that is now Saskatchewan and Alberta. He took part in the North-West Rebellion of 1885, and on May 16, 1893, was promoted to the commissioned ranks.

He continued his service in the northwest, then at Depot Division, and then back north in the Yukon. One of his more notable patrols took place from January 4, 1897, to April 1897 when—along with Constable Samuel Hetherington (#894), a guide, and dog teams—he travelled from Fort Saskatchewan[44] via Lac La Biche to Fort McMurray. He returned via Fort Vermillion, Battle River,

Arthur Jarvis's 3,220-kilometre patrol, 1897

Peace River, Lesser Slave Lake, and Athabasca Landing, covering a total distance of over 3,220 kilometres.

Jarvis also served in the Boer War in 1900, and on March 21, 1911, he left service on a compulsory retirement because of chronic synovitis in his left knee. He was granted a pension of $1,178 per year. With the outbreak of the First World War, he was back in service as an assistant provost marshal. On June 27, 1925, he was committed as insane to a hospital at Guelph, Ontario. He died in 1930 at Montreal, Quebec, and was buried at Toronto, Ontario.

Two of his brothers also served in the NWMP: Constable Steven Murray Jarvis (#347), from 1879 to 1887, and Constable Frederick Starr Jarvis (#1058), from 1884 to 1903.

Jarvis Street, Red Deer, Alberta, is named after Constable William Morley Puncheon Jarvis, NWMP #2083.

See the preceding entry: **Jarvis Bay Village**.

Jarvis Street, Whitehorse, Yukon, is named after Inspector Arthur Murray Jarvis, NWMP and RNWMP O.104.

See the preceding entry: **Jarvis River**.

Joy (Cape Joy), Nunavut (Lat: 73°39'00"N, Long: 83°13'00"W), on the Borden Peninsula at the north end of Baffin Island, was named by the fifth Thule expedition after Inspector Alfred Herbert Joy, RNWMP and RCMP O.221.

See also **Joy River** entry.

Joy Island, (Lat: 55°54'00"N, Long: 80°07'00"W), in Hudson Bay just north of James Bay, is named after Inspector Alfred Herbert Joy, RNWMP and RCMP O.221.

See also **Joy River** entry.

Joy (Mount Joy), Nunavut (Lat: 63°16'00"N, Long: 69°38'00"W), on Baffin Island adjacent to Joy River, was named in 1932 after Inspector Alfred Herbert Joy, RNWMP and RCMP O.221.

See also **Joy River** entry.

Joy (Mount Joy), Yukon (Lat: 63°45'00"N, Long: 132°55'00"W), is the highest peak (2,235 m) in the Lansing Range. While mapping the geology of this region in 1909, Joseph Keele, a geological surveyor for Canada, named this peak after Staff Sergeant Geoffrey Beeston Joy, RNWMP #3045.

Joy served from April 24, 1894, until December 17, 1928, in Depot, "K," "M," and "E" Divisions. On March 19, 1901, while posted in the Yukon, he experienced the displeasure of his Officer Commanding Inspector Starnes, who fined him two dollars for "being late on departure to his detachment." Joy died in West Vancouver on October 13, 1946.

Joy Range, Devon Island, Nunavut (Lat: 79°15'00"N, Long: 87°20'00"W), was named in 1970 after Inspector Alfred Herbert Joy, RNWMP and RCMP O.221.

See following entry.

Joy River, Nunavut (Lat: 63°13'00"N, Long: 69°40'00"W), near Frobisher Bay on the southern tip of Baffin Island, was named in 1946 after Inspector Alfred Herbert Joy, RNWMP and RCMP O.221.

He was engaged with the Force on April 19, 1909, as #4919 and served in Divisions "K," "F," "G," "K," "O," and Headquarters before being promoted to the commissioned ranks on September 15, 1927. He then served in "G" again and Headquarters, Ottawa, where he died April 29, 1932, while still in service.

*The travels of Joy in 1929 (See **Stallworthy***
for more information regarding this map)

In the north, Joy made some notable patrols by dog team. In 1920 he accompanied Inspector J.W. Phillips (O.173) on a lengthy patrol of the Belcher Islands in southeast Hudson Bay for a murder investigation. On April 22, 1926, with Corporal Robert Garnett (#10119) and an Inuit guide, he journeyed from Craig Harbour to Grethasoer Bay and Axel Heiberg Island via Jones Sound and the west coast of Ellesmere Island, returning on May 31, 1926—a distance of 1,570 kilometres. He opened the first detachment at Bache Peninsula in 1927. In 1929, with Constable Reginald Taggart (#10303) and an Inuit guide, he patrolled the Sverdrup Islands from Dundas Harbour to Bache Peninsula, covering a distance of 2,735 kilometres in 81 days. On this trip, he and the others had the harrowing experience of being attacked by a polar bear in their night igloo.

See also **Phillips Channel**.

Jumbo Butte, Saskatchewan, about six kilometres east of Eastend, is named after a NWMP drayman named Jumbo.

Jumbo disappeared while driving between Eastend and another small post. His horse and buckboard, along with his neatly folded uniform, were found on top of the butte named after him, but Jumbo was never seen again.

Kearney Cove, Nunavut (Lat: 74°44'00"N, Long: 90°46'00"W), on the south shore of Devon Island, is named after Staff Sergeant Henry Kearney, RCMP #10368.

Kearney served from 1919 to 1921 in the Coldstream Guards, and from 1921 to 1926 in the Military Foot Police, before moving to Canada. He then served in the Force from December 2, 1927, to December 1, 1956. Throughout his career he served in "M," "K," "J," "C," and "G" Divisions, as well as in Headquarters, Ottawa.

While in the north early in his service, he was posted to Dundas Harbour on Devon Island. In the commissioner's 1931 annual report to government, it was mentioned that he and Constable William Mowat (#6588) retrieved the body of an American tourist from Marble Canyon in Banff National Park.

After his retirement, Kearney was employed in security work with the Distant Early Warning (DEW) radar line across northern Canada. In his later years he worked in the communications office of the West Vancouver City Police.

He died March 18, 1974, at North Vancouver, B.C.

Kendall Place, Calgary, is believed to have been named after Sergeant Ralph Selwood Kendall, RNWMP #4351.

He was born in England and served in South Africa with the 22nd Imperial Yeomanry before coming to Canada. In the Boer War he saw action in the Transvaal, Orange Free State, and Cape Colony, where he suffered a leg wound.

Kendall served from March 31, 1905, to March 30, 1910, mainly in Calgary, Banff, and Laggan (later Lake Louise). From 1911 to 1924 he served in the Calgary City Police as sergeant in charge of the mounted squad, and in this position he met many visiting dignitaries, including the Prince of Wales (later Edward VIII) and Canada's Governor General, Lord Byng. From 1924 to 1939 he was a court orderly at Calgary.

Kendall was also an author. In 1918 he wrote *Benton of the Royal Mounted* and in 1920 *The Luck of the Mounted*. He died February 25, 1941, at Calgary and was buried in the Union Cemetery.

Kennedy Point, Nunavut (Lat: 64°00'00"N, Long: 94°19'00"W), on Baker Lake, was named in 1950 after Constable Alfred Baldry Kennedy, RNWMP #5626, who made sketch maps of the district while in this area in 1916.

Kennedy had previously served for ten years in the Royal Navy before serving in the Force from July 9, 1913, to January 31, 1918. He served in "K" and "D" Divisions. Between 1914 and 1917 he was involved in the Baker Lake patrols during which he made his explorations. He later served in "F" Division before taking his discharge.

He also suggested "Schooner Cove" and "South Channel" as names for nearby features. These suggestions were accepted and are later entries herein. He died on April 18, 1953, at Huddersfield, England.

Kerr Road, Canadian Police College, Rockcliffe, Ontario, is named in honour of Constable John Randolph Kerr, NWMP #3040, Honour Roll #22.

Kerr served from April 14, 1894, until his death on May 28, 1897, when he was killed in the Minnichinas Hills, Northwest Territories (Saskatchewan), during the shootout with Almighty Voice. (For full details see the **Hockin Avenue** entry.)

On April 4, 1896, he appeared in Orderly Room at Depot Division, charged with "allowing a prisoner to escape." He was fined eighteen dollars and seven days with hard labour.[45]

He was buried in St Mary's Cemetery at Prince Albert.

Ketchen, Saskatchewan, between Sturgis and Kelvington on the Canadian National Railway line, is named after Brigadier-General Huntley Douglas Brodie Ketchen, commander of Winnipeg military district. He had earlier served as a staff sergeant in the NWMP as #3002.

See following entry.

Ketchen Avenue, Calgary, is named after Brigadier-General and Staff Sergeant Huntley Douglas Brodie Ketchen, NWMP #3002.

Ketchen served in the Force from January 1, 1894, to April 2, 1901, including his service with the Lord Strathcona's Horse Regiment in South Africa from 1900 to 1901. He had been in the "F" Division pay office before going overseas.

At the end of the Boer War, he was granted a free discharge to join the South African Constabulary. In the First World War he was a brigadier-general, commanding the 6th Canadian Infantry Brigade. He died in 1959 at Winnipeg, Manitoba.

Kettles Creek, Alberta (Lat: 49°29'50"N, Long: 113°55'28"W), which flows into Pincher Creek about 80 kilometres southwest of Lethbridge, is named after Sub-Constable Charles Kettles, NWMP #491 (Original Series), #184 (New Series).

Kettles began his adult life in the Canadian militia. He then served in the Force from June 7, 1876, to June 14, 1879, mainly in what is now southern Alberta. Early in 1879, along with

91

Superintendent Albert Shurtliffe (O.12), he helped establish the Pincher Creek detachment and the nearby NWMP horse farm. For his three years' good service he was awarded Land Warrant #0236.

He left to homestead near Pincher Creek and in 1883 opened a butcher shop in the town. With the outbreak of the North-West Rebellion in 1885, he served in the Rocky Mountain Rangers with former Sub-Constable John Herron, NWMP #378 (Original Series).

See also **Herronton**.

King Close, Red Deer, Alberta

King Close, Red Deer, Alberta, is named after Sub-Constable George Clift King, NWMP #304 (Original Series).

In the early years King owned a store in Red Deer.

See following entry.

King (George Clift King Home), Calgary, Alberta, is named after Sub-Constable George Clift King, NWMP #304 (Original Series).

King served from April 28, 1874, to June 15, 1877. He experienced the 1874 March West and then served in what is now Alberta. In 1875 he was in "F" Troop, which was sent to the Red Deer River to meet Sir Selby Smith, head of the Canadian militia. The troop then turned south to build a post at the confluence of the Bow and Elbow Rivers. King was assigned to find a suitable northern ford across the Bow River, so he became the first member of the Force to set foot on the site of what would become Fort Calgary.

After being discharged from the NWMP in 1877, he managed the I.G. Baker Company store at Fort Calgary. He became the first postmaster for the Town of Calgary and served as its second mayor from 1885 to 1887. On April 17, 1886, he was one of 24 former members to meet and form the NWMP Veterans' Association.

He died July 18, 1935, at Calgary and was buried in the Union Cemetery.

Kinney (Mount Kinney) (1,729 m), Yukon (Lat: 65°02'00"N, Long: 137°04'00"W), east of the Hart River, was named in May 1973 after Constable George Francis Kinney, RNWMP #4582, Honour Roll #36.

Constable Kinney served in the Yukon from May 3, 1907, until his death in February 1911. He died on the Peel River, 56 kilometres from Fort McPherson, on the ill-fated "Lost Patrol." The mountain named in his honour lies just east of the patrol's route to Dawson. He was buried at Fort McPherson.

See also the **Fitzgerald Settlement** entry.

Kirk Lake, Northwest Territories (Lat: 63°43'00"N, Long: 109°05'00"W), northeast of Great Slave Lake, is named after Corporal Ernest Archibald Kirk, RCMP #10035.

Kirk served from November 21, 1923, to May 14, 1950, in "G," Depot, "G," "E," "K," "D," Depot, "M," and then "E" Divisions, retiring as corporal.

In 1938 he received the Commissioner's Commendation for saving a starving family in the north. He was then stationed at the Old Crow detachment when he received word that an isolated family was in serious distress. Since another member was away on patrol with the police dog team, he borrowed a team, loaded supplies, and headed out. He travelled to the Blue Fish Lakes, approximately 112 kilometres south of Rampart House, and managed to locate the family of Charles Thomas, which was near starvation. He nourished them, left supplies, and returned to his detachment.

He retired in Burnaby, B.C., where he died February 8, 1958.

Kittson Butte, Saskatchewan (Lat: 49°34'00"N, Long: 109°53'00"W), in the Cypress Hills near Fort Walsh,[46] is named after Surgeon John George Kittson, NWMP O.21.

Kittson was appointed to the commissioned ranks of the NWMP on April 3, 1874, as the first doctor/surgeon in the Force. He accompanied the March West in 1874 as far as present-day Fort Macleod[47] and then returned with Commissioner French to Dufferin for the winter of 1874/75. In 1876 the Headquarters of the Force was established in the west, so he returned to Fort Walsh until

Dr. John G. Kittson second from the left, 1889

1879. In 1879 the Department of Indian Affairs began paying half of his salary for the work he did with the Indian population.

He resigned January 24, 1882, to go into private practice in St. Paul, Minnesota, where he died two years later on May 10, 1884.

Klondike River, Yukon, entering the Yukon River from the east, was known in the early days by many different names. Inspector

Charles Constantine (O.79), who was also the mining recorder at Fortymile, made the name "Klondyke" official with the discovery on Bonanza Creek. It was later changed to "Klondike" in 1898.
See also **Constantine (Mount Constantine)** entry.

Lambert Avenue, Calgary, Alberta, is believed to be named after Constable James Smith Lambert, NWMP #2320.
Lambert served in the Force from May 30, 1889, to May 17, 1898, mainly as a carpenter. In 1891 he built the Fort Macleod detachment building and in 1893 the Boundary Creek detachment building.
From 1898 to 1900 he was in the Yukon. Then he joined the Lord Strathcona's Horse for service in the Boer War. During the First World War, from 1914 to 1919, he was a captain in the 13th Canadian Mounted Rifles. He then returned to contracting and built several business blocks in Lethbridge as well as the municipal hospital at Fort Macleod. He later lived in Calgary and became a building contractor. He died on January 8, 1948, at Calgary, Alberta.

Larsen (Henry Larsen Building), Yellowknife, Northwest Territories, was named for Superintendent Henry Asbjorn Larsen, RCMP O.347. This building, completed in 1970, houses "G" Division headquarters and the Yellowknife detachment.
See following entries.

Larsen (Cape Larsen), Northwest Territories (Lat: 69°47'00"N, Long: 117°15'00"W), on Wallaston Peninsula of Victoria Island, was named after Superintendent Henry Asbjorn Larsen, RCMP O.347, by Lieutenant Baggild, Royal Canadian Navy, while on a voyage on the *St. Roch* in the western Arctic in 1948.
See following entries.

Larsen **(Coast Guard Vessel *Henry Larsen*)** is a Canadian Coast Guard vessel named after Superintendent Henry Asbjorn Larsen, RCMP O.347, who was made a Fellow of the Royal Geographical Society of Canada and also awarded a Polar Medal with Bar.
See following entries.

Larsen (Henry Larsen Elementary School), Ottawa, Ontario, is named after Superintendent Henry Asbjorn Larsen, RCMP O.347, of *St. Roch* fame.
See following entry.

Larsen Sound, Nunavut (Lat: 70°30'00"N, Long: 98°45'00"W), on the Boothia Peninsula, was named on January 5, 1965, by the Department of Mines and Technical Surveys in honour of Superintendent Henry Asbjorn Larsen, FRGS, PmB, LLD, RCMP O.347. Larsen's name was chosen in recognition of his role on the RCMP's *St. Roch*, when he navigated the Northwest Passage from west to east from June 1940 to October 1942 and from east to west from July 1944 to October 1944.

Henry Larsen of St. Roch fame

Henry Larsen grew up in Norway and began his adult life serving in the Royal Norwegian Navy. In 1925 he signed on as a crewmember aboard the *Maid of New Orleans*, under Captain C. Klengenberg,[48] for a supply trip to the north.

Larsen joined the RCMP on April 16, 1928, as #10407, and after training was posted to "E" Division, Vancouver, B.C. In 1940, as the sergeant in charge of the RCMP northern supply vessel *St. Roch*, he was ordered to sail from Vancouver to Halifax by way of the Northwest Passage. Larsen sailed the little wooden vessel from Vancouver around Alaska into the Arctic Ocean. The ship reached Walker Bay on Victoria Island in late September 1940, and it wintered there until July 1941. In 1941 Larsen continued east until he was frozen in again for the winter at Pasley Bay. In 1942 he picked his way through Bellot Strait and into open water, reaching Halifax October 11, 1942. This was the first vessel to navigate the Northwest Passage from the west to the east.

His crew on this historic trip included the following: M.F. Foster (#8406); W.J. Parry (#7756), cook; A.J. Chartrand (#10155); F.S. Farrar (#10607); G.W. Peters (#12704); P.G. Hunt (#12740); and E.C. Hadley (#13013). Each received the Polar Medal.

In 1944 Larsen reversed the trip and completed the 11,740 kilometres in 86 days. His crew on the return trip were the following: Corporal G.W. Peters (#12704), engineer; Corporal P.G. Hunt (#12740); J.M. Diplock (#14583); Special Constables O. Andreasen, L.G. Russill, R.T. Johnsen, W.M. Cashin, J.S. McKenzie, F. Matthews, and G.B. Dickens.

Larsen was promoted to the commissioned ranks on December 1, 1944, as O.347. In his last years of service as a superintendent he was the commanding officer of "G" Division (Northwest Territories).

He received these awards: Fellow of Royal Geographical Society of Canada, Patrons Medal of the Royal Geographical Society of London, Massey Medal (first recipient), Polar Medal and Bar, and a honorary degree of Doctor of Laws from Waterloo University.

Following his retirement, he authored two books: *The Northwest Passage* and *The Big Ship*. He died on October 29, 1964, at Vancouver, B.C., and was buried in the Depot Division Cemetery.

See also these entries: **St. Roch Island, Chartrand Star, Farrar (Cape Farrar)**, and **Andreasen Head.**

Larsen Street, Depot Division RCMP, Regina, Saskatchewan, is named in honour of Corporal Ole Roust Larsen, RCMP #25876, Honour Roll #167.

Corporal Larsen served from July 1967 until his death on August 11, 1981, at Climax, Saskatchewan. On August 9, 1981, Larsen attended a family dispute, which ended when the husband, Keith Sipley, departed angrily. Two nights later, a car drove by Larsen's home twice, squealing its tires. Larsen recognized the vehicle as Sipley's and went out unarmed in the police car to check him. At first Sipley ignored the siren and flashing lights, but then he stopped abruptly on the main street in front of a hotel. Larsen turned off the emergency lights and siren and got out of the police car as Sipley, armed with a .22 calibre rifle, got out of his car. Without warning, he shot Larsen several times. Larsen struggled back to the police car to turn the siren on for help, and as he was getting into the police car, Sipley shot him two more times in view of witnesses. Sipley then got back into his own car and drove away.

While attempting to drive across the U.S. border through back fields, Sipley's car became immobilized. He then walked into an American farmer's yard, got into a pickup truck, and began driving crazily around the farmyard. The farmer came out, but by that time Sipley had shot himself dead.

Larsen was buried with full honours at the RCMP Cemetery at Depot Division, Regina.

Latta Bridge, Edmonton, Alberta, is named after Constable David Gilliland Latta, NWMP #2442.

Latta served in the Force from April 30, 1890, until April 20, 1893. In 1902 he opened a blacksmith shop at Edmonton, and in 1906 he served as an alderman. Constable Latta died at Edmonton on November 11, 1948.

Laughland Street, Depot Division RCMP, Regina, Saskatchewan, is named in honour of Sergeant Kenneth Morley Laughland, RCMP #17368, Honour Roll #121.

Laughland served from November 15, 1951, as a pilot in the RCMP Air Services with several years of flying experience. On July 13, 1963, he was piloting a Force aircraft, CF-MPO (de Havilland Beaver on floats), with three other members and a prisoner aboard for a short flight from Mayo to Carmacks, Yukon. Laughland circled to look for obstacles, then banked to land in the river. The plane struck some wires and crashed into the ground, burning fiercely upon impact. The probable cause of the crash was a wing stall occurring during the approach to landing. The other members aboard were Corporal Robert William Asbil (#19626, Honour Roll #122), Constable Proctor L.A. Malcolm (#18570, Honour Roll #123), and Constable William J.D. Annand (#19206, Honour Roll #124).

Sergeant Laughland was buried at Cedar Valley Memorial Gardens, Nanaimo, B.C.

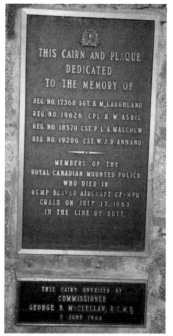

Cairn erected at Carmacks, Yukon, in memory of K.M. Laughland and others

Lavoie Island, Nunavut (Lat: 62°42'00"N, Long: 69°34'00"W), off the south coast of Baffin Island, is named after Constable Joseph Adolphe Arthur Lavoie, RCMP #10332.

Lavoie served in the Force in "A," "G," and "N" Divisions from July 4, 1927, to October 15, 1941.

Early in his service with "A" Division, he was another one to run afoul of regulations. On May 3, 1928, he appeared in Orderly Room for having missed a parade and was fined one dollar!

He died on April 9, 1968, at Mont-Joli, Quebec.

Layton Hills, Saskatchewan (Lat: 49°22'00"N, Long: 106°04'00"W), sixteen kilometres from St. Victor, are named after Constable David Fred Layton, NWMP #3637.

Layton served briefly in the Force from April 12, 1900, to August 12, 1903, in southern Saskatchewan. No information has been found on his later life.

Lee Point, Nunavut (Lat: 76°23'40"N, Long: 82°16'00"W), on the southeast tip of Ellesmere Island, is named after Constable Herbert Patrick Lee, RCMP #9754.

Lee served for almost four years in the Force from February 10, 1921, to January 3, 1925. He appeared in Orderly Room while in training. Records indicate that he and three other recruits were caught playing poker for money, and they each lost five dollars to the government pot!

The remainder of Lee's service was in the north. In 1922 he was one of nine members under Inspector Charles E. Wilcox (O.194) to erect detachment buildings at new posts on Baffin and Ellesmere Islands.

When he left the Force he moved to the U.S. and became a prolific author of novels based loosely on his service in the north. In 1928 he published *Policing the Top of the World*, then in rapid succession came *Baffin's Gold*, *Heritage of the North*, *The Girl from Baffin Island*, and *Hell's Harbour*. In 1936 he published *North of the Stars* while working at the same time as a reporter for the *New York Sun*. He was killed on November 11, 1936, when he was struck by a freight train in Long Island City, New York.

Lemsford, Saskatchewan, a hamlet midway between Swift Current and the Alberta border on Highway #32, was named after Constable William Leonard "Tillie" Lawton, NWMP #3556.

Constable Lawton served with the NWMP in the Yukon from April 3, 1900, to July 30, 1902. He left the Force in Whitehorse to work for the White Pass and Yukon Railway. He then turned to farming in the Lemsford area, adjacent to the South Saskatchewan River, where there was a natural ford. This point soon became known locally as "Len's Ford," but when the Geographical Survey established the place name it was listed as "Lemsford."

William Lawton died at Vancouver, B.C., in 1965.

Lowry Place, Depot Division RCMP, Regina, Saskatchewan, is named in honour of Corporal William Hay Talbot Lowry, NWMP #907, Honour Roll #12.

Lowry served in the NWMP from June 7, 1883, until he was killed on May 3, 1885, during the Battle of Cut Knife Hill in the North-West Rebellion.

On May 2, 1885, during the North-West Rebellion, Superintendent William M. Herchmer (O.37) and Superintendent Percy Neale (O.34) led a force of 319 men, including 74 members of the NWMP, from Battleford to Cut Knife Hill about 61 kilometres distant. In the battle that ensued at Cut Knife Hill, three members of the NWMP were killed: Corporal William H.T. Lowry (#907, Honour Roll #12), Constable Patrick Burke (#402 Honour Roll #11), and Corporal Ralph Sleigh (#565, Honour Roll #10). Sergeant John Ward (#36) was wounded.

Lowry was buried at Battleford. In his memory, his parents later donated the font that is in the Force Chapel at Depot Division.

See also **Burke Lake** and **Sleigh Square**.

McBeth Fiord, Nunavut (Lat: 69°32'20"N, Long: 69°10'00"W), between Cape Raper and Henry Kater Peninsula on the east coast of Baffin Island, was named in 1982 after Sergeant Hugh Alexander "Hughie" McBeth, RCMP #7850.

See following entry.

McBeth River, Nunavut (Lat: 69°32'00"N, Long: 70°02'00"W), which flows into the head of McBeth Fiord, was named in 1950 after Sergeant Hugh Alexander "Hughie" McBeth, RCMP #7850.

Hughie joined the RNWMP on June 6, 1919, after having served in the 26th Battalion Canadian Expeditionary Force during the First World War. He served until June 5, 1945, with the RCMP in Divisions "D," "O," "HQ.," "G," "D," "J," "O," and "G."

In 1943, during his time at Pond Inlet, he made a patrol by dog team from Pond Inlet to Home Bay on Baffin Island: a round trip of at least 1,285 kilometres. Also while at Pond Inlet—possibly in connection with the same patrol—an Inuk named Kooneeloosie reported finding the body of an Inuk woman named Kudloo at the lead end of what is now called McBeth Fiord. A third Inuk named Kyak went with McBeth on the investigation, with Kooneeloosie leading them to the body.

In 1966, in memory of the Inuk woman, a nearby lake was named Kudloo Lake (Lat: 69°38'00"N, Long: 70°05'00"W). A second lake nearby, at the head of McBeth Fiord, was named Kyak Lake after McBeth's guide, and a third lake (Lat: 69°34'00"N, Long: 70°09'00"W) was named Kooneeloosie Lake for the Inuk who found Kudloo's body.

The fiord and river were named in recognition of McBeth's long service with the Inuit of the eastern Arctic. He died on November 27, 1985, at Charlottetown, Prince Edward Island.

MacBrien (Mount Sir James MacBrien), Northwest Territories (Lat: 62°07'00"N, Long: 127°41'00"W), is named after Sir James Howden MacBrien, DSO, CMG, KCB, RNWMP and RCMP O.240. Mount MacBrien is the highest point in the Mackenzie Mountains (2,762 m), located near the Yukon border north of the Nahanni National Park and east of Tungsten, Yukon.

MacBrien was born in Ontario, raised on a farm, and began his adult life in 1896 by enlisting in the 34th Ontario Regiment, Canadian Militia. He remained only a short time before joining the RNWMP.

MacBrien accomplished several firsts for the Force. He was the first commissioner to have earlier served in the ranks. He joined the RNWMP April 7, 1900, as #3588, volunteering for service in the contingent of the Lord Strathcona's Horse bound for the Boer War. While in South Africa, he received a free discharge to serve in the South African Constabulary and did so for six years as #1392, ending as sergeant-major and second in command in the Northern Transvaal.

He returned to Canada in 1906 to a commission in the Canadian militia (Royal Canadian Dragoons). In 1914 he attended the British Staff College and was there when the First World War began. He joined the Canadian Expeditionary Force and by 1915 was the commander of the Canadian Infantry Brigade. He was wounded and awarded the Distinguished Service Order (DSO). In 1916 he was promoted to brigadier-general in charge of the 12th Brigade. On his return to Canada he was appointed as chief of staff, Department of National Defence, and promoted to major-general. In this post he established the Royal Canadian Air Force (RCAF). He left this position in 1927.

At this time his attention turned back to an earlier interest—flying. He became the director of Inter-Provincial Airways, was an advocate of flying clubs, and was soon elected president of a growing flying club association. He was also now a trained aircraft pilot and received his first airplane in 1929.

On August 1, 1931, at the retirement of Commissioner Starnes, he was appointed commissioner of the RCMP as O.240. He is credited with moving the Force to the modern age, even to the extent of suggesting that "Mounted" be dropped from the name "Royal Canadian Mounted Police." This was one idea that did not "fly," perhaps fortunately, as the prestige it has brought to the Force—and to Canada—by mere mention of the name continues.

He saw the Force through the rapid changes and growth of the 1930s. The Preventive Service and several provincial police forces were absorbed. Provincial policing duties were assumed in Prince

Edward Island, Nova Scotia, New Brunswick, Manitoba, and Alberta. He also established the first police dog service sections, radio-equipped cars, patrol vessels, and the first aircraft.

The first official duty flight in the Force was in 1928 when the RCAF transported Sergeant A.P. Colfer (#5099) to the west coast of James Bay to bring out a mental patient. Seven years earlier, in 1921, Sergeant Thorne (#4290) had flown from Edmonton to Fort Simpson, returning to the detachment as a passenger in the Imperial Oil Company's Junkers Tri-Motor, although this was not credited as an official flight.

Commissioner MacBrien was an ardent pilot and is to be credited with the creation of the air section and the purchase of the first aircraft for the Force: four de Havilland Dragonfly aircraft in 1937. He had another earlier first on June 6, 1935, when, flying back to Ottawa from a conference in the U.S., his aircraft was forced down in Ohio, resulting in the first known "ex gratia payment"[49] being made for damage caused to a farmer's crop at Fayette, Ohio. The payment was ten dollars.

During this same period he brought the forensic laboratories into the modern age, sponsored "up-and-coming" members to full-time university for law degrees, and established the Mounted Police Museum at Depot Division. He was knighted by King George V in 1935 as a member of the Order of the Bath, receiving the honour of Knight Commander Most Honourable Order of the Bath (KCB), accompanying his earlier appointment as a companion to the Order of St. Michael and St. George (CMG).

One can only speculate where he may have taken the Force if he had not also been the first commissioner to die while in office, which—sadly—happened in Ottawa on March 5, 1938. Three of his sons also saw public service: Constable James Ross MacBrien (#11742), who served in the Force from 1932 to 1936, then left to join the British army, and Special Constable William Ross MacBrien (#S1288), who served from 1932 to 1934. A third son was killed in an air crash on January 1, 1941, while serving in the Royal Canadian Air Force.

McCutcheon Drive and **McCutcheon Place**, Medicine Hat, Alberta, are named after Sergeant Robert McCutcheon, NWMP #458 (Original Series).

McCutcheon served from May 7, 1875, until May 15, 1878, at Fort Macleod and Fort Walsh. As was usual in those days of extreme discipline, he had his brushes with the Orderly Room. On December 12, 1875, he was charged for "failing to give up a shovel, when ordered" and was admonished. On February 12, 1876, he was charged for being "absent at watch setting" and fined one dollar.

On November 14, 1879, he was in the search party that found the body of Constable M. Graburn, who had been murdered near Fort Walsh. He died September 28, 1943, and was buried in the Burnsland Cemetery, Calgary, Alberta.

See also **Graburn Walk**.

Macdonell Three of the following entries are for the Macdonell family that was a dynasty within the Force. The family relationships and ranks are listed here.

(a) Superintendent Alexander Roderick Macdonell, NWMP#26 (Original Series), O.39, who served from 1876 to 1895 and was an uncle to (c). Note: When in the ranks, his surname was shown as "MacDonnell"; upon promotion to commissioned ranks, his surname was shown as "MacDonell."

(b) Lieutenant-General Sir Archibald Cameron Macdonell (NWMP and RNWMP Superintendent O.95), who served from 1889 to 1907. Cousin of (d), (e), and (f), and possibly (a).

(c) Superintendent Albert Edward Crosby Macdonell, NWMP and RNWMP #543, O.117. He served from 1881 to 1917 and is father of (d), (e), and (f). Note: Service files record his name as McDonell.

(d) Chief Superintendent Cortlandt Benfield Macdonell, RCMP #10170, O.367, who served from 1926 to 1966. Also father of (g), brother of (e) and (f).

(e) Constable Donald Ross Macdonell, RCMP #10399, Honour Roll #50, who served March 9, 1928, until his death April 19, 1931.

(f) Staff Sergeant Albert Macdonell, RCMP #12532, who served from 1934 to 1961.

(g) Assistant Commissioner Cortland I.C. Macdonell, RCMP #18851, O.840, who served from 1955 to 1993, retiring as the commanding officer of "F" Division.

MacDonnell Avenue, Calgary, Alberta, is named after Lieutenant-General Sir Archibald Cameron Macdonell, KCB, CMG, DSO, NWMP and RNWMP O.95.

Superintendent Macdonell attended the Royal Military College in Kingston, Ontario, and then served in the Force from September 28, 1889 (NWMP), until March 4, 1907 (RNWMP). He served mainly at Depot Division, which was then the headquarters for the Force. During this service he also served—and was wounded—in the Boer War.

On April 19, 1906, he was granted six months leave to again attend the Royal Military College to qualify for a permanent position in the Canadian militia. At completion, he resigned his RNWMP commission to join the Lord Strathcona's Horse and, in 1912, took command. At the outset of the First World War he was lieutenant-colonel, and in 1915 he took command of the 7th Canadian Infantry. In 1916 he was wounded. He commanded the 1st Canadian Division in 1917 and was promoted to lieutenant-general. In 1919 he was knighted by the king, and from then until his retirement in 1925, he was commandant of the Royal Military College, Kingston, Ontario. He died on December 23, 1941, at Kingston, Ontario.

Macdonell Drive, Depot Division RCMP, Regina, Saskatchewan, is named in honour of Constable Donald Ross Macdonell, RCMP #10399, Honour Roll #50.

Constable Macdonell served from March 9, 1928, in "F" and "D" Divisions until his death on April 19, 1931. Like many before him, he did not escape that dreaded Orderly Room and made his appearance on July 21, 1928, charged with "negligence." Assistant Commissioner Worsley fined him two dollars.

In April 1931, when posted to the Port Nelson detachment, Constable Macdonell set out on a dog team patrol with Special Constable Norman Massan. On April 18 they camped for the night on a small island at the mouth of Fourteen Mile River. During the night a sudden thaw caused water to flow over the ice, threatening to flood the island. Leaving their dogs and equipment behind, they began to wade to the main shore and higher ground. It is not known exactly what then happened, but the first indication of trouble came a few days later when some of their dogs returned to Port Nelson.

Sergeant (later Sergeant-Major) John Molloy (#6737) set out to search for them, and on April 27, 1931, he found Massan's body. A few days later the body of Macdonell was found. Both were frozen under newly formed ice. Constable Macdonell was buried in the Union Cemetery in Edmonton, Alberta.

McDonnell (Mount McDonnell), B.C. (Lat: 50°57'00"N, Long: 117°41'00"W), south of Glacier National Park, is named after Superintendent Albert Edward Crosby Macdonell, NWMP and RNWMP O.117.

He joined the Force on June 7, 1881, and was first posted to present-day Saskatchewan, then to that part of the Northwest Territories which is now Alberta. In the North-West Rebellion of 1885 he served in Steele's Scouts[50] and took part in the Battle of Cut Knife Hill on May 2 of that year.

During the policing of the construction of the Canadian Pacific Railway in 1885–86, he was the first member of the Force in charge of the most westerly detachment at Farwell (present-day Revelstoke, B.C.). As sergeant-major in 1897, he was in the NWMP contingent to England for Queen Victoria's Jubilee celebrations.

He next served in the Yukon and was promoted to commissioned ranks as O.117 on August 1, 1900. He retired May 31, 1917, and then organized the Alberta Provincial Police for the Province of Alberta. He died April 8, 1938, at Calgary, Alberta, and is buried in the Union Cemetery.

McGibbon Bay, Saskatchewan (Lat: 55°08'00"N, Long: 105°15'00"W), the southwest portion of Nut Bay in Lac La Ronge, is named after Assistant Commissioner John Alexander McGibbon, NWMP, RNWMP, and RCMP O.62.

McGibbon joined the NWMP on June 25, 1880, as #427 and served in what is now Saskatchewan. At the time of the North-West Rebellion of 1885 he was posted to Prince Albert, so he took part in the actions under Superintendent Crozier.[51] He was promoted to the commissioned ranks as O.62 on September 15, 1885, and continued to serve in Saskatchewan and then Alberta. In his last years of service he was at Depot Division. He retired October 1, 1920, to the West Coast and died at Vancouver, B.C., on March 28, 1939.

He was the first of three generations to serve in the Force, each member retiring as an assistant commissioner. His son was Douglas Lorne McGibbon (#9775, O.312), who served from 1921 to 1956. In turn, Douglas Lorne's son Douglas William McGibbon (#15547, O.573) also served from 1948 to 1983.

McIllree River, Saskatchewan (Lat: 55°07'00"N, Long: 105°46'00"W), which flows into Lac La Ronge from the south, is named after Assistant Commissioner John Henry McIllree,[52] NWMP O.13.

McIllree joined the Force on October 2, 1873, within days of its inception, receiving regimental #6 (Original Series). On April 1, 1874, before the 1874 March West began, he was promoted to the commissioned ranks as a sub-inspector (O.13) and became the first member to receive a commission from the ranks. On the

March West he was the assistant officer in charge of "E" Division. He kept a daily journal of the events of the March West, and those diaries are now preserved in the Glenbow Archives at Calgary, Alberta. He then served in that part of the Northwest Territories that became the province of Saskatchewan in 1905, and at the Headquarters of the Force. At the outset of the North-West Rebellion in 1885 he was the officer in charge of Maple Creek district, known then as "A" Division.

John McIllree, on the white horse, is leading a NWMP patrol at the time of the North-West Rebellion

McIllree served in the Force until March 21, 1911, retiring as an assistant commissioner with an annual pension of $1,925. He then moved to the West Coast and in 1915 became a charter member of "A" Division's RNWMP Veterans' Association. He died in 1925 at Victoria, B.C.

Note: His wife was an accomplished artist, and many of her paintings are in the RCMP Museum at Depot Division, Regina.

McIntosh Creek, Yukon (Lat: 61°57'00"N, Long: 137°17'00"W), which flows into the Nisling River, was named in 1965—at the request of G.W. Rowley—after Constable George Whitfield Cameron McIntosh, NWMP #3518.

See following entry.

McIntosh (or MacKintosh) Lake, Yukon—the official record names McIntosh Lake, Yukon, after Constable George Whitfield Cameron McIntosh, NWMP #3518. In our search, however, no such lake was located, but we found one named "MacKintosh" (Lat: 61°34'25"N, Long: 136°58'45"W). It is probable that the name was spelled incorrectly.

McIntosh served in the Force from March 22, 1900, to 1902 at Maple Creek and in the Yukon, leaving the Force from Whitehorse. He later lived at Bear Creek Trading Post, Yukon. He died November 29, 1939, at an unknown location in the Yukon, possibly at Bear Creek.

MacKay Hill, Saskatchewan (Lat: 50°46'00"N, Long: 103°48'00"W), near Fort Qu'Appelle, is named after Constable Robert Hugh MacKay, NWMP #368.

MacKay served in the Force from June 9, 1879, until August 13, 1883, beginning his service with the usual long passage west through the U.S. He travelled first by train to the end of the steel, then aboard the steamer *Red Cloud* on the Missouri River, and finally overland to Canada.

He served mainly at Fort Walsh and Fort Qu'Appelle, as recorded by his appearances in the Orderly Room for the usual problems of those days. At Fort Walsh on September 24, 1879, he was charged with "disobeying an order" and was admonished by Superintendent Crozier. On September 23, 1880, at Fort Qu'Appelle, he was charged by Inspector Steele with "being intoxicated, however slightly, on guard duty" and was fined one month's pay and confined to barracks for an additional three months. On December 16, 1881, Inspector Steele charged him again with "being intoxicated, however slightly," fined him fifteen dollars, and confined him to barracks for one month.

When MacKay left the Force he homesteaded three miles west of Fort Qu'Appelle on top of the hill that now bears his name. In winters he freighted supplies by ox team to Prince Albert. He died on March 6, 1948, at Qu'Appelle, Saskatchewan.

McKellar Bay, Nunavut (Lat: 62°45'00"N, Long: 69°30'00"W), on the south coast of Baffin Island, is named after Corporal Alexander McKinlay McKellar, RCMP #10272.

McKellar served in the Force from April 27, 1927, to May 31, 1934, first in "D" Division (Manitoba) and then in "G" Division (eastern Arctic).

During his first year of service at Winnipeg, he had a mishap while working as a guard at the offices of the Receiver General of Canada; he somehow managed to discharge his revolver, shattering a window. The Orderly Room parade cost him a fine of five dollars for the "oops" and a further eight dollars for the window.

He was then transferred north and spent the majority of his remaining time on the south coast of Baffin Island. We have been unable to learn what became of him since leaving the Force in 1934.

Macleod Drive, Lethbridge, Alberta, is named after Commissioner James Alexander Farquharson Macleod, NWMP O.4.

See the **Macleod Island** entry.

Macleod (Colonel Macleod Elementary School), Calgary, Alberta, is also named after Commissioner James Alexander Farquharson Macleod, NWMP O.4.

Macleod (Colonel Macleod Manor), Fort Macleod, Alberta, is named in honour of Commissioner James Alexander Farquharson Macleod, NWMP O.4.

Macleod (Fort Macleod), Alberta, the site of the present town of Fort Macleod, was the first established NWMP fort in 1874, named by Commissioner French after its founder, Assistant Commissioner James Alexander Farquharson Macleod, NWMP O.4.

Fort Macleod, Alberta

Macleod Gazette, Fort Macleod, Alberta, was owned and named by Constable Charles Edward Dudley Wood, NWMP #466.

Wood served in the Force from August 21, 1880, to July 24, 1882, mainly at Macleod, and was invalided from service after being injured when he was thrown from a horse.

He borrowed money and started the first newspaper in the area, the *Macleod Gazette*, which published until about 1910. In 1886 he was one of 23 ex-members to meet and form the NWMP Veterans' Association. By 1924 he had moved to Weyburn, Saskatchewan, where he became a judge. He died in 1925 at Weyburn, Saskatchewan.

Macleod Island, Alberta (Lat: 49°44'00"N, Long: 113°22'00"W), 40 kilometres west of Lethbridge in the Oldman River, is named after second permanent commissioner James Alexander Farquharson Macleod, CMG, NWMP O.4. This island was the site of the original establishment of Fort Macleod, named after the founder. The fort was soon moved to the main shore because of repeated flooding.

In 1860 Macleod passed his law exams and was called to the Bar of Upper Canada. He served as major in the 1870 Red River Expedition and was promoted to a lieutenant-colonel in the militia. On September 25, 1873, he was appointed superintendent as the fourth officer in the fledgling NWMP and was promoted to assistant commissioner just prior to the 1874 March West, making him the second in command for the march.

Upon their arrival at their destination in western Canada, the troops' primary task was to find a suitable site for winter quarters, as fall was advancing. Commissioner French assigned this task to Macleod and their recently acquired guide, Jerry Potts. Potts led Macleod to an ideal spot on the Oldman River. There was good pasture for their spent horses and groves of tall cottonwoods for building materials. Construction of the most necessary buildings began immediately. Soon after they had arrived, Sub-Constable Godfrey Parks (#364, Original Series) died of typhoid, contracted on the March West. His was the first burial in the new cemetery.

On July 22, 1876, with the resignation of Commissioner French, Macleod was appointed as the second permanent commissioner, and then on November 15, 1876, he was appointed stipendiary magistrate for the Northwest Territories, in addition to his primary role. He must be singularly credited with the overall peaceful and generally violence-free settlement of the west. In his four years as commissioner he established a peaceful understanding with the Blackfoot Confederacy and enjoyed a respectful personal relationship with the principal chiefs, who called him "Stamix Otokan" (Bull's Head).

On November 1, 1880, Macleod resigned as commissioner to become a full-time magistrate, and in 1886 he was appointed to the Supreme Court for the Northwest Territories. He continued until his death—caused by Bright's disease—on September 5, 1894. He had been awarded the Commander of the Order of St. Michael and St. George (CMG) for his service to Canada. He was buried in the Union Cemetery at Calgary, Alberta.

See also the **Potts (Jerry Potts Street)** and **French Lake** entries.

Macleod Mall, Calgary, Alberta. See previous entry.

Macleod Plaza, Calgary, Alberta. See **Macleod Island**.

Macleod Trail, Alberta, the highway (Highway #2) between Calgary and Fort Macleod.
　　See **Macleod Island**.

Makinson Inlet, Nunavut (Lat: 77°16'00"N, Long: 79°40'00"W), on the eastern shore of Ellesmere Island leading inland from Smith Bay, was named in 1962 after Sergeant George Tingley Makinson, RCMP #9994.

Makinson was educated in the Nova Scotia Agricultural College and then spent two years as an entomologist and orchard inspector. He then served with the Force from September 5, 1923, to September 3, 1943, in "HQ", "N," "D," "G," "E," "K," and "F" Divisions, retiring from the Swift Current detachment. During 1927–28 he was stationed on Ellesmere Island; it was during that time that he discovered the inlet named after him. From 1933 to 1936 he served aboard the *St. Roch* supply vessel.

In the 1860s his grandfather, George Makinson, purchased a farm south of Clarke's Beach, Conception Bay, Newfoundland. Over the ensuing years, three roads converged at the farm and the locale became known as "Makinsons," which has since grown into a small community. The farm remained in the family, so upon his retirement, Sergeant Makinson returned to the family dairy business. For many years the farm supplied dairy products to the U.S. Naval Base at Argentia.

After Newfoundland joined Confederation in 1949 as Canada's tenth province, Makinson was elected in the first provincial assembly as a Liberal member of the House of Assembly for the riding of Port de Grave. He died at Makinsons, Newfoundland, on February 18, 1986.

See also the **St. Roch Island** entry.

Marshall Ranch, Saskatchewan, on Highway #18 a few miles east of Big Beaver, and also the site of the Big Muddy detachment and the cairn for the Last Mounted Police Horse Patrol,[53] is named after Constable James Marshall, NWMP #1470.

Hailing from St. John, New Brunswick, Marshall joined the NWMP on June 11, 1885, and served to July 28, 1896. In his early days he was stationed at Wood Mountain, then under the command of Depot Division. He then served at Battleford and took part in the North-West Rebellion of 1885. After leaving the Force, he ranched at Big Muddy.

Constable Marshall is buried in the family plot a few feet away from the ruins of the Big Muddy detachment. This area is still known locally as the Marshall Ranch. He was the uncle of Constable William H. Marshall (RCMP #10725, who served from 1929 to 1935), granduncle to both Corporal Douglas F.W. Marshall (RCMP #19043, who served 1955 to 1975) and Sergeant Donald R. Marshall (RCMP #21009, who served 1959 to 1981), and finally, great-granduncle of Constable John R. Marshall (RCMP #41560, who is serving in the Force as of 2001).

Masinasin Post Office, Alberta (Lat: 49°09'00"N, Long: 114°00'00"W), 150 kilometres southwest of Medicine Hat near Coutts, was named by an unknown RNWMP member of Milk River detachment in 1909.

The name "Masinasin" is said to be Cree for "Writing on Stone," which is the name of a nearby Provincial Park. See the **Police Creek** entry.

Mast House, 209 Elliot Street, Whitehorse, Yukon, is named after Sergeant Ivor Mast, RCMP #11195.

This frame cottage was built about 1901 and was first occupied by Doctor F.J. Nicholson, who was the superintendent of the first hospital in Whitehorse. From 1931 to 1935 Sergeant Mast served in the Force, mainly in the north. Upon retiring from the Force he took employment with the Department of Corrections at Whitehorse, and he purchased this house from the territorial government. Ivor and his wife Martha lived in the house from 1961 to 1985 before fully retiring and moving to the West Coast.

The home has since been declared a heritage site and named "the Mast House."

Maunsell, Alberta, in the southwestern area of the province, is named after Sub-Constable Edward Herbert Maunsell, NWMP #380 (Original Series). The official Geographical Survey records his regimental number as 125, which was a file number assigned to him by the comptroller of the Force in Ottawa and was not his regimental number.

See following entries.

Maunsell Close, Calgary, Alberta. See the next entry.

Maunsell Street, Fort Macleod, Alberta, is also named after one of two brothers who served in the NWMP (#380 or #386).

There is some confusion as to which street was named for which brother, so we have taken the easy way out and do not provide the answer. We can provide what is known about both men.

Sub-Constable Edward Herbert Maunsell, NWMP #380 (Original Series), was born in 1854 and served in the Force from June 11, 1874, to June 25, 1877. In 1874 he was a member of the first troop to arrive where Fort Macleod was built. He had joined the Force at St. Paul, Minnesota, with a contingent that was moving west. For his three years' good service, he received Land Warrant #0098. Edward died in 1923 and is buried in the Union Cemetery, Fort Macleod.

Sub-Constable George Maunsell, NWMP #386 (Original Series), served from February 25, 1875, to May 31, 1878, and for his three years' good service he received Land Warrant #0188. George died in 1919.

Both men left the Force to take up ranching in partnership with a third brother, Harry. They established the IV Ranch, adjoining the Peigan Reserve near Fort Macleod. By 1886 the Maunsell brothers' ranch was running over 10,000 head of cattle. Harry Maunsell and his wife Mary retired to Calgary in 1935, and for the next twelve years Harry became a familiar figure at the Calgary Stampede and Exhibition.

Medicine Hat, Alberta, in southeastern Alberta on Highway #1, received its first known official mention in a report of the NWMP in 1882.

"Medicine Hat" is a translation of the Blackfoot "saamis," which means "the headdress of a medicine man." Several stories exist on the origin of the name: from a battle between the Cree and Blackfoot in which a Cree medicine man lost his war bonnet; from the appropriation of a fancy hat worn by a settler; or from the shape of a hill east of the city that resembles a medicine man's hat.

Despite these variations, the translation remains constant and the first known record is that of the NWMP report. The following year the town was founded and marked by a railway point of the advancing Canadian Pacific Railway. Also in 1883, the site appeared on a Department of the Interior map.

Mellor, Northwest Territories (Lat: 60°42'50"N, Long: 114°56'30"W), a railway point between Hay River and Pine Point, was named in 1963 by the Canadian National Railway for its proximity to Mellor Rapids.

See following entry.

Mellor Rapids, Northwest Territories (Lat: 60°46'15"N, Long: 114°57'05"W), on the Buffalo River, was named after Sergeant Arthur Howard Llewellyn Mellor, RNWMP and RCMP #3970, O.201.

Mellor joined the Force on January 27, 1903, and served in "K" Division and then "G" Division where, in 1911, he almost lost his life in the rapids later named after him. During the First World War he volunteered for the "A" Squadron cavalry draft and served as a quartermaster sergeant in Canadian Expeditionary Force (#2684279). On his return from overseas he was promoted to the commissioned ranks as inspector. He then served in "F," "K," and "D" Divisions before his final transfer to Headquarters, Ottawa. He retired August 1, 1938, as the assistant director of criminal investigations for the Force.

He retired to Victoria, B.C., and died there on June 19, 1950.

Mihaluk Lake, Nunavut (Lat: 64°08'45"N, Long: 96°17'45"W), southwest of Qamanaugaq Lake between Baker Lake and Tehek Lake, was officially named in 1980. The true origin of the name is unknown, but was derived from RCMP patrol maps that had contained the name "Meesaluk," Inuktitut for "shallow waters."

Milburn Crescent, Swift Current, Saskatchewan, is named after Corporal William Milburn, NWMP #1894. Corporal Milburn served in the NWMP from January 22, 1887, to January 21, 1892, completing his five-year term of service. He served mainly at Maple Creek, where he was the head cook for the Division headquarters that was located there. Following his service he moved to Swift Current, and he was—over the years—a merchant, rancher, Dominion land agent, sheriff, Justice of the Peace, and town councillor. He retired to Oak Bay beside Victoria, B.C., and died there on August 1, 1947.

Millar Road, Calgary, Alberta, may have been named after Constable Malcolm Tanner Millar, NWMP #429.

See following entries.

Millarville, Alberta, a town west of Calgary, is named after Constable Malcolm Tanner Millar, NWMP #429.

See following entry.

Millarville Ranchers' Hall, Heritage Park, Calgary, Alberta, is named after Constable Malcolm Tanner Millar, NWMP #429.

The Ranchers' Hall was built about 1895 on land donated by Joseph Fisher about 25 kilometres southwest of Millarville. The district was named after Malcolm Tanner Millar, a former member of the NWMP, who took up land there in 1886.

Millar served from June 25, 1880, to July 27, 1885, through the areas that are now Alberta and Saskatchewan. On December 6,

1880, while stationed at Fort Walsh, he appeared in Orderly Room and was confined to barracks for seven days for "using threatening language to an NCO."[54] In 1884 he took part in the "Craig Incident,"[55] a precursor to the North-West Rebellion. Craig, an employee on Poundmaker's Reserve, had been assaulted. Superintendent Crozier, Inspector Antrobus, and 27 men responded. Millar was stationed at Battleford as the North-West Rebellion began in 1885, so he saw some of the action that ensued there.

After leaving the Force in 1885, he was the first settler and postmaster of Millarville. He also ranched at Priddis, Alberta. He died in Calgary, Alberta, on June 22, 1937.

Millen Creek, Northwest Territories (Lat: 67°40'00"N, Long: 135°42'00"W), near Fort McPherson, was named in 1978 after Constable Edgar Millen, RCMP #9669, Honour Roll #51. A cairn at this creek commemorates the death of Constable E. Millen at—or near—the site of his murder in January 1932.

See following entries.

Millen Lane, Depot Division RCMP, Regina, Saskatchewan, was named in honour of Constable Edgar Millen, RCMP #9669, Honour Roll #51.

See **Millen Street** entry.

Millen (Mount Millen), Yukon (Lat: 67°28'00"N, Long: 136°25'00"W), northeast of Lapierre House, was named in 1973 after Constable Edgar Millen, RCMP #9669, Honour Roll #51.

See **Millen Street** entry.

Millen Park, Edmonton, Alberta, is the site of a park and memorial to Constable Edgar Millen, RCMP #9669, Honour Roll #51.

Edgar Millen Park, Edmonton, Alberta

Millen Street, Inuvik, Northwest Territories, is named after Constable Edgar Millen, RCMP #9669, Honour Roll #51.

"Newt"[56] Millen served from November 22, 1920, until his death January 31, 1932, in what has become internationally known as

"The Case of the Mad Trapper of Rat River"—a case that has spawned books and "B" movies.

Millen served briefly in "D" Division before being posted north to "G" Division, Northwest Territories. Between 1928 and 1931 a man calling himself Albert Johnson was seen from time to time in various locations in the territories and was reported as appearing "odd." Constable Millen had an opportunity to talk to him in July 1931, but found him "unco-operative and uncommunicative." In December 1931, some Indians reported that he was stealing furs from their traplines.

On December 26, 1931, Constable Alfred "Buns" King (#10211) and Special Constable Bernard went to investigate. They located Johnson's cabin, but he would not answer the door. King returned with Constable Robert G. McDowell[57] (#10269) and also a search warrant. At their approach, Johnson shot through the door, seriously wounding King[58] in the chest. Constable McDowell drove their dogs for twenty hours non-stop to get the injured Constable King to the nearest medical help at Aklavik.

The officer in charge of the area, Inspector Alexander N. Eames (O.209), returned with McDowell, Millen, two special constables, two trappers, and 42 dogs. A two-day siege ensued without success. Johnson was shooting from gun-port slits at ground level in his cabin. The police even dynamited the cabin roof, but the explosion did not dislodge him. The police group withdrew to Aklavik for more supplies, and on their return found the cabin abandoned. It was now clear why they had not been successful, as Johnson had been well dug in below ground level.

The new posse added ex-Constable John A. Parsons (#4848) as well as Staff Sergeant Hersey and Sergeant Riddell of the Army Signals Corps with Aklavik Radio. The group split up to search separate areas. On January 31, 1932, Johnson surprised both Constable Millen and Sergeant Riddell when—from an ambush—he shot and killed Millen.

More joined in the hunt, including Constable William S. Carter (#10186), ex-Constable Arthur N. Blake (#4481), and ex-Constable Constant Ethier (#10233). Famed bush pilot W.R. "Wop" May was engaged, flying the supplies and doing an aerial search for any signs of the wanted man. Meanwhile, Constable Sidney W. May (#10521) and two special constables were searching east from the Yukon.

Snowshoe tracks not covered by fresh snowfalls were finally found, and on February 7, 1932, Johnson was spotted on the Eagle River. He took cover behind his pack in the snow and commenced firing on the advancing posse, seriously wounding Staff Sergeant

Hersey. Firing continued from both sides until Johnson's return fire ceased. He was dead. In his possession was a mixture of Canadian and American cash totalling $2,410, a few pearls, some gold dental fillings (not his), a .22 Winchester rifle, a 30-30 Savage rifle, a sawed-off Ivor Johnson shotgun, and 127 rounds of ammunition. The weapons and his snowshoes are now in the RCMP Museum at Depot Division. As the final solemn rite to this case, Constable Millen was laid to rest in the Beechmount Cemetery, Edmonton, Alberta.

Despite a widespread investigation, and suggestions from around the world, the true identity of Johnson remained a mystery. After 57 years the 1989 book *Trackdown*, written by Dick North, finally offered some very convincing information that Johnson was actually John Konrad Jonsen, a man with a criminal record in the U.S.

See map page 64.

Millet, Alberta, was named after August Millet by Father Lacombe. At various times Millet was under contract to the NWMP at Fort Saskatchewan.

Mitchell School (Junior High School), Winnipeg, Manitoba, is named after Staff Constable[59] (later Colonel) James Bertram Mitchell, NWMP #156 (Original Series).

Mitchell served from April 1, 1874, to May 31, 1877. He was in "E" Division on the 1874 March West. For his three years' good service he received Land Warrant #0097. He became an architect and settled in Winnipeg, practising his profession for over 36 years. He was also a commissioner of school buildings.

He died in Winnipeg on November 14, 1945.

Monson Lake, Yukon (Lat: 60°10'00"N, Long: 131°19'00"W), near Swift River, is named after Constable George Thomas Monson, NWMP, RNWMP, and RCMP #3406.

See following entry.

Monson (Mount Monson), Yukon (Lat: 62°08'10"N, Long: 136°24'15"W), southwest of Whitehorse, is named after Constable (later Corporal) George Thomas Monson, NWMP, RNWMP, and RCMP #3406.

Monson was in the Force from 1899 to 1907, serving first in Alberta and then the Yukon. He had his difficulties with authority as early in 1899 he appeared in Orderly Room at Calgary, where he was fined one dollar for "neglecting to obey an order." In 1901 he was back in Orderly Room and fined one dollar for "making a false statement." He then went north and served in the Yukon.

His whereabouts were unknown after 1907 until he joined the Canadian Expeditionary Force and served overseas in the First World War. Following the war in 1919, he reengaged with the Force and was posted again to "K" Division (Alberta) as a corporal. Almost immediately he was in trouble, as in Blairmore on September 22, 1919, he was charged in Orderly Room with being "intoxicated, however slightly," and was demoted to constable. He left the Force on July 26, 1920.

Monson died at Athabasca, Alberta, in 1976.

Moodie Island, Nunavut (Lat: 64°37'00"N, Long: 65°26'00"W), near southeast Baffin Island at the entrance to Cumberland Sound, was named in 1945 after Superintendent John Douglas Moodie, NWMP and RNWMP O.66.

See following entry.

Moodie Lake, Manitoba (Lat: 58°39'30"N, Long: 94°22'08"W), near

J.D. Moodie

McClintock on the Canadian National Railway line to Churchill, is named after Superintendent John Douglas Moodie, NWMP and RNWMP O.66.

Moodie came to Canada from England in 1880 and farmed near Brandon, Manitoba. On September 15, 1885, he was commissioned an inspector in the NWMP and first served in that part of the Northwest Territories that became the provinces of Alberta and Saskatchewan in 1905. In 1900 he served in the contingent that went to the Boer War, where he was wounded.

On his return in 1903, he was appointed governor of Hudson Bay with instructions to take possession of all islands to the north for Canada. He built posts at Fullerton, Chesterton, and Fort Churchill.

After retiring from the Force as a superintendent on September 15, 1917, he ranched at Eastend, Saskatchewan, and later moved to Maple Creek, Saskatchewan, where he was Justice of the Peace and coroner until 1932. He retired to Calgary, Alberta, in 1944. He died there on December 6, 1947, and was buried in Burnsland Cemetery.

Note: His wife, Geraldine, was a noted photographer, and a collection of her photographs are held in the British Museum.

Moody Lake (spelling error), Manitoba (Lat: 55°05'44"N, Long: 100°42'59"W), southwest of Burntwood Lake, was named after a son of the "first Mountie in the Hudson Bay area," Superintendent John Douglas Moodie, NWMP and RNWMP 0.66.

Geological records of 1921 indicate that B.W. Waugh named the lake after an old settler, but the settler himself stated it was named after Superintendent Moodie's son—a statement that was accepted in 1968.

Moore (Mount Moore), Nunavut (Lat: 63°09'00"N, Long: 69°40'00"W), north of Lake Harbour on Baffin Island, was named in 1946 for Constable Gifford Paul Colclough Moore, RCMP #10352.

Moore served from September 22, 1927, to September 21, 1947, in "N," "G," Depot, and "K" Divisions. During his service in the north he was stationed at the Lake Harbour detachment and on the RCMP schooner *St. Roch*.

He died on December 31, 1979, at Edmonton, Alberta.

See also the **St. Roch Island** entry.

Moriarty Road, Depot Division RCMP, Regina, Saskatchewan, is named in honour of Corporal Michael Moriarty, RNWMP and RCMP #6352, Honour Roll #55.

Moriarty had a varied police career. From 1908 to 1911 he served in the Glasgow City Police, Scotland, and from 1911 to 1913 he was in the London Metropolitan Police. By 1914 he had come to Canada, as he joined the Force on October 20, 1914, and began his service in "F" Division. He left in 1917 to join the Saskatchewan Provincial Police and then, in 1918, the newly formed Alberta Provincial Police. He was still with the Alberta Provincial Police on April 1, 1932, when the RCMP absorbed it, returning him to the Force. He then continued serving in Alberta until his death on April 26, 1935.

On that day, near the town of Rosebud, a man named David Knox had threatened a bailiff when he was served with an eviction notice. Moriarty, with Constable Albert R. "Jeekie" Allen (#11811), returned to the Knox farm with a summons. When Moriarty got out of the car to open the gate, he was shot in the back. Allen tried to remove him while under fire, but without success. He had the detachment notified, and soon five armed members arrived with several armed farmers. A short time later, Knox was seen running across a field. The posse attempted to corner him with cars, but he retreated to a granary and began firing at them. Shots were returned. Knox held the posse at bay for two hours until his shooting finally ceased. After a lull, a member drove by the granary, using his car as a shield, and saw that Knox had committed suicide.

Moriarty was not married, and his nearest relative lived in New York State. At his relatives' request, he was buried at Lackawanna, New York.

Moses Hill, Yukon (Lat: 67°19'00"N, Long: 136°49'00"W), twelve kilometres from Lapierre House, was named in 1973 after RCMP Special Constable John Moses.

Moses was the Indian special constable who drove dog teams for the RCMP in their hunt for Albert Johnson.

See **Millen Street** entry for details of this manhunt.

Mounted Police Museum, Depot Division RCMP, Regina, Saskatchewan.

The Force first opened its privately owned[60] museum on June 28, 1933, as a project for the 50th anniversary of the Force. It had a rather humble beginning in the "A" Block of Depot, which was used primarily as the headquarters' administration offices for policing Saskatchewan and for Depot Training Division. As the museum included the history of three major phases, from the NWMP, through the RNWMP, and then the RCMP, the name of "Mounted Police Museum" was chosen to represent all three.

Through time and difficulties of space, the museum was moved to the basement of "C" Block (Barracks) at Depot and later to this building's main floor. The present-day separate building for the museum at Depot was a Centennial gift to the Force from the federal government in recognition of its 100 years of service to the Canadian people. It was officially opened in 1973.

By the early 1980s, the museum again faced problems. It needed more display space, updating of displays, some office facilities, as well as more urgent requirements for climate-controlled storage for many delicate artifacts, and for funding—the primary necessity. The museum holds thousands of items, including uniforms, weapons, vehicles, and exhibits from historical cases in the Force's 128 years of service, but it had no space to display the majority of its holdings.

Members of the Regina Veterans' Association met and formed the "Friends of the Mounted Police Museum" in 1988 to support and raise funds for "our" museum. They began, and continually carry on, a busy program of raising funds for new displays and—ultimately— for a new museum building. They opened and continue to maintain the "Scarlet and Gold" gift shop within the museum, selling a wide range of Mounted Police mementos, police-related books, and so forth. They are assisted by a summer students program, by a volunteer group in the busy tourist season, and by recruit cadets, who act as guides and pose in Review Order Uniform for the ever-present cameras. The Friends also sell membership in their society and issue a quarterly newsletter of their projects and progress.

On June 2, 2000, the Natural Resources minister announced a federal grant of $25 million for a new Visitor's Reception Centre and Museum to be built at Depot. Our understanding is that the museum portion is contingent upon the Friends of the Mounted Police Museum raising a certain amount as well. At last it seems that the museum may be coming to the recognition it truly deserves.

Nash Field, Depot Division RCMP, Regina, Saskatchewan, is named in honour of Sub-Constable John D. Nash, NWMP #135 (Original Series), Honour Roll #1.

Nash served from October 1, 1873, until his accidental death March 11, 1876. He took part in the historic March West of 1874 and then served in the Fort Macleod area. While his death was not the first in the Force, it was the first one attributed to duty-related causes.

He was hauling logs with a team of horses for the construction of buildings at Fort Macleod, riding on top of the load. About ten kilometres from the fort, while going down a hill, the load spilled; falling logs fatally crushed him. Sub-Constable Nash was buried in the Union Cemetery at Fort Macleod.

Although his service was not quite three years, a Land Warrant (#0183) was granted in his name and given to his mother in Halifax, Nova Scotia.

Nicholson Building, RCMP Headquarters, Ottawa, was the name chosen for the Headquarters Building as part of the 125th Anniversary celebrations of the Force (1873–1998) to honour Commissioner Leonard Hanson Nicholson, MBE, OC, GCStJ, LLD, RCMP O.264.

Nicholson joined the Force as regimental #10049 on December 14, 1923, but he purchased his discharge in 1926 to join the New Brunswick Provincial Police. There he rose to the rank of inspector before moving to the Nova Scotia Provincial Police, where he remained until the RCMP absorbed them on April 1, 1932. He was now back with the Force as Inspector O.264.

At the outbreak of the Second World War, the Force was given the task of setting up the #1 Provost Corps (military police), and Nicholson was assigned to supervise. More volunteers than could be handled came forward from the ranks, so the Corps was soon in full operation with men already trained for the majority of their anticipated roles. Nicholson was appointed provost marshal and served in that capacity throughout the war. He later wrote about the history of the provost corps in the book entitled *Battle Dress Patrol*. For his services in the Second World War, he was made a Member of the British Empire (MBE).

At war's end he returned to the Force as director of criminal investigations with the rank of assistant commissioner. He was in this role when Commissioner S.T. Wood (O.171) retired on April 30, 1951. Nicholson was then appointed the ninth permanent commissioner of the Force.

In response to a serious strike in Newfoundland in 1959, Nicholson planned to send in a contingent of members; however, the federal government of the day overruled him, so he resigned on principle. He remained in Ottawa following his retirement and died there on March 22, 1983. He was buried in the Force Cemetery at Depot Division. Note: For those of us who met him personally, he was a true gentleman!

Nicholson Circle, Canadian Police College, Rockcliffe, Ontario, is named in honour of Sergeant Richard Henry Nicholson, RNWMP and RCMP #5611, Honour Roll #49.

See following entry.

Nicholson Field, Depot Division RCMP, Regina, Saskatchewan, is named in honour of Sergeant Richard Henry Nicholson, RNWMP and RCMP #5611, Honour Roll #49.

Sergeant Nicholson was one of another extended family in the Force. His brother-in-law was Staff Sergeant John "Taffy" Jones (#5649), who served from 1913 to 1927. His nephews were trumpeter David Jones (#10038), who served from 1923 to 1926; Staff Sergeant John J. Jones (#10139), who served from 1925 to 1947; and Constable Thomas Jones (#10351), who served from 1927 to 1948. Finally, his great-grandson, Constable William R. Marlow (#40054), is presently serving (as of spring 2002).

Nicholson joined the Force on June 17, 1913, and was posted to the Yukon. With the need for additional men in the First World War, he became one of many to volunteer, reporting to Depot Division to join the newly formed "A" Squadron (cavalry) for service in France. His Canadian Expeditionary Force number was #2683716.

At war's end he returned to Depot Division and became the third chauffeur of the Division's one and only car.[61] By 1926 he had been posted to "D" Division[62] and was in charge of the Brandon detachment. It was here that he experienced the displeasure of Inspector Mellor in Orderly Room. He was reduced to the foot of the Seniority Roll of Sergeants for "disgraceful conduct by failing to report the absence of a subordinate." In other words, he hadn't reported one of his men having a hangover.

On December 31, 1928, accompanied by Constable J. Watson of the Manitoba Provincial Police, he went to search for a "moonshine still" on William Eppinger's farm near Molson, Manitoba, about 61 kilometres east of Winnipeg. Their approach surprised Eppinger at the still site, which was in a heavily bushed area; Eppinger grabbed his rifle, which was close at hand. Nicholson leapt forward and struggled with Eppinger for control of the weapon, which, in turn, discharged into Nicholson's leg. Eppinger immediately fled as Nicholson fell. Constable Watson tried to staunch the flow of blood and carried Nicholson to a nearby farmhouse, but Nicholson bled to death before the doctor arrived.

Eppinger was arrested the following day and was sentenced to five year's imprisonment for manslaughter. Sergeant Nicholson was buried in the Force Cemetery at Depot Division.

Nicholson River, Northwest Territories (Lat: 62°48'00"N, Long: 114°12'00"W), north of Wood Buffalo Park near Pine Point, is named after Staff Sergeant John Daniel Nicholson, NWMP and RNWMP #1709.

As in the previous entry, Nicholson was a member of another Force family. His nephews were Staff Sergeant James Archibald Cawsey (#6367), who served from 1914 to 1951, and Sergeant John Nicholson Cawsey (#11462), who served from 1932 to 1944 and was also the first dog master in the Force. His grand-nephews were Staff Sergeant Lorne Cawsey (#12807), who served from 1935 to 1964, and Constable Robert Allan Cawsey (#13839), who served for the year 1941 and later became a judge in Alberta.

John Nicholson served from December 14, 1885, to 1911, mainly in Alberta. By 1894 he was a sergeant, but he was demoted to constable when he allowed a prisoner to be an assistant cook, and the prisoner took the opportunity to escape.

By 1908 he was a staff sergeant and became widely known for the "Clover Bar Murder Case." In this case he arrested William King for horse theft. While endeavouring to bargain his situation, King led Nicholson to the body of a murder victim and implicated an associate as the killer. Nicholson left the prisoner in the custody of another member, and while he made further enquiries, King escaped. Both members were then demoted to constable. King was later arrested in Edmonton. Through Nicholson's good work, King was found guilty of the murder and was hanged. The demoted members' ranks were reinstated.

In 1911 Nicholson left the Force to be a detective for the Alberta government. When the Alberta Provincial Police was formed in 1917, he joined too, and by 1919 he was second in charge of that department.

As an aside, Nicholson worked tirelessly on behalf of the veterans of the RNWMP to have their pensions adjusted to the cost of living. In 1945 J.W. Horan published his biography entitled *On the Side of the Law.*

Nicholson died May 10, 1945, at Victoria, B.C., and was buried in the Royal Oak Burial Park.

See also the **Cawsey Drive** entry.

Nicolle Flats, in Buffalo Pound Provincial Park, Qu'Appelle Valley, Saskatchewan, is named after Superintendent Charles Nicolle, NWMP O.23½.[63]

Nicolle was engaged with the Force on April 29, 1874, as #324 (Original Series). Just as preparations for the commencement of the 1874 March West were in the final stages, Quartermaster Joseph Forget (O.23) resigned on June 20, 1874. Nicolle was promoted to the commissioned ranks on June 17, 1874, to replace him.

On July 15, 1875, his services were "dispensed with." His duties were handed over to Percy Neale (#2, Original Series), and he was granted one month's pay as gratuity. He then moved back to eastern Canada.

In 1881 he returned to the Qu'Appelle Valley and began homesteading. He staked a claim around Buffalo Pound Lake and began farming, naming his place "Mapleford." Disaster struck in the winter of 1906–07 when he lost 400 horses to the severe conditions. His son Douglas was the last member of the family to live on the original ranch. The house is still standing today and serves as a tourist attraction.

See also the **Osborne** entry.

Oldman River, Alberta, was named by Jerry Potts, a NWMP scout and interpreter.

"The River the Old Man Played On" was the interpretation of the Blackfoot name. Potts shortened it to the Old Man River. Now the name is displayed as one word, "Oldman."

See also **Potts (Jerry Potts Street)**.

Oliver Crescent, Depot Division RCMP, Regina, Saskatchewan, is named in honour of Constable Peter Seddon Oliver, RCMP #12572, Honour Roll #72.

Plaque commemorating P.S. Oliver in France

Oliver joined the Force on June 22, 1936, and served in "D" Division. At the outbreak of the Second World War in 1939, he volunteered for the #1 Provost Corps, which was being formed from members of the Force. His Canadian Army Provost Corps number was C.42026. He went overseas as a lance corporal and by 1942 had been commissioned as a lieutenant. He was then transferred to #2 Provost Company.

The #2 Provost Company was led by Captain Stevenson (RCMP #12370). Oliver was second in command, but he was killed in action during the raid on Dieppe on August 19, 1942. The raid was code-named "Operation Jubilee" and became an infamous operation in war history that was—with hindsight—an ill-advised and poorly prepared attack on the German fortress of Europe. There were 41 members of the Force in that raid. Oliver was the only member of the Force to die that day; he was also the first member of the Force to be killed in action in the Second World War.

Lieutenant (Constable) Oliver was buried in the Dieppe Canadian War Cemetery at Hautot-sur-Mer, France.

Osborne, Manitoba, a community and school district north of Morris on the Canadian Pacific Railway line and first noted on a Department of the Interior map in 1884, is named after temporary first commissioner Colonel W. Osborne Smith, NWMP O.2½.[63]

Osborne was named a Canadian Pacific Railway point in 1883. A post office followed in 1911, but it ceased operations in 1970. With the modernization of railroads, the railway station no longer exists.

Osborne Smith was a lieutenant colonel in the Canadian Militia at the time of the formation of the NWMP. On September 25, 1873, he was appointed as temporary commissioner of the NWMP until the federal government decided upon a permanent commissioner. With the appointment of Commissioner French, Smith's temporary appointment was cancelled on October 16, 1873. In 1874 he was in command of the militia troop escort of William Morris at the negotiations of Treaty Number Four at Qu'Appelle. He commanded the Winnipeg Light Infantry in the North-West Rebellion of 1885.

See also the **Nicolle Flats** entry.

Owens (Mitch Owens Road), Ottawa, Ontario, a boundary road between the city of Gloucester and Osgoode Township, is named after Corporal Mitchell "Mitch" George Owens, RCMP #14455.

Mitch served in the Force from 1942 to 1963 in "G" Division (Northwest Territories) and Headquarters, Ottawa. He made the west to east passage on the *St. Roch* in 1944–45. Following his retirement from the Force he was connected with the Gloucester city council for 25 years, so they recognized his community work by naming this road in his honour.

Parker Avenue, Medicine Hat, Alberta, is named after Inspector William Parker, NWMP and RNWMP #252 (Original Series), #28 (New Series), and O.132.

Parker served from April 14, 1874, until November 1, 1912. He was in the March West of 1874 and then served in what is now Alberta. He took part in the quelling of the 1885 North-West Rebellion, having arrived from Fort Saskatchewan where he was then posted. He was promoted to the commissioned ranks on March 1, 1903, as O.132 and continued his service in Alberta.

He took time out to serve in the First World War, then returned to the Force and retired from the Medicine Hat detachment on May 31, 1928. He then sold real estate in the Medicine Hat area and authored the manuscipt entitled *38½ Years Service and Experience in the Mounties*. The book was later published in 1973 under the title *William Parker, Mounted Policeman*.

William Parker died at the age of 91 at Medicine Hat on May 16, 1945, and was buried in the Hillside Cemetery. His diaries are now in the Glenbow Archives, Calgary, Alberta.

Parsons Lake, Northwest Territories (Lat: 68°57'00"N, Long: 133°38'45"W), in the Mackenzie Delta, is named after Constable John Ambrose Parsons, RNWMP #4848.

Parsons served in the Force from April 24, 1909, until April 23, 1916, in "F," "K," and "G" Divisions. He left the Force from Herschel to join a whaling company on Herschel Island. In 1932 he was in Aklavik at the time of the hunt for the "Mad Trapper,"[64] so he was called back to assist in tracking the fugitive.

Later, from 1950 to 1965, he managed a store at Codroy, Newfoundland. He died on October 5, 1974, at Halifax, Nova Scotia.

Patrol Avenue, Medicine Hat, Alberta, is named in honour of the NWMP barrack situated nearby.

Paynton, Saskatchewan, situated on Highway #16 between Battleford and Lloydminster, is named—in part—after Constable Peter Paynter, NWMP #743.

Three former members of the NWMP were supposedly the earliest, or at least among the earliest, settlers of the "Paynton" district west of Battleford.

Constable Peter Paynter served in the Force from April 3, 1882, to April 2, 1890, at Fort Macleod and Battleford. On leaving the force, he homesteaded at the present-day location of Paynton and died there in 1934. Sub-Constable John W. Shields (#258) served in the Force from 1877 to 1880 and soon settled in the same area. Constable James McCreedy (#1285) served from 1885 to 1890 before settling in this area. All three were said to have become prosperous farmers.

By 1903 a group of 2,000 colonists from England came to a huge tract of land in the area, which was secured by Reverend Isaac Barr. By 1905 it became an organized village. Hearsay is that the original name proposed was "Paynterton," to honour Paynter as the original settler, but then it was changed to "Paynton" to honour two men. The "Paynt" contains the first part of Paynter's name, and the "nton" includes the last part of prominent Barr colonist William Thornton's name.

Pearkes (G.R. Pearkes Recreation Centre), Saanich, B.C., located in the municipality of Saanich in Greater Victoria, is named after Major-General (Constable) George Randolph Pearkes, RNWMP #5529, who was also a lieutenant-governor of B.C.

See following entries.

Pearkes (Coast Guard Vessel *George R. Pearkes*), a Canadian Coast Guard ship, is named after Major-General George Randolph Pearkes, RNWMP constable #5529. This vessel, a light icebreaker, was built in 1986 by the Versatile Pacific Shipyards, Victoria, B.C. Its home port is in Quebec City, and it is manned by a crew of 25.

See following entry.

Pearkes (Major-General George Pearkes Building), National Defence Building, Ottawa, is named after Major-General George Randolph Pearkes, VC, DSO, MC, CdeG, and former RNWMP constable #5529.

Constable Pearkes served in the Yukon from February 13, 1913, to February 19, 1915, when he purchased his discharge to join the army in the First World War. During his short stint in the Yukon he was—for a time—paid 50 cents extra per day to be the town patrolman of Whitehorse.

He went on to a distinguished military career, rising to major-general. In his later years he also served as lieutenant-governor for the province of B.C. He retired, finally, in Victoria, B.C., where he died on May 30, 1984. General Pearkes was buried next to the Holy Trinity Church in West Saanich, B.C.

As an aside, on January 15, 1935, Order-in-Council 168/30 ordered a refund of 50 dollars to be paid to Lieutenant-Colonel Pearkes—being the amount he had paid to purchase his discharge from the RNWMP to enable him to join the Canadian Mounted Rifles on March 2, 1915—some twenty years later!

Pearson Welding Training Centre, Canadian Forces Base Borden, Ontario, is named after Constable William Oliver Pearson, RNWMP #6849. Pearson's name was actually chosen because of his military service rather than for his service in the Force.

He joined the Force on April 26, 1918, as part of the "A" Squadron Cavalry (as #2683830) in order to perform duties in France during the First World War. With demobilization at the war's end, he was discharged from the Force on June 18, 1919.

In the Second World War he enlisted as a welder with the 3rd New Brunswick Coast Brigade. He was transferred to the Royal Canadian Ordnance Corps and then Royal Canadian Electrical and Mechanical Engineers. On October 25, 1944, he was awarded the Bronze Cross. During the battle of Wousche Plantage in Holland, when under direct fire, he spent two hours welding a tank to get it back into action.

On November 25, 1994, in recognition of Pearson's war service as a welder, Canadian Forces Base Borden named the new Welding Training Centre after him.

He died in Burnaby in 1962 and was buried in the Forest Lawn Cemetery.

Pedley, Alberta, an unincorporated place on Highway #16 some eleven kilometres east of Hinton, is named after Sergeant Albert Reuben Pedley, NWMP, RNWMP, and RCMP #3613.

See following entry.

Pedley Reservoir, near Pedley, Alberta (above).

Pedley served from April 18, 1900, to April 17, 1924, within Alberta. He made a most notable patrol from December 17, 1904, to January 7, 1905. This 21-day patrol began with Pedley setting out in blizzard conditions by dog team, escorting an insane man from Fort Chipewyan to Fort Saskatchewan, Alberta, and then covering a distance—"as the crow flies"—of 612 kilometres. En route, on December 31, 1904, he complicated the journey by arresting three men at Lac La Biche; however, he still arrived with them at Saddle Lake on January 4, 1905, and handed them over for trial. He then continued on to Fort Saskatchewan with only the mental patient. In 1952 Metro-Goldwyn-Mayer produced a movie titled *The Wild North* that was billed as being based on this epic patrol, but there was no similarity to fact.

Following his retirement from the Force in 1924, Pedley moved to England and died on June 3, 1959, at Salisbury, England. His son, Corporal George Albert Pedley (RCMP #10609), also served from 1929 to 1955.

Peebles District, southeast of Fort Saskatchewan, Alberta, is named after Constable Albert "Charlie" Peebles, NWMP #1335.

Peebles served from April 28, 1885, until April 27, 1890, in what are now "F" and "K" Divisions. He left the Force from Fort Saskatchewan and settled locally.

On July 11, 1892, he was appointed trustee of the first school district at Agricola (south of Fort Saskatchewan) and on May 30, 1895, became a trustee of the first school district at the Partridge Hill School (southeast of Fort Saskatchewan), which was named after him. He died on November 24, 1932, and is buried at Fort Saskatchewan.

Pelletier Bay, Nunavut (Lat: 63°44'30"N, Long: 91°48'00"W), near Chesterfield Inlet on the west side of Hudson Bay, is named after Inspector Ephrem Albert Pelletier, NWMP and RNWMP O.122.
See following entries.

Pelletier Lake, Manitoba (Lat: 58°37'10"N, Long: 94°26'29"W), near McClintock on the railway line to Churchill, is named after Inspector Ephrem Albert Pelletier, NWMP and RNWMP O.122.

Pelletier Point, Nunavut (Lat: 63°44'00"N, Long: 91°45'00"W), on Baker Foreland south of Chesterfield Inlet, was named in 1979 after Inspector Ephrem Albert Pelletier, NWMP and RNWMP O.122. The name was given in recognition of Pelletier's 1908 patrol from Alberta to Chesterfield Inlet.

Pelletier previously served as a lieutenant in the 2nd Battalion of the Canadian Mounted Rifles during the Boer War. He was appointed inspector in the NWMP on January 1, 1901, and served until June 1, 1910, when he resigned. His reason for resignation is unknown, but from review of his service in the Force it could well be he was tired of walking and paddling his way back and forth across western Canada!

On July 5, 1907, he was transferred from Depot Division, Regina, to Churchill with Sergeant George Butler (#2412) and Constables Lyman Caldwell (#4526) and Cyril Travers(#4570). They travelled by Canadian Pacific Railway to Winnipeg, Manitoba, then by narrow-gauge railway to Selkirk, where the Dominion Fish Company's steamer took them to Lake Winnipeg. They continued their trip on the boat *Keewatin* on Lake Winnipeg and down the Nelson River to Norway House. Here they boarded York boats and journeyed to Split Lake. They then travelled with three canoes and ten dogs for eighteen days, canoeing and portaging up the Deer River, over to the Churchill River, then along it to Churchill, arriving on August 20. They had endured 46 days of unpleasant travelling just to be transferred.

By 1908 he was back west at Fort Saskatchewan, for it was then he was instructed to establish a link between the eastern and western Arctic. Accompanied by three other members, including Constable Robert Walker (#3829) and Constable Patrick Conway (#4217), he went from Fort Saskatchewan, Alberta, to Athabasca Landing and then—by way of the Hudson's Bay Company's boat—across the lake and down the Slave River to Fort Smith on the Alberta–Northwest Territories border. From here they used canoes to cross the Great Slave Lake, then paddled down the Hanbury and

Route of Pelletier's 1908 trip

Thelon Rivers to Baker Lake, and then to Chesterfield Inlet on the western shore of Hudson Bay. They were met there by a whaleboat. That winter they returned south by dog team to Churchill, Norway House, and finally Gimli, Manitoba—in all, over 4,830 kilometres. It was for this feat that the point was named after him.

Inspector Pelletier died in 1952, but we have not learned where. See also **Conway Point** and **Walker Island** entries.

Perry Building, "A" Block–Administration Building, Depot Division RCMP, Regina, Saskatchewan, was dedicated to Commissioner Aylesworth Bowen Perry, NWMP, RNWMP, and RCMP O.44.

See following entries.

Perry Lake, Saskatchewan, is named after Commissioner Aylesworth Bowen Perry, NWMP, RNWMP, and RCMP O.44. Ottawa records list Perry Lake, Saskatchewan, without directions from any landmark or coordinates. There are three Perry Lakes and we have not been able to determine which one is named after Commissioner

Perry. Their locations are as follows: near the south end of Reindeer Lake (Lat: 56°54'00"N, Long: 102°43'00"W); adjacent to Lake Athabasca (Lat: 59°54'00"N, Long: 108°29'00"W); and near Govan (Lat: 51°29'00"N, Long: 104°10'00"W).

See following entry.

Perry River, Nunavut (Lat: 67°43'00"N, Long: 102°14'00"W), flowing from MacAlpine Lake to the Arctic into Queen Maud Gulf, was named in 1953 after Commissioner Aylesworth Bowen Perry, CMG, NWMP, RNWMP, and RCMP O.44.

Perry had previously served in the Royal Engineers when he was appointed to the commissioned ranks in the NWMP on January 24, 1882. Only three years later he was superintendent at Fort Macleod when the North-West Rebellion broke out.

On April 18, 1885, he led twenty men with a nine-pound field gun en route to Edmonton to join General Strange's Force. They reached Calgary in three days, having travelled 170 kilometres. They then went through seven days of very bad weather to get to Red Deer, where they constructed a raft and used 365 metres of picket ropes to cross the river. The raft, loaded with the field gun, broke free. Superintendent Perry and Constable Diamond (#910) swam to shore to retie the ropes. The raft was finally secured. They continued on, cutting road here and there, until they reached Edmonton. It had taken them a total of thirteen days, including almost four days to cross the river at Red Deer.

On August 1, 1900, Perry went from the rank of superintendent to that of the fifth permanent commissioner, succeeding Herchmer, who had retired. Over the following 22 years he guided the Force through some significant changes. The provinces of Alberta and Saskatchewan came into being in 1905, and with that their responsibility for self-policing, although there was a provision for the Force to carry out provincial policing by contract. Within a few years the two provinces formed their own provincial police forces.

In 1911 Perry led a contingent of the Force to England for the Coronation of King George V. Then it was back to more changes at home, for soon the First World War had its profound impact on the Force. In 1920, with the absorption of the Dominion Police and its duties, the Force's federal roles were now a Canada-wide responsibility.

Commissioner Perry retired on March 31, 1923. He marked his career with not only his police work but also with the Companion Most Distinguished Order of St. Michael and St. George.

He died February 14, 1956, in Ottawa and was buried at Lachute, Quebec.

See also the **Gladys Lake** entry.

Phillips Channel, Northwest Territories (Lat: 67°52'00"N, Long: 135°04'00"W), in the Mackenzie River delta, is named after Assistant Commissioner John Willett Phillips, NWMP, RNWMP, and RCMP O.173.

Phillips joined the NWMP on June 1, 1898, as #3300 and served in "K" Division. He was promoted to the commissioned ranks on April 1, 1913, as O.173. He then served in "G" Division (Northwest Territories), "O" and "A" Divisions (Ontario), and finally "E" Division (B.C.), where he retired December 31, 1935, as the commanding officer.

On July 22, 1918, when stationed in the north, a routine patrol became a life-threatening experience. He departed Herschel Island with Corporal William A. Doak (#4396) and Constable Eric H. Cornelius (#5369) on a boat to get their mail. During a sudden storm their boat became wrecked in floating ice. The men were forced to abandon the boat and jump from one tippy floe to another, endeavouring to reach solid ice. They eventually came to open water and had to swim in the frigid ocean to reach shore. Cornelius set out, soaking wet, to Herschel some nineteen kilometres away, while Phillips and Doak sought shelter in driftwood on the shoreline. By the next morning, with Doak now delirious, they had the good fortune of attracting the attention of a whaleboat passing by and were rescued. When Constable Cornelius was found, he was still struggling valiantly—his clothing frozen—toward his destination.

In 1920, accompanied by Sergeant Alfred H. Joy (#4919), he made a lengthy patrol of the Belcher Islands (in southeast Hudson Bay) on a murder investigation.

Assistant Commissioner Phillips died on November 8, 1959, at Belleville, Ontario.

See also **Doak Island** and **Joy River** entries.

Pierlet (Roger Pierlet Bridge), Cloverdale–Surrey, B.C., is named in honour of Constable Roger Emile Pierlet, RCMP #29984, Honour Roll #147.

Pierlet had served from 1967 to 1972 in the Canadian Forces Artillery before joining the Force on August 9, 1972. He was at his first field posting when he was murdered. In the early morning hours of March 29, 1974, John Miller and Vincent Cockriell from

R.E. Pierlet

nearby Langley were drinking and decided to kill a policeman. They drove to nearby Cloverdale where they drew attention to themselves by throwing a bottle through a window of the Justice Building and driving erratically. Constable Pierlet stopped them, and as he was talking to the driver, the passenger shot him from less than two metres away with a 30-30 rifle. The bullet struck him in the chest and tore through his heart.

Constable William J. Mead (#27648), en route as backup, found Pierlet within minutes. Prior to stopping the car, Pierlet had radioed in the licence plate number, so the police at least knew the vehicle they were seeking. The car was soon found, and a wild high-speed chase ensued before Constables Larry Misner (#27652) and Blaine Everett (#29646) finally stopped it. Miller and Cockriell were charged with murder, convicted, and sentenced to life imprisonment. By 1995 Cockriell was already receiving day passes from prison.

Constable Pierlet is buried in the Force Cemetery at Depot Division, Regina, Saskatchewan.

Pincher Creek, Alberta, is a name with an NWMP connection. History suggests the town got its name when prospectors accidentally dropped a pair of pincers in the creek about 1868. A party of NWMP supposedly recovered the pincers in 1875 when they were establishing a hay camp at Pincher Creek.

Pincher Creek, Alberta

The name was firmly on our maps when, in 1879, Inspector (later Superintendent) Albert Shurtliffe (O.12) with a sergeant and seven constables—Sergeant William Parker (#20), Constables William Reid (#102), Alfred Lynch-Staunton (#241), James Bruneau (#216),[65] David Grier (#226), John Johnston (#230), Peter McEwen

(#233), and Sub-Constable Charles Kettles (#184)—established a horse-breeding farm and detachment at this point.

See also **Kettles Creek** entry.

Pinhorn, Alberta (former site), 115 kilometres southwest of Medicine Hat, is named after Veterinary Staff Sergeant Gerald Charles Pinhorn, RNWMP #4462. While this site no longer exists, it is entered here because it may still be a common reference point in the local area.

Pinhorn only served in the Force one year—from June 11, 1906, to June 30, 1907. He was transferred to Alberta on July 1, 1906, to serve as a veterinarian. He left the Force to be a veterinary inspector for the Department of Agriculture in southern Alberta, and he ran a quarantine station on the U.S. border for the movement of cattle between Canada and the U.S.

A post office was established at the described location on January 1, 1914, but was closed permanently on February 25, 1948.

Pinhorn retired to Victoria, B.C., and died there on May 28, 1951.

Police Creek, Alberta (Lat: 49°05'00"N, Long: 111°38'00"W), in Writing-On-Stone Provincial Park, is in the southeast corner of Alberta.

This is a conservation area of aboriginal pictographs from early history and the site of an early NWMP post. There is now a reconstruction of the NWMP detachment here.

Police Creek, Yukon (Lat: 64°24'25"N, Long: 135°20'00"W), the north fork of the Beaver River, was named in 1905. This was one of the trails used by the RNWMP on the Dawson–McPherson patrols, running along this creek from Dawson via the Little Wind River.

Police Flat, Northwest Territories (Lat: 69°49'00"N, Long: 122°41'00"W), on Cape Lyon adjacent to the Arctic Ocean, was so named by the Hydrographic Service and accepted in 1970. It is the site of an RCMP patrol cabin originally situated on this topographical feature.

Police Flats, Alberta (Lat: 49°33'30"N, Long: 114°18'20"W), 60 metres north of Highway #3 and about four kilometres east of Bellevue, was in 1881 a temporary NWMP post established near Burmis and Passmore to combat an epidemic of cattle rustling.

Sergeant John Daniel Nicholson (#1709) was in charge there in 1900–1901.

See also **Nicholson River** entry.

Police Island, Northwest Territories (Lat: 64°51'00"N, Long: 125°11'00"W), in a small lake in the Franklin Mountains north of Fort Norman and west of Fort Franklin, was accepted in 1981 from a proposal by warden R.C. Timmins, as it was the name already in local use.

Police Lake, Manitoba (Lat: 58°46'53"N, Long: 94°14'06"W), nine kilometres west of Churchill, was the name first applied in 1916 on a Department of the Interior map, which showed an RCMP post on the east shore.

Police Lake, Nunavut (Lat: 63°20'20"N, Long: 90°43'00"W), at Chesterfield Inlet on the west side of Hudson Bay, was so named as it was the lake from which the Force detachment obtained its fresh water supply. It is 1.6 kilometres from the hamlet.

Police Outpost Provincial Park, Alberta, in southern Alberta at the Montana border, is the site of an early NWMP outpost.

The detachment was established in the 1890s to prevent smuggling in the vicinity. Outpost Lake (Lat: 49°01'00"N, Long: 113°28'00"W) forms a part of the boundary of the park, and the original NWMP post was on its southern shore.

The park is nineteen kilometres west from Cardston on Highway #5, then a further eighteen kilometres south from there.

Police Point, Northwest Territories (Lat: 70°11'00"N, Long: 124°45'00"W), on Cape Parry in the Arctic Ocean, was named in 1952.

Police Point Drive, Medicine Hat, Alberta, extends from Parkview Drive through a residential area to the Police Point Park Interpretive Centre.

Police Point Park, Medicine Hat, Alberta, is the former location of an NWMP barracks.

Policeman Creek, Canmore, Alberta, is located in front of the NWMP Museum on Main and 8th Street.

Policeman's Point Road, Yukon, 30 kilometres northwest of Whitehorse on Highway #2, was the name suggested by the Yukon Department of Highways to honour the NWMP's temporary detachment at Lake Laberge. The detachment was organized in 1898 as a checkpoint on the supply road to the steamboats.

Pollock Coulee, Saskatchewan (Lat: 49°38'00"N, Long: 108°58'00"W), in southwest Saskatchewan about seventeen kilometres from Eastend, is named after Constable Daniel Houston Pollock, NWMP #1104.

Pollock served in the NWMP from 1884 until 1896. He died in 1932 at Eastend, Saskatchewan.

See **Anxiety Butte** entry for details of Pollock's service.

Port Mann Freeway Patrol is an RCMP Trans-Canada Highway patrol through Burnaby, Coquitlam, and Surrey in the Lower Mainland of B.C.

This unit was previously known as the Lower Fraser Valley Freeway Patrol, then Unit "B" Freeway Patrol. The present name was suggested by Staff Sergeant William J. Hulgaard (#17856) and authorized by District 1 commanding officer, Assistant Commissioner H. Jensen (O.642).

The area of Port Mann was originally named after Sir Donald Mann, co-builder of the Canadian Northern Railway. Staff Sergeant Hulgaard was in charge of this patrol when it opened in 1965. He left on transfer in 1966, returned in 1973, and served there until 1988, serving a total of sixteen years at this detachment. His final year, prior to retirement, was at Vancouver Headquarters as the "E" Division traffic supervisor.

Potato Creek, Yukon (Lat: 68°09'00"N, Long: 140°23'00"W), a tributary to Surprise Creek and the Old Crow River, is the name that was reported in 1949 by Corporal Ernest A. Kirk, RCMP #10035. The name "Schaefer Creek" had been applied mistakenly by the International Boundary Survey crew in 1911 and continued being shown as such on maps until 1950.

See also **Kirk Lake** entry.

Potts (Jerry Potts Boulevard), Lethbridge, Alberta.
See following entry.

Jerry Potts information sign near Warner, Alberta

Potts (Jerry Potts Street), Fort Macleod, Alberta, is named after the famous scout for the NWMP.

The son of a Blood Indian woman named Crooked Back and Andrew Potts, a Scottish fur trader with the American Fur Company, Jerry Potts was ideally suited to being a scout. At the end of the March West of 1874, Major Macleod had the task of re-supplying the column and establishing winter quarters. He journeyed south to Fort Benton, Montana, for the supplies. There he met and hired Potts in October 1874 as a guide and interpreter, as he had knowledge of the intended NWMP post's area.

Potts led the Force back into Canada to Fort Whoop-Up and then to an ideal location for the winter, which is the present location of Fort Macleod.

Potts had a name as a warrior, having grown up with his mother's people and fighting with the Blackfoot in battles against their enemies. In 1877 he acted as an interpreter at the signing of Treaty Number Seven and continued his valuable and faithful role until his death on July 14, 1896. He received a full military funeral at Fort Macleod.

Several of his descendants have since served, or are now serving, in the Force. Those known include Constable Henry Potts (#43363), who served from 1978 to 1995 and died on September 4, 1999, at Fort Macleod; Constable Tyronne P. J. Potts (#43380), who is now serving; and Constable Janet Potts (#43382) who is also serving as of 2001.

See also **Macleod Island**.

Primrose Lake, Yukon (Lat: 60°06'00"N, Long: 135°41'00"W), a nineteen-kilometre-long lake east of the Takhini River, was named by George White-Fraser of the Department of the Interior while setting out monuments on the Yukon–B.C. boundary in 1900. He named it after Inspector Philip Carteret Hill Primrose, NWMP O.56, who was in charge of the Tagish Post and district at the time.

See following entry.

Primrose Subdivision, Edmonton, Alberta, is named after Superintendent Philip Carteret Hill Primrose, retired RNWMP member (O.56) and lieutenant-governor of Alberta.

Primrose attended the Royal Military College in Kingston, Ontario, and then received his commission in the Force on August 1, 1885. He served in the territories (now Saskatchewan and Alberta) and then the Yukon before finishing his service at Depot Division.

On March 17, 1898, during the Yukon gold rush, he established the Stikine detachment on the Boundary Post known as Moors Landing, Stikine River. His party travelled from Regina to Vancouver, B.C., on the Canadian Pacific Railway and then sailed on the S.S. *Tees* to Fort Wrangell, Alaska. He had twenty men, ten horses, 25 dogs, and 80 tons (72,575 kilograms) of supplies. From Fort Wrangell they travelled on the Hudson's Bay boat *Glenora* to Cottonwood Island in the mouth of the Stikine River. From there they went upstream 56 kilometres to their destination.

Primrose retired on April 15, 1915, and was then a magistrate at Edmonton, Alberta, until 1935. On the advice of Prime Minister William Lyon Mackenzie King, he was appointed lieutenant-governor of Alberta, effective October 1, 1936. He died on March 17, 1937, and was buried in the Edmonton City Cemetery. He was also a son-in-law of Superintendent Deane. (See **Deane House** entry.)

Pringle Lake, Yukon (Lat: 60°08'00"N, Long: 136°59'00"W), on the west side of Haines Junction near Dalton Post, is named after Constable James Albert Pringle, NWMP #2702.

Pringle served in the Force from July 6, 1891, until February 24, 1901, mainly in the Yukon at Dawson Trail Post and at Tagish. He remained in the north and died at Dalton Post, Yukon, on July 14, 1945.

Profit River, Yukon, near the Alaska Highway, is named after Corporal J.A. Profit, NWMP #3708.

Profit served from April 27, 1900, to April 26, 1908, in Battleford, Saskatchewan. On August 4, 1901, he appeared before Superintendent

Griesbach in Orderly Room and was fined two dollars for "overstaying his pass." From 1905 to 1907 he took part in the Peace–Yukon Trail[66] project through part of B.C. and the Yukon. Details of his later life are unknown.

Prongua, Saskatchewan, a town northwest of Battleford, is named after Sub-Constable Anthony Jefferson Prongua, NWMP #278.

Prongua was an American and had previously served in the Missouri Regiment of the Confederate Army during the American Civil War. He served in the NWMP from April 16, 1875, to April 16, 1881, mainly in the Battleford area. For his good service he received Land Warrant #0202. In 1876 his was the first wedding at Battleford. He then ranched about sixteen kilometres west of Battleford, near the town that now bears his name. In the North-West Rebellion of 1885 he served as sergeant in the Battleford Home Guards #2 Company. Later he was also the Indian agent, store owner, and Pool elevator agent in the town.

By 1891 his fortunes—or outlook on life—had changed somewhat. He was apparently operating an illicit still and doing a bit of rustling. In February a neighbouring farmer, Emil Richards, and his hired man, Peter Dacotah, visited Prongua to partake in some of his homemade spirits. Edward Fletcher, a recent arrival from Montana, was also present. As the drinking progressed, Fletcher pulled out a revolver and shot Dacotah because he "talked too much." Richards walked to Battleford to report the crime. Inspector William D. Antrobus (O.36) with Sergeant John R. Clisby (#265), Corporal John D. Nicholson (#1709), and several constables rode out to investigate. Fletcher was eventually found guilty of murder, while Prongua was fined $50 for liquor offences, convicted of cattle theft, and sentenced to five years imprisonment in Stony Mountain Penitentiary.

On his release, Prongua returned to "his" town, and again he reversed his behavior; in 1904 he served as the first chairman of the Prongua School District #1117. In 1905 he petitioned for a post office for his area, and upon its establishment he served as postmaster for seven years. He died February 7, 1922, and was buried in the Prongua Cemetery.

Putnam Island, Manitoba (Lat: 52°22'47"N, Long: 97°04'47"W), near the eastern shore of Lake Winnipeg between Berens and Pigeon Rivers, is named after Corporal Edward Frederick Putnam, RCMP #10709.

Putnam served from September 28, 1929, until November 30, 1954, in "D" (at Berens River detachment), "K," "G," and "N"

Divisions. He also served with the Provost Corps in the Second World War as #C.42056. Corporal Putnam died at Ormond Beach, Florida, on February 3, 1989.

Ralls Lane, Depot Division RCMP, Regina, Saskatchewan, is named in honour of Corporal Leonard Victor Ralls, RNWMP #6177, Saskatchewan Provincial Police, and RCMP Honour Roll #52.

L. V. Ralls was murdered near this bridge at Foam Lake, Saskatchewan

Corporal Ralls served from September 9, 1914, in "F" Division until 1923, when he left to join the Saskatchewan Provincial Police (SPP). In 1928, when the SPP was absorbed into the RCMP, he returned to the Force and continued to serve in Saskatchewan in "F" Division. In 1932 he was in charge of the Foam Lake detachment until his death on July 5, 1932.

Through the early summer of 1932, there had been several burglaries along the highway through Yorkton. Just after midnight on July 5, 1932, Constable Michael Novakowski (#11159)[67] tried to stop a suspicious car that failed to yield to his directions. When he attempted to pass it, the driver tried to cut him off, and then the occupants began shooting at the police car. He stopped at the next village, phoned ahead to Corporal Ralls at Foam Lake, described the situation, and asked for a roadblock.

Ralls parked his car on a convenient bridge to prevent passage. The wanted car soon arrived, stopped, and—in the darkness—one occupant slipped out. As Ralls approached the car, he was suddenly shot at from two directions. Ralls was mortally wounded, but managed to return fire and retreat toward his own car. The fugitives then tore the ignition wires from the police car and sped away. Ralls managed to call out for help. A nearby neighbour, awakened by the gunfire, came to Ralls' aid and drove him to the local doctor. Although Ralls died soon after arrival, he did report that his assailants had fled to the east.

Word of the corporal's murder spread rapidly, probably because his wife had been notified of a shooting, learned it was her husband, and attended the doctor's office.

The officer in charge of that area, Inspector William J. Moorhead (O.206), came from Yorkton to Foam Lake to take charge of the search. A radio station in Regina was called upon to alert surrounding areas. Within a day, three aircraft were scouring the countryside, and many armed farmers volunteered their assistance. Constable Novakowski and Constable Walter E. Hutchinson (#10773) found the abandoned stolen car, with stolen property inside, hidden in thick bush near the village of Lintlaw. Several sightings of possible suspects were being received.

On July 7 three horses were stolen from a farm near Kelvington, and the police posse moved closer to its quarry. Constable (later Superintendent) Joseph Parsons (#10851) and the Wadena town constable found three horses tied to a tree near Kinloch. As they crept closer, Mike Kurulak walked over to the horses; he was promptly arrested. The town constable held the prisoner while Constable Parsons approached a nearby farmhouse. Suddenly two men came out. When they were ordered to stop, they drew guns, commenced shooting, and fled into some nearby bush.

The Saskatchewan roads and towns where Corporal Ralls' murderers fled and were finally found

The main group of one posse soon arrived, led by Sergeant (later Superintendent) Norman J. Anderson (#6495). The police learned from the arrested suspect that the remaining fugitives were Mike's older brother Bill Kurulak and Bill Miller. Both had criminal records. A careful search of the bush land was now underway.

On July 8 Bill Kurulak went to a farm near Green Water Lake and asked for a place to sleep. He was arrested as he slept by Corporal George S. Nutt (#6163), Constable Peter Nightingale (#10949), and Constable Frank Newman (#10904). The owner had given him a bed, then quietly went to a neighbouring farm and called the police. Kurulak had a loaded revolver under his pillow, but he was in police hands before he had a chance to reach it.

Miller, the last fugitive at large, was spotted several times throughout the day, but each time he fled in an exchange of gunfire. Late in the afternoon he was finally surrounded in a large bushy area; there was considerable gunfire from both sides. After a reasonable lull in Miller's shooting, members cautiously entered the bush and found Miller lying dead. He had two serious wounds from police bullets, but had committed suicide with his own revolver.

The Kurulak brothers were charged with murder. Bill Kurulak was sentenced to hang on December 29, 1932, while Mike received fifteen years in the penitentiary for manslaughter. Corporal Ralls was buried at St. Mary's Cemetery in Prince Albert, Saskatchewan.

Ranger Seal Bay, Nunavut (Lat: 63°45'00"N, Long: 91°42'00"W), at Chesterfield Inlet on the western shore of Hudson Bay, was named in 1955 from a chart supplied by the RCMP, showing their locally applied name of "Kakeyeaseeoovik," Inuit for "Ranger Seal Bay."

Ransom Street, Depot Division RCMP, Regina, Saskatchewan, is named in honour of Second Class Constable[68] George Herbert Edward Ransom, RCMP #19915, Honour Roll #96.

Ransom served in "O" Division in southern Ontario from April 15, 1957, until his death on June 8, 1958, when he and four other members drowned in Lake Simcoe. The others members were: Corporal Herbert M. Smart, #14588, Honour Roll #92; Second Class Constable Maurice Melnychuk, #19469, Honour Roll #93; Second Class Constable Glen F. Farough, #19478, Honour Roll #94; and Constable David M. Perry, #19879, Honour Roll #95.

On June 7, 1958, Corporal Smart and his patrol had arrested four men for some offence under the Indian Act. The five policemen were then observed at about 10:30 p.m. near Jackson's Point on Lake Simcoe, launching a 4.25-metre police boat with a 35 hp outboard motor into the lake. The weather was calm.

After midnight, now June 8, a sudden and violent electrical storm swept across the lake. When the patrol had not returned, a search was undertaken. At about noon the boat was found in the middle of the lake, floating upside down. The body of Corporal Smart was found later that day. In a continuing search, the bodies of Melnychuk and Farough were found next—on June 26. On June 30 the body of Perry was found, and Ransom's body was finally found on July 9.

We do not know the purpose of this late-night patrol with a maximum load for the size of boat and have to make the presumption that it had something to do with their earlier arrests.

We also presume that whatever happened came without much warning, for although there were life jackets in the boat, they were not being worn.

Constable Ransom was buried at Melville, Saskatchewan.

RCMP Celebrations Museum, Fairview, Alberta, is—despite its name—not an RCMP Museum. It is located in a house formerly occupied by an RCMP officer.

This museum demonstrates the typical pioneer home and exhibits an early-day school room and general store, as well as the original 1928 home and jail of the RCMP.

RCMP Centennial Library, Fort Macleod, Alberta, is named in honour of the RCMP.

RCMP Park, Athabasca, Alberta, is a park named in honour of the RCMP.

RCMP Point, Manitoba (Lat: 53°59'22"N, Long: 97°49'10"W), on the north shore of Fort Island in Little Playgreen Lake (at the north end of Lake Winnipeg), was once the location of an RCMP detachment and barracks.

Red Coat Trail, from Emerson, Manitoba, to Fort Macleod, Alberta, is a "signed" network of highways that generally follows the original route of the March West in 1874. The main highways of the route are Highway #2 in Manitoba, Highway #13 in Saskatchewan, and Highways #3, #4, and #61 in Alberta.

One of the distinguishing features of the Force was the scarlet tunic, hence the name "Red Coat" or "Red Jacket."

Red Coat Trail School Division, Assiniboia, Saskatchewan, is the headquarters for a provincial school division.

Red Coat Inn, Colonel Macleod Boulevard, Fort Macleod, Alberta, is a 28-unit motel located in a town with historic RCMP connections.

See the **Macleod Island** entry.

Red Jacket, Saskatchewan, a village west of Moosomin on Highway #1, commemorates one of the NWMP's stopping places in the early days.

Regina Roughriders, Regina, Saskatchewan, is a rugby team that took its name from an earlier NWMP team. In 1891 the NWMP in Regina had a rugby club known locally as the "Rough Riders." About 1910 the local newspaper—when referring to the Regina Rugby Club—used the name "Roughriders" informally for the first time because of their rough game. There was another athletic team—possibly a lacrosse team—that was also called the "Roughriders." When that team disbanded, the rugby team then used the name exclusively from November 1924 on. The name stuck. Although there was never any known formal adoption of it, according to one source, it originated in Regina with the NWMP team.

Rhodeniser Road, Canadian Police College, Rockcliffe, Ontario, is named in honour of Constable Willis Edward Rhodeniser, RCMP #12690, Honour Roll #62.

See following entry.

Rhodeniser Road, Depot Division RCMP, Regina, Saskatchewan, is named in honour of Constable Willis Edward Rhodeniser, RCMP #12690, Honour Roll #62.

Constable Rhodeniser served from July 2, 1935, in "K," "F," "K," and "F" again, as a police dog master, until his death on August 26, 1939.

This tragedy began with Nelson Sammy having a family dispute. His wife left their house with their two small children, and he suspected they would have gone to her parents' house nearby on the Indian Reserve. He took his rifle and went to their house, where he shot both his mother-in-law and father-in-law. He continued to search the reserve for his wife. He eventually saw her through the window of her sister's home and fatally shot her.

A number of police arrived in response to the shootings. In the darkness, Rhodeniser took up Sammy's trail with police dog "Tell," the other members following behind. He had tracked Sammy about 1.6 kilometres with the dog "off leash" when suddenly the dog barked, indicating that he had located his quarry. Concerned for his dog's safety, Rhodeniser switched on his flashlight and was promptly shot. Despite his mortal wound, he was able to return fire and wound Sammy before dying.

Those following him then arrested Sammy. He was charged with four counts of murder and was hanged at Regina, Saskatchewan, July 4, 1940.

Rhodeniser's body was returned to his parental home in Nova Scotia and buried in Parkdale Cemetery, Farmington, Nova Scotia.

Richardson Crescent, Regina, Saskatchewan, is named after Sergeant Major Arthur Herbert Lindsey Richardson, VC, NWMP and RNWMP #3058.

Richardson served from May 7, 1894, to November 12, 1907, mainly out of Depot Division. With the outbreak of the Boer War he volunteered and went overseas with the Lord Strathcona's Horse. He was awarded the Victoria Cross.[69] The *London Gazette* of September 14, 1900, gives this account of Richardson's bravery:

> On the 5th of July 1900 at Wolve Spruit, a party of Lord Strathcona's Corps, only 38 in number, was engaged at close quarters with a party of the enemy. When the order to retire had been given, Sergeant Richardson rode back under very heavy cross-fire and picked up a trooper whose horse had been shot and who was wounded in two places, and rode with him out of fire. At the time when this act of gallantry was performed, Sergeant Richardson was within 300 yards of the enemy and was himself riding on a wounded horse.

After his return to Canada in 1902, Richardson was among those in the NWMP contingent to attend the Coronation of King Edward VII in London, England. Upon leaving the Force in 1907, he served for just over a year as the chief of police at Indian Head, Saskatchewan. He then returned to England where he worked as a cinema attendant and tramway worker. While he lived in relative obscurity, a Scotsman lived on his name and fame. He impersonated Richardson throughout England, even to the extent of attending the King's garden party and receiving military honours at his funeral. Richardson died, almost unnoticed, December 16, 1932, at Liverpool, England.

Rivett Crescent, Yellowknife, Northwest Territories, is named after Corporal Albert Thomas "Bing" Rivett, RCMP #10496.

"Bing" served in the Force from September 17, 1928, to October 18, 1948, in "F," "G," and "E" Divisions. While in the north ("G" Division), a part of his service was spent in Yellowknife.

He died June 22, 1990, at Lanzville, B.C.

Rouleau Lake, Alberta (Lat: 49°25'00"N, Long: 113°42'00"W), in the Pincher Creek area, was named by field topographer J.A. MacDonald after Constable Achille Rouleau, NWMP #497.

Rouleau served from September 22, 1880, until September 22, 1885, then ranched at Fish Creek (Fishburn area) near Pincher

Creek with ex-Constable William Hill Metzler (#432). He died at Pincher Creek, Alberta, on June 15, 1936.

Metzler had served from June 25, 1880, to June 25, 1885, and died in 1954, also at Pincher Creek.

Routledge Lake, Saskatchewan (Lat: 55°05'00"N, Long: 104°21'00"W), near Wappawekka Lake, is named after Assistant Commissioner Walton Henry Routledge, NWMP and RNWMP O.85.

Routledge joined the NWMP as #465 on August 21, 1880, and served mainly at Depot Division until promoted to the commissioned ranks as an inspector on May 1, 1887. He authored the first book of *Rules, Regulations and Orders*, bringing together the "scattered" regulations then in place into a single manual that continued— with amendments—until the 1960s.

He then served in "K" Division. In 1892 he testified at the commission of inquiry into the conduct of Commissioner Herchmer and was subjected to a scathing attack in the *Macleod Gazette* newspaper on his evidence. While still in "K" Division, he made a patrol—from December 16, 1897, to March 26, 1898—of some 3,495 kilometres from Fort Saskatchewan to Fort Simpson and back. He then served in "M" Division (Yukon), and while there he authored a manual, *Handbook for the Yukon Territory*.

He was then transferred south to Saskatchewan and promoted to assistant commissioner. In the fall of 1919 he was granted a (sick) leave of absence. En route south to San Diego, he died aboard a train at Portland, Oregon, on November 6, 1919.

His son, Staff Sergeant Major Walton W.J. Routledge (#12548), also served in the Force from 1935 to 1963.

See also **Herchmer Street** and *Macleod Gazette*.

Rykerts, B.C., a Customs port of entry at the Canada–U.S. border south of Creston, is named after Sub-Constable John Charles Rykert, NWMP #461 (Original Series).

Rykert's history is first known in 1873, when he worked on a survey crew for the Canadian Pacific Railway right-of-way in the Great Lakes area of Ontario. He served in the Force from May 21, 1875, until May 11, 1877, when he obtained a substitute.[70]

He had his brushes with discipline for we find that he was in Orderly Room on February 22, 1876, charged with being "insolent to a senior member." He was fined 75 cents and, in the same circumstance, another three dollars for "giving a false statement."

When he left the Force, Rykert joined the Canada Customs Service, and by 1881 he was a Canada Customs officer on ships plying between San Francisco, California, and Victoria, B.C. In 1883 he established a Customs office where the Kootenay River re-enters Canada, serving not only as a Customs officer, but also as an immigration inspector, gold commissioner, and registrar of shipping. This point of entry became known as the "Port of Rykerts."

He died at Rykerts, B.C., on January 19, 1931.

St. Roch Basin, Nunavut (Lat: 69°15'00"N, Long: 95°00'00"W), between King William Island and Boothia Peninsula at the southern limit of James Ross Strait, was named in 1960 after the RCMP patrol vessel that passed through the area in 1941 while traversing the Northwest Passage from west to east.

See following entries.

St. Roch Harbour, Nunavut (Lat: 66°55'00"N, Long: 62°06'00"W), a small bay at the northern side of the head of Reid Bay on eastern Baffin Island, was named in 1942 by Inspector H.A. Larsen, RCMP O.347; the name was approved in 1950.

See also **Larsen Sound**.

The St. Roch *in Vancouver*

St. Roch Island, Northwest Territories (Lat: 69°26'00"N, Long: 132°59'00"W), near McKinley Bay and the Tuktoyaktuk Peninsula, is named after the RCMP patrol vessel that took shelter here from the ice field in September 1944.

The *St. Roch* was the first ship to sail through the Northwest Passage from west to east (1940–1942), skippered by Staff Sergeant (later Superintendent) Henry A. Larsen, RCMP #10407, O.347. She again sailed through the Northwest Passage from east to west (1944), again skippered by Larsen. In addition, the *St. Roch* was the first to circumnavigate North America (1950), skippered by Inspector Kenneth W.N. Hall RCMP #11814, O.372.

See also **Larsen Sound**.

Sam (Stick Sam Walk), Depot Division RCMP, Regina, Saskatchewan, named is in honour of Special Constable Stick Sam, NWMP Honour Roll #26.

Stick Sam was one of the earliest special constables hired by the Force in the Yukon. On July 29, 1903, Constable Sam was on a patrol with Inspector Albert E.C. Macdonell (O.117) and Constable William J. Povoas (#3653), returning to the Dalton Trail from a new gold strike on the Alsek River.

As they forded the Kaskawulsh River on horseback, they blundered into deep water. In midstream, Sam's horse plunged into the deep water and in its struggle it either reared or rolled over backwards. Both horse and rider disappeared momentarily. Stick Sam broke surface once and was then lost from sight. In spite of an extensive search, Constable Sam's body was never recovered. He left a young widow and infant daughter.

Sanders (Colonel Sanders Elementary School), Calgary, Alberta, is named after Colonel[71] (Superintendent) Gilbert Edward Sanders, DSO, CMG, NWMP and RNWMP O.52.

Sanders was born in B.C. in 1863. He attended the Royal Military College in Kingston, Ontario, and then received a commission in the NWMP on September 1, 1884. He was posted at Fort Macleod, then Calgary. By the outset of the North-West Rebellion he was at Prince Albert. He also served in the Boer War and retired from the Force on March 1, 1912.

Sanders then served in the First World War as lieutenant-colonel in command of the 2nd Pioneer Battalion, earning the Distinguished Service Order and the Companion Most Distinguished Order of St. Michael and St. George. Following the war, from 1919 to 1932, he was a police magistrate in Calgary, Alberta. He also helped found the Calgary Corps of Commissionaires.

His father-in-law was Surgeon Augustus Jukes, NWMP O.47. Colonel Sanders died in the Colonel Belcher Hospital,[73] Calgary on April 19, 1955, and was buried in the Union Cemetery.

Sanderson Avenue, Medicine Hat, Alberta, is named after James Francis Sanderson, a NWMP guide, scout, and interpreter.

Saskatchewan (Fort Saskatchewan), Alberta, situated on the North Saskatchewan River about 32 kilometres northeast of Edmonton, was the first NWMP post north of Calgary. It was erected in 1875 under the direction of Inspector William Drummer Jarvis (O.2) as "The Fort on the Saskatchewan." The location was not popular with the citizens of Fort Edmonton as they felt it was too far away to supply adequate protection.

Fort Saskatchewan, Alberta

The area had been locally known as Birch Hills since the plentiful supply of birch bark made it a popular canoe-building area for the Indians. As early as 1795 the Northwest Company had a trading fort known as Fort Augustus in the same area, and there were permanent settlers in the area by 1872. Today the "little fort on the river" has grown into a bustling town.

See also **Jarvis Crescent**.

Scarlet And Gold Inn, Fort Macleod, Alberta, situated at 23rd Street and 7th Avenue, gets its name from the traditional colours of the Force.

Scarlet and Gold was the name chosen for a magazine published by the "A" Division Veterans' Association from 1919 until the 1990s, and it may be from this source that the name was taken for the motel.

Schooner Cove, Nunavut (Lat: 63°59'00"N, Long: 94°16'00"W), in Baker Lake, was named in 1951 from a suggested name found on a rough chart drawn in 1916 by Constable Alfred Baldry Kennedy, RNWMP #5626.

See **Kennedy Point**.

Schrader-Anson Sport Field, Depot Division RCMP, Regina, Saskatchewan, is named in honour of Sergeant Robert J. Schrader, RCMP #15445, Honour Roll #141, and Constable Douglas Bernard Anson (#21129, Honour Roll #142).

Sergeant Schrader, who had served from June 10, 1948 in "E" and "F" Divisions, and Constable Anson who had served since October 21, 1959, were involved in a particularly tragic incident when they let their guards down in an always potentially dangerous family dispute.

They were working out of the Prince Albert detachment on October 9, 1970, when a radio call about a domestic dispute came in. It was alleged that Wilfred Robertson had fired a shot past a man found with his wife. Schrader and Anson volunteered to attend the scene as they were already in the general area.

They drove to the Robertson residence, near Macdowall, about 24 kilometres south of Prince Albert. Both men got out of the police car. For some unknown reason, Schrader left his Sam Browne[16] and revolver in the car. While Anson went to knock on the door, Schrader checked out Robertson's truck, which was parked in the yard.

Mrs. Robertson opened the door for Anson, who was immediately shot by Wilfred Robertson with a heavy calibre rifle from within the house. The impact knocked Anson backward and spun him around, and he was shot a second time in the back. Schrader now found he was cut off from his car and revolver. He sought shelter behind a tree and attempted to reason with the assailant. Robertson calmly shot three times, the first shot hitting the tree, and the others fatally injuring the sergeant. Robertson retrieved Constable Anson's revolver from his holster, ate a meal, and then drove off in the police car.

A massive manhunt ensued. The car was quickly found, but without a trace of Robertson. The following spring his frozen body was found about 1.5 kilometres from the house where he had taken his own life.

Sergeant Schrader and Constable Anson were buried side by side in the Force Cemetery at Depot Division.

Seigel Place, Depot Division RCMP, Regina, Saskatchewan, is named in honour of Constable Harold Stanley Seigel, RCMP #22976, Honour Roll #145.

Constable Seigel had served in the Force since January 24, 1963 in "D" Division. In the late afternoon of September 26, 1971, near Ile Des Chenes, Manitoba, Seigel, Staff Sergeant Edward J. M. Webdale (#15397), and Constable Floyd Rushton (#24455) answered a complaint about a shooting incident.

Apparently Jean D'Auteuil had barricaded himself with a .22 rifle in the bathroom of the family home. When his father tried to reason with him, he shot through the door, narrowly missing his father.

As the members took seemingly appropriate cover, Webdale negotiated with D'Auteuil, using a loud hailer. Through a period of over two hours, Webdale tried to convince D'Auteuil, who was rambling and incoherent, to come out. It was apparent that he was mentally unstable. Finally, Webdale threw a tear gas grenade into the house to flush him out. The response was one shot, and Seigel, who had taken cover in the garage, was found dying from a gunshot wound to his head. Constable Rushton sped him to the nearest medical care, but he died en route.

The assailant was finally overcome by gas at about two the following morning and was arrested. D'Auteuil was charged with capital murder, but he was found to be insane and committed to the Selkirk Mental Hospital.

Constable Seigel was buried in the Chapel Lawn Memorial Gardens at Winnipeg, Manitoba.

Seller Lake, Manitoba (Lat: 54°59'59"N, Long: 94°30'59"W), northwest of God's Lake, is named after Constable Leslie Ellsworth Seller, NWMP and RNWMP #3504.

Seller served from March 20, 1900, to April 4, 1907, when he purchased his discharge. He first served in present-day Alberta and was then transferred to the Hudson Bay district.

In February 1906, while stationed at Fullerton, he and a special constable and Inuit interpreter travelled by dog team 800 kilometres north from Fullerton to locate the vessel *Ernest William* and make a Customs inspection of its cargo at Repulse Bay. They carried 526 kilograms of meat just for the dogs.

Seller died in 1917 at an unknown location. His brother, Constable William Morely Seller (#3510), also served briefly in 1900.

Shaw Street, Depot Division RCMP, Regina, Saskatchewan, is

named in honour of Constable John George Shaw, RCMP #11582, Honour Roll #56.

The murder of Constable Shaw was either the first or second murder in this tragedy that saw four policemen murdered and their three assailants killed.

Shaw's adult life began in the First World War with service in the British Expeditionary Force Durham Light Infantry. He was wounded in action, returned to England, and after he recovered, was in training for the Royal Flying Corps at

John George Shaw

war's end. Following the war, he served for four and a half years in the Middlesbrough Constabulary before coming to Canada. He joined the Manitoba Provincial Police in 1930 and then became a member of the RCMP when that Force was absorbed on April 1, 1932. Still in "D" Division, in 1934 he received a commendation for his investigation of a particular break, enter, and theft.

On October 4, 1935, he was with Benito's town constable Wainwright, investigating a series of burglaries and robberies. They checked a car containing three young men: Joseph Posnikoff, John Kalmakoff, and Peter Voiken. They were clean-cut, well-dressed, and recognized as being from the Doukhobor sect (noted for abstinence and non-violence). Nevertheless, the police searched their car, found nothing of interest, and departed. The policemen later learned these men were suspects wanted by the Pelly detachment, so they returned to look for them. They located the three men and placed them in the police car, apparently without searching them first.

En route to Pelly, the three men in the back seat suddenly attacked the two policemen. At least one had a knife since both policemen suffered slash wounds to their heads and necks, as well as defensive cuts to their hands. The prisoners managed to wrest Wainwright's gun away and shoot both him and Shaw at point-blank range. In the struggle, the police car went into the ditch. The three men dragged the bodies of the two policemen out of the car and into a slough by the road. After stripping them of valuables, they drove away in the unmarked police car.

When neither policeman showed up as expected, a search was begun. On October 7 a farmer found the two bodies, and a hunt was organized across the prairie provinces. Constable George Campbell Harrison (#10946, Honour Roll #57) had seen the car earlier west of Calgary, but before any news broadcast of the murders. By now the fugitives had reached Banff National Park, about 100 kilometres west of Calgary, Alberta; however, not having the park's two-dollar entrance fee, they turned back east. At nearby Exshaw they purchased one dollar of gas, at which time the attendant's wife recognized the Manitoba licence plate from a just-released radio news broadcast. She called the police at the Canmore detachment. In turn, they alerted the Banff detachment, so Sergeant Thomas Wallace[72] (#11326, Honour Roll #58) and Constable George "Nipper" Coombe (#11732) started east to intercept the stolen car. A roadblock was set up. Soon Constable Harrison, Constable Alexander G. Campbell (#11764), and Corporal John P. Bonner (#8500) joined them.

In the meantime, the fugitives had stopped a car and robbed an elderly couple of their valuables, then continued to follow their victims

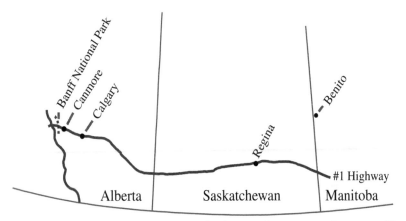

The manhunt for three fugitives, which went from Manitoba to Banff National Park, involved four policemen being murdered and their assailants being killed

back west toward Banff Park. It was now dark when the victims reached the roadblock; they urgently told the police that the people in the car following them had just robbed them. Sergeant Wallace and Constable Harrison started walking toward the following car, lit by its headlights, when they were met with a hail of gunfire. Harrison was able to shoot out the headlights before collapsing, and despite a mortal wound Wallace also shot back as he retreated. During the gunfire, the three fugitives fled into the surrounding woods. Constable Campbell loaded the two wounded policemen into his car and raced to the nearest medical aid at Canmore.

Meanwhile, back at the scene, Constable Coombe saw a movement in the heavy bush and shot. When he advanced, he found he had killed Joseph Posnikoff, who was carrying Constable Wainwright's stolen police revolver. In the stolen Manitoba police car they found an RCMP holster bearing the printed #11414 (the regimental number of ex-Constable George Hivey), which was the holster Constable Shaw had been using.

The highways were closed off and every moving car was checked. A second roadblock was set up just east of the Banff Park gate, partially manned by Banff National Park wardens. More members arrived on scene, including Inspector Arthur Birch (O.291), Constable Alexander Brown (#9225), Constable Gordon McGlynn (#11082), and Constable James Moffatt (#11967). Following soon after, more arrived: Constable R. Fenn (#10561), Constable Donald MacAdam (#12691), and Constable John Cawsey (#11462) with police dog "Dale." The armed teams were now separately searching likely areas for the wanted men.

On October 8, near Seven Mile Hill, one of the small search teams was fired on from the roadside forest. Unfortunately for the fugitives, this posse included Banff Park warden (and former member of the Force—#7718) William "Dickie" Neish. Neish, an excellent marksman, shot back, heard a scream, then saw a movement, and shot again. The remaining two fugitives had now been mortally wounded. They were driven to Banff Hospital and placed under guard by Constable Melville Eaton (#11760). Both were unconscious and died shortly afterward.

Sergeant Wallace and Constable Harrison had also died earlier that day in the Colonel Belcher[73] Hospital at Calgary. Constable Shaw was buried in Birchwood Cemetery, Swan River, Manitoba. Town constable Wainwright was buried in Benito, Manitoba. Sergeant Wallace was buried in the Union Cemetery, Calgary, Alberta, and Constable Harrison was buried in the Banff Cemetery.

Shoal Lake, Manitoba, a village northeast of Winnipeg, was an early site (1876) of an NWMP post, as it was a strategic position where several trails came together. The name was taken from a nearby lake of the same name.

Shwaykowski Track, Depot Division, Regina, Saskatchewan, is named in honour of Constable Dennis Modest Nicklos Shwaykowski, RCMP #25308, Honour Roll #152.

Constable Shwaykowski served from December 3, 1966, in "A" Division (Ontario) and then "K" Division, where he was serving at the Red Deer City detachment at the time of his death.

Stan Hicks and his girlfriend had broken up. On the night of April 6, 1977, Hicks had spotted her in a pub in a shopping mall and apparently went home for weapons. The police office received a call to the effect that there

D.M.N. Shwaykowski

was a "looney" at the pub with a shotgun and that he was now driving around the mall in his pickup truck. Constable Shwaykowski and Constable Dave Guy (#27461), who were in plain clothes, responded to the call. They spotted the truck and recognized the driver. Constable Shwaykowski motioned Hicks to stop, which he did. Shwaykowski then told him to get out, but instead, Hicks drove off. Constable Shwaykowski jumped on the running board of the moving truck and attempted to arrest Hicks by grabbing his shirt. By now the truck had reached a speed of about 80 kilometres per hour and was heading towards a landscaped area of rocks and shrubbery. When the truck struck the curb, Shwaykowski was thrown from his position; he struck his head on some boulders and died instantly.

A search was begun, but almost immediately Hicks phoned the police office from a service station to surrender. On arrival, police found him in his truck, in possession of a rifle and shotgun. He was charged with first-degree murder. That charge was later stayed, and a guilty plea was entered on a criminal negligence charge. He was sentenced to three years imprisonment.

Constable Shwaykowski was buried in Birchwood Cemetery at Swan River, Manitoba. He left a widow and three young children. A plaque in his honour was installed at Red Deer City Hall as he was the first police officer to die on duty in that city.

Sid Lake, Northwest Territories (Lat: 62°16'00"N, Long: 104°04'00"W), between Whitefish and Mosquito Lakes and emptying into the Thelon River, was the name first applied on an RCMP sketch map of a patrol from Stony Rapids to Dubaunt Lake. The date of the patrol, or members involved, was not shown. The name was accepted in 1951 from a submission of the surveyor general.

Sifton (Fort Sifton), Yukon, is the site where the NWMP built one of their more important posts in the Yukon. It was called Fort

Sifton after the Minister of the Interior. Following an edict laid down by Superintendent Samuel B. Steele (NWMP O.40), every traveller passing this point was required to register his party and boat. The Customs officer, and sometimes the police, examined all "outfits" to ensure the traveller had enough supplies to be self-sufficient. The name of the post was

Fort Sifton (across river), Yukon

later changed to Tagish. In 1898 a small range of hills about 24 kilometres northeast of Champagne was named the Sifton Range.

Siksik Hill, Northwest Territories (Lat: 72°24'00"N, Long: 125°12'00"W), at Cape Parry, was named in 1965 after a former RCMP special constable.

See following entries.

Siksik Lake, Northwest Territories (Lat: 72°23'00"N, Long: 125°05'00"W), at Cape Parry, is a local name given because of the lake's proximity to Siksik Hill and Siksik Point, which were both named in 1965 after a former special constable of the RCMP.

Siksik Point, Northwest Territories (Lat: 72°25'00"N, Long: 125°26'00"W), at Cape Parry near Banks Island, was named in 1954 after a former special constable of the RCMP.

There has never been a special constable in the Force by the exact name of "Siksik," but there was a special constable named Arsene Sikinik (#S1605), who was a guide in the Chesterfield Inlet area until 1938. It is presumed this was the member after whom the three landmarks were named.

Sintaluta, Saskatchewan, a village located on the Trans-Canada Highway #1 some eighteen kilometres east of Indian Head, was named by Major James Morrow Walsh, NWMP O.7. He assigned the name from an Indian word meaning "the end of the fox's tail." At that time, the valley was known as Red Fox Valley, and the Red Fox Creek ran through the area, emptying into a slough about one kilometre from the present-day townsite. Thus, the village was interpreted as being "the end of the fox's tail."

See also **Walsh Trail**.

Sittichinli (Mount Sittichinli), Yukon (Lat: 67°11'00"N, Long: 136°15'00"W), south of Rat River, is named after Lazarus Sittichinli, an RCMP special constable. He drove one of the dog teams in the famous 1932 search for Albert Johnson, the "Mad Trapper of Rat River."

See the **Millen Street** entry for details of the Albert Johnson manhunt.

Sleigh Square, Depot Division RCMP, Regina, Saskatchewan, is named in honour of Corporal Ralph Bateman Sleigh, NWMP #565, Honour Roll #10.

Corporal Sleigh served in the Force from June 7, 1881, to his death on May 2, 1885, in the North-West Rebellion. He had earlier served in that portion of the Northwest Territories that became the province of Alberta in 1905, and by the time the rebellion broke out in 1885, was posted to the Frog Lake detachment.

In 1884 he was involved in the "Craig Incident," which was a precursor to the North-West Rebellion. During the rebellion, Sleigh met his death in the Battle of Cut Knife Hill on May 2, 1885. On that day, Superintendent William M. Herchmer (O.37) and Superintendent Percy Neale (O.34) had led a force of 319 men (including 74 members of the NWMP) from Battleford to Cut Knife Hill, about 61 kilometres distant. In the battle there, three members of the NWMP were killed: Corporal Sleigh, Constable Burke (#402, Honour Roll #11), who died following day, and Corporal William H.T. Lowry (#907, Honour Roll #12). Sergeant John Ward (#36) was wounded.

Corporal Sleigh was buried at Battleford, Saskatchewan.

See also **Crozier Lake**, **Burke Lake**, and **Lowry Place** entries.

Slippery Point, Nunavut (Lat: 63°59'00"N, Long: 94°09'00"W), between Baker Lake and Chesterfield Inlet, is the name—approved in 1966—taken from RCMP maps of 1953, and which members serving earlier in that area had given to the location.

The name was translated from "Kuasanaktok," which is Inuit for "Slippery Point."

South Channel, Nunavut (Lat: 64°02'00"N, Long: 94°35'00"W), on Baker Lake, was named in 1980 from a suggested name on a sketch map done by Constable Alfred Baldry Kennedy, RNWMP #5626, when he was exploring this area in 1916.

See also **Kennedy Point**.

Spalding Lake, Saskatchewan (Lat: 57°14'00"N, Long: 103°20'00"W), near Nokomis Lake, is named after Deputy Commissioner James Wilson Spalding, NWMP, RNWMP, and RCMP O.166.

Spalding joined the NWMP on April 23, 1900, as #3667 and first served in "F" Division, and then from 1905 to 1907 on the Peace–Yukon Trail project.[74] He then returned to "F" Division and was promoted to the commissioned ranks April 1, 1912. He continued to serve in Saskatchewan until he was appointed as deputy commissioner of the Force in Headquarters, Ottawa.

He retired on April 23, 1937, to the West Coast and died on July 4, 1961, at White Rock, B.C. His son, Assistant Commissioner Frank Spalding, RCMP #11745, O.366, served from 1931 to 1968.

Stackhouse Circle, Canadian Police College, Rockcliffe, Ontario, is named in honour of Constable Donald Gilbert Stackhouse, RCMP #12108, Honour Roll #83.

Constable Stackhouse served from January 8, 1934, in "A" Division, then "F" Division, where he was stationed at the Estevan detachment before volunteering for the #1 Provost Corps that was being organized for service in the Second World War. He was briefly posted to "N" Division—where the corps members were assembling to undergo initial training—and received his military #L.22013.

D.G. Stackhouse

He landed in Italy with the Allied invasion, and on May 31, 1944, was on a motorcycle patrol when he hit a buried teller mine and was killed instantly. He was buried in the Cassino War Cemetery.

Stallworthy (Cape Stallworthy), Nunavut (Lat: 81°23'00"N, Long: 93°30'00"W), the most northerly tip of Axel Heiberg Island, was named in 1946 after Corporal (later Sergeant-Major) Henry Webb Stallworthy, FRGS, OC, RNWMP and RCMP #6316.

Stallworthy served in the Force from September 25, 1914, to February 28, 1946. He began his career in Alberta and then went to the Yukon. For one to retire as a sergeant-major—who is typically the perfectionist for punctuality and parades—Stallworthy had a lapse in the beginning. On March 17, 1916, he was paraded into Orderly Room at Dawson and fined three dollars for being "absent from parade."

When the "A" Squadron cavalry draft was called for service in France during the First World War, he was one of seventeen to volunteer from the Yukon and served as Canadian Expeditionary Force #2684351. On return from overseas, he served briefly in Headquarters; then he went back north to the Yukon and Northwest Territories.

On September 20, 1924, Stallworthy and a local priest had the stressful task of amputating the leg of the wife of Staff Sergeant Clay (#4279), who had been badly mauled by sled dogs. We next find him stationed at the Bache detachment on Ellesmere Island in 1932. Word was received of an overdue German Arctic expedition led by Doctor E. Krueger. In searching for them, Stallworthy made a 65-day, 2,253-kilometre patrol by dog team across Ellesmere Island and around Axel Heiberg Island. He did not locate the expedition, but he did find a record they had left at Peary's Cairn on the cape of the island. At that time, this was the most northerly patrol made by any member of the Force.

For his service in the north, he was made a Fellow of the Royal Geographical Society of Canada. Next, he was transferred to B.C., and later he served again at Headquarters Ottawa, in New Brunswick, and at Toronto, Ontario. He was awarded the Order of Canada for his services to the nation.

He died at Comox, B.C., on December 25, 1976.

See also **Clay Point** and **Joy River** entries.

See map page 89.

Starnes Creek, Ontario (Lat: 49°04'00"N, Long: 89°12'00"W), northwest of Thunder Bay, is named after Commissioner Cortlandt Starnes, NWMP, RNWMP, and RCMP O.71.

See following entries.

Starnes Fiord, Nunavut (Lat: 76°37'00"N, Long: 82°10'00"W), on the southeast coast of Ellesmere Island, was named in 1941 after Commissioner Cortlandt Starnes, NWMP, RNWMP, and RCMP O.71.

Starnes Lake, Ontario (Lat: 49°05'00"N, Long: 89°15'00"W), northwest of Thunder Bay, is named after Commissioner Cortlandt Starnes, NWMP, RNWMP, and RCMP O.71.

Starnes Street, Lethbridge (now 15th Street North), was named after Commissioner Cortlandt Starnes, NWMP, RNWMP, and RCMP O.71.

Previous to his service in the Force, Starnes had served as a captain in the 65th Mount Royal Rifles and as an adjutant he took part in the North-West Rebellion of 1885. On March 1, 1886, he received commission as inspector in the NWMP at an annual salary of $1,000. He replaced Inspector Arthur F.J. Gautier (O.70), who had died.

Starnes saw service in what are now "K" and "M" Divisions, and at Headquarters. In 1928 he acted for the Force in negotiations with the Province of Saskatchewan to absorb its provincial police force and assume the policing of that province by contract.

He was appointed the sixth permanent commissioner on April 1, 1923, and served in that capacity to July 31, 1931. He died in 1934 at St.Hilaire, Ontario.

Sir Samuel Steele Memorial Building, Orillia, Ontario

Steele Avenue, Calgary, Alberta, is named after Superintendent Samuel Benfield Steele, NWMP Superintendent O.40.

See following entries.

Steele Barracks, Edmonton, Alberta, was reassigned and renamed on May 11, 2000, from the former Namao or Lancaster Park Air Force Base to the new army base for Western Canada called Steele Barracks, after the legendary Sir Samuel Benfield Steele.

See **Steele Street** entry for details on his service.

Steele Civic Building, Orillia, Ontario, a civic building on Peter Street South in Orillia, is to be known officially as the "Sir Samuel Steele Memorial Building."

Steele once resided in Orillia while attending school within one half-block of this building.

See **Steele Street** entry for details on his service.

Steele Creek, Yukon (Lat: 63°36'30"N, Long: 139°01'25"W), west of Pelly Crossing, is named after Superintendent Samuel Benfield Steele, NWMP O.40.

See **Steele Street** entry for details on his service.

Steele Creek, Yukon (Lat: 61°23'50"N, Long: 139°43'35"W), in the Kluane National Park Reserve, is named after Superintendent Samuel Benfield Steele, NWMP O.40.

See **Steele Street** entry for details on his service.

Steele Crescent, Battleford Trail subdivision, Swift Current, Saskatchewan, is named after Superintendent Samuel Benfield Steele, NWMP O.40, who led Steele's Scouts in the North-West Rebellion of 1885.

See **Steele Street** entry for details on his service.

Steele Crescent, Regina, Saskatchewan, is named after Superintendent Samuel Benfield Steele, NWMP O.40.

See **Steele Street** entry for details on his service.

Steele (Colonel Sam Steele Street), Fort Macleod, Alberta, 4th Avenue, is named after Superintendent Samuel Benfield Steele, NWMP 0.40.

See **Steele Street** entry for details on his service.

Steele (Fort Steele), B.C., situated near the town of Cranbrook, was established by Superintendent Samuel Benfield Steele, NWMP O.40, in 1887 as "Kootenay Post." The town's residents renamed it "Fort Steele" a year later.

Fort Steele, B.C.

This site, as established by the government of B.C. on March 6, 1961, is now the Fort Steele Provincial Heritage Park, and consists of 150 hectares about sixteen kilometres northeast of Cranbrook on Highway #93. There are now about 50 buildings: some have been restored on their original sites and others were moved from other locations. The park includes the Wild Horse Theatre, a museum, and a re-creation of the original NWMP troops' quarters.

See **Steele Street** entry for details on his service.

Steele Glacier, Yukon (Lat: 61°15'00"N, Long: 140°10'00"W), in Kluane National Park Reserve, is named after Superintendent Samuel Benfield Steele, NWMP O.40.

See **Steele Street** entry for details on his service.

Steele Height Subdivision, Edmonton, Alberta, is named after Superintendent Samuel Benfied Steele, NWMP O.40, and his brother, James Bond Steele. James Bond Steele was the first schoolteacher in the area, so this subdivision was named in honour of the two brothers.

See **Steele Street** entry for details on his service.

Steele (Mount Steele) (5,073 m), Yukon (Lat: 61°05'30"N, Long: 140°18'35"W), in the Ice Field Ranges of the St. Elias Mountains and in the northwest corner of Kluane National Park, was named by J. J. McArthur while surveying the International Boundary Line. He named this peak after one of the most outstanding men in the history of the Yukon: Superintendent Samuel Benfield Steele.

See **Steele Street** entry for details on his service.

Steele Narrows, Saskatchewan (Lat: 54°02'00"N, Long: 109°19'00"W), ten kilometres from Loon Lake village, is named after Superintendent Samuel Benfield Steele, NWMP O.40.

While leading Steele's Scouts at this location in 1885, Steele was engaged in a battle with the Métis and Cree during the North-West Rebellion.

See **Steele Street** entry for details on his service.

Steele Narrows, Saskatchewan

Steele Narrows Provincial Park, Saskatchewan (Lat: 54°02'20"N, Long: 109°19'10"W), located at Steele Narrows (see above) and named after Superintendent Samuel Benfield Steele, NWMP O.40.

See **Steele Street** entry for details on his service.

Steele Park, Fort Saskatchewan, Alberta, at 92nd Avenue and 87th Street, is named after Superintendent Samuel Benfield Steele, NWMP O.40.

See **Steele Street** entry for details on his service.

Steele (Sir Sam Steele Junior Public School), 131 Huntsmill Boulevard, Toronto, Ontario, is named after Superintendent Samuel Benfield Steele, NWMP O.40.

See the next entry.

Steele Street, Whitehorse, Yukon, is named after Major-General Sir Samuel Benfield Steele, KCMG, CB, MVO, NWMP Superintendent O.40.

If the average Canadian could name only one member of the NWMP, that member would most surely be Sam Steele. His fame, in the minds of those that know the name, would be from his time as a superintendent in the NWMP, despite the fact that he went on to a military life in which he rose to major-general and received a knighthood. To adequately report his service, even in the Force, would take a book unto itself, so we beg your indulgence for this fleeting glance at a complex man and his history-making career.

Raised in Ontario, Sam began his teenage life with military service. He served in the militia against the Fenian raids when only fourteen years old. At age fifteen, he was appointed ensign with the 35th Regiment of the Canadian Militia.

When the unrest took place in the Red River colony, Sam Steele was again at the fore. At the time of Confederation in 1867, arrangements were made for the transfer of the Northwest Territory (Rupert's Land) to the Dominion of Canada. The Hudson's Bay Company had held sway in the west for almost 200 years and now agreed to annul its charter. The transfer was slated for December 1, 1869, but as survey parties began laying out the lands in sections, the Métis were offended and a number of them, under Louis Riel, stopped their work. The Métis then formed a provisional government and forbade entrance of the appointed lieutenant-governor. Threats were made and sides taken. In the end, a military contingent was sent, and Steele took part as a private in the 1870 Red River Expedition.

When the NWMP was born in 1873, Steele was a sergeant in "A" Battery Royal Canadian Artillery. By chance, he met Major Walsh (O.7), a friend of the family, who was recruiting for the new mounted police force for western Canada. Steele agreed to go with him, as sergeant-major of the first "A" Division, if he could obtain a discharge. He returned to Kingston, obtained his discharge, and left for Brockville by steamer to meet the first group. He took over his new duties on October 1, 1873.

This first contingent of recruits included Sam's two brothers. The first was Sergeant Richard Elmes Steele (#7, Original Series, and #18, New Series), who served from October 2, 1873, to 1882 and died in 1926 at Battleford, Saskatchewan. The second brother was Constable Godfrey MacNeal Steele (#43, Original Series, and #18A, New Series), who served from October 2, 1873, to 1878 and died in 1928 at Westbank, B.C. They joined at Collingwood, Ontario, on October 2, 1873.

Sam Steele now commenced the long trip west for a second time, having made the trek three years earlier on the Red River Expedition. They travelled west via steamer on the Great Lakes and then overland for 725 kilometres to arrive at Lower Fort Garry, Manitoba. On November 3 they made their attestations before the Force even had an official name. It was simply referred to as the "Mounted Police Force." Soon regimental numbers were assigned, and Sam became #5 (Original Series). Due to his military background he was appointed as sergeant-major of a troop. He was also a riding instructor before the time of the March West in 1874. In 1878, when the New Series numbers were issued, Sam was given #1, probably as the ranking non-commissioned officer. On September 10, 1878, he was promoted to the commissioned ranks as the 40th commissioned officer of this fledgling Force. Inspector Sam Steele (O.40) now began to create history in western Canada.

In 1882 the Canadian Pacific Railway asked the government for help in policing its rail line's construction. It had thousands of labourers who brought the expected gambling, prostitution, liquor, and serious assaults, any of which could interfere with building a railway. The Force was called on and organized a detachment of only 25 men to police construction under Inspector Sam Steele. He was soon bouncing from one trouble spot to another. A federal statute entitled "An Act for the Preservation of Peace in the Vicinity of Public Works" was passed, and—among other things—it prohibited drinking or gambling within sixteen kilometres of either side of the line. This provided Steele with the authority he needed to deal with just about any problem as it arose.

There had been a strike near Moose Jaw that precipitated the foregoing federal statute. Now, in 1885, he was facing another one boiling up at Beaver Crossing between Golden and Revelstoke, B.C. About 1,200 men walked out over a pay dispute. Sergeant Peter Kerr (#704) had made an arrest, and a mob rescued the prisoner. Sergeant William Fury (#333) managed to re-arrest the man and retreat back over a footbridge to the police camp while the mob advanced. Steele had been sick in bed, but upon hearing the commotion, he arose, armed himself, and confronted the growing mob, reading them the riot act and issuing a stern warning. A few brave souls continued to advance, but as one was wounded in the shoulder, the mob dispersed.

Through his time with the railroad construction difficulties, Steele lost only one man and that was most indirectly when Constables Ernest Percival (#557) and William Ross (#760) were patrolling the railway at Palliser, midway between Golden and Field, B.C. Ross died by his campfire on December 31, 1884, becoming the first member of the Force to die while on duty in B.C. He may possibly have died from exposure, but there is an inference that some New Year's celebration may have contributed. He was buried beside the railroad at Golden. In 1953, Constable John W. White (#16721), the co-author of this book, found the grave and commenced the paperwork for a proper interment in a cemetery. This came to fruition in 1955, when Corporal Al Jensen (#14891), then in charge of the Golden detachment, removed Ross's remains to the Golden Cemetery.

During his duties with the railway construction, in the spring of 1885, the North-West Rebellion broke out and Steele was recalled from Beaver River to Calgary. Here he was gazetted a major in the Canadian militia and called on to raise a mounted corps of the Alberta Field Force that, in turn, was named "Steele's Scouts" in his honour. At Edmonton, he swore in his three brothers—Richard, Godfrey, and James—as scouts. They saw action in the rebellion, and—again—served well.

Following the rebellion in 1886, Steele was called upon to hunt down Big Bear and his followers, who had massacred nine people at Frog Lake. After defeating them at Loon Lake, Steele was mentioned in dispatches.

By 1887, now as superintendent, Steele was in command of "D" Division at Fort Macleod. The Kootenay Indians, under Chief Isadore, were in a dispute with the settlers near present-day Cranbrook, B.C., which culminated with a raid on the local jail at Wild Horse Creek and the release of an Indian charged with the murder of two miners. The B.C. government, fearing a serious uprising, called on the federal government in Ottawa to send in the NWMP. The Force assigned the task to Steele. He set out on June 3, 1887, with three officers and 75 men via the Canadian Pacifc Railway to Golden. There he suffered a setback, when Sergeant-Major Thomas Lake (#13) committed suicide with his service revolver. Lake had been suffering from neuralgia and was in considerable pain. He was buried, in Steele's words, "among the pine trees by the camp."[75]

They then moved south 240 kilometres by way of the Columbia River to the junction of the Kootenay River and Wild Horse Creek. Here, Steele's men built their fort very close to the present-day site of Fort Steele. In late August Steele sent for Chief Isadore and ordered him to hand over the suspect from the earlier murders. He then gave the arresting constable eight days to organize his evidence. The hearing was held on September 5, 1887, and due to insufficient evidence, Steele set the accused Indian free. Within a few months, Steele had restored peace, and by June of 1888 his Division withdrew to Fort Macleod by way of the Crow's Nest Pass. Steele regretted that he had to leave behind four men who had died of "mountain fever" (typhoid). These four, who were buried at Fort Steele, are the following: Constable Henry Lasenby (#1848), who died September 22, 1887; Constable James Mason (#1788), who died October 20, 1887; Constable Abraham Fisher (#1787), who died October 24, 1887; and Constable Herbert Michell (#1836), who died on December 16, 1887.

Near the end of the century the gold rush was on in the Yukon, where there was no on-scene government in any form. The Force was again called on to fill the breach; men were sent north by 1895 in anticipation of what was to come. In 1898 Steele was sent north to replace Superintendent Constantine,[76] who had fallen ill. Superintendent Steele was in command of "B" Division, with headquarters at Dawson, while Superintendent Z.T. Wood[77] had "H" Division at Tagish.

When he first arrived, Steele found streams of ill-prepared people pouring in "to the lure of riches" in the gold fields. They were without provisions, adequate clothing, or knowledge of the north. He promptly established Customs ports in the White and Chilkoot Passes, raised the Union Jack, and issued the proclamation, "No entry into Canada unless in possession of two months provisions and 500 dollars or six months provisions and 200 dollars." At Lake Bennett he imposed restrictions on boats after the misfortune of several drownings from inadequate craft; all vessels had to be inspected and registered before they were allowed to set out on the

Yukon River. Additionally, women and children were required to walk around several dangerous parts of the river.

Steele established reliable mail service and acceptable sanitation rules at Dawson. Officials tried to have him removed because he would not accept their less-than-legal practices. They didn't count on the people rallying to his cause, even with a petition. Again, he soon had the major problems solved and in 1899 was relieved by Superintendent A.B. Perry.[78] When Steele left to go south, the wharf was crowded with "well wishers" from the elite to the dancehall girl—all wishing him well.

Steele's next challenge came with the outbreak of the Boer War. Canada sent troops, and members of the NWMP were given leaves of absence if they wished to volunteer. Many did, joining the Lord Strathcona's Horse, which was commanded by Steele. When the war was over, Steele remained—by agreement of the Force—to organize and lead the South African Constabulary. He took retirement from the Force on March 1, 1903.

Steele returned to Canada and to the military in 1907 with command of Military District #13 at Calgary, Alberta. In 1914 he authored the book *Forty Years in Canada–Reminiscences of the Great Northwest*. Then he went to war again.

In the First World War Steele raised and commanded the 2nd Canadian Division and rose to major-general. At war's end he received the Knighthood of the Order of St. Michael and St. George (KCMG). Other decorations that he received were the Companion Most Honourable Order of the Bath (CB) and a Member Royal Victoria Order—Class IV (MVO). With his life's work done, he died on January 30, 1919, at Putney, England. Steele's body was brought back to Canada to be buried in St. John's Cemetery at Winnipeg, Manitoba.

Stewart Point, Manitoba (Lat: 52°22'38"N, Long: 97°03'59"W), on the eastern shore of Lake Winnipeg, is named after Sergeant Hugh Alexander Stewart, RNWMP and RCMP #6461.

Stewart joined the Force on October 4, 1915, and first served in "F" Division, then "M" in the Yukon. With many members then serving in the First World War, the Force's position on discipline was moderated. This moderation was demonstrated by the events following a prisoner's escape from Stewart's custody. On August 28, 1916, Stewart was charged in Orderly Room for allowing the "escape" and was sentenced to two month's hard labour; it was also recommended that he be dismissed from the Force. On September 16, after he had served 31 days of imprisonment, the commissioner remitted his remaining sentence and did not approve the recommendation for dismissal, as there was a shortage of men.

When "A" Squadron cavalry draft was called in 1918, he volunteered and served in France as Canadian Expeditionary Force #2684356. At war's end he was posted to "D" Division (Manitoba), where he served until retiring on October 3, 1940.

He then promptly joined the Royal Canadian Air Force and served as Chief Investigations Officer for the Western Air Command as a flight lieutenant. He later retired to Vancouver, B.C., and died there on December 7, 1973.

Strathcona Creek, Yukon (Lat: 63°47'00"N, Long: 139°32'00"W), a tributary of the Indian River from the north, was named on January 5, 1902, by Fred Envoldsen and C.W. Williams. The men had found gold, staked a claim, and named this stream—probably in honour of the Lord Strathcona's Horse, a Canadian cavalry regiment raised and first commanded by Colonel Samuel Benfield Steele of the NWMP. The regiment served with great distinction in the Boer War from 1899 to 1902.

See **Steele Street** entry.

Strickland Lake, Yukon (Lat: 63°52'50"N, Long: 138°07'00"W), midway between Stewart Crossing and Dawson, is named after Inspector D'Arcy Edward Strickland, NWMP and RNWMP O.99.

See following entries.

Strickland (Mount Strickland) (4,212 m), Yukon (Lat: 61°14'15"N, Long: 140°40'00"W), in the Ice Field Ranges of the St. Elias Mountains, is named after Inspector D'Arcy Edward Strickland, NWMP and RNWMP O.99.

Strickland Street, Whitehorse, Yukon, is named after Inspector D'Arcy Edward Strickland, NWMP and RNWMP O.99.

Strickland was commissioned as an inspector in the NWMP on November 15, 1891, having previously served as lieutenant in the Prince of Wales Dragoons.

He served in what are now "F," then "M," and finally "K" Divisions. In 1895 he was in the first party of the NWMP to the Yukon, and following his service in the north was posted to Fort Saskatchewan as the officer in command. He died March 20, 1908, while in that role and was buried at Fort Saskatchewan in the Force Cemetery.

See **Constantine (Mount Constantine)** for details of early NWMP service in the Yukon.

Taggart Lake, Nunavut (Lat: 78°27'00"N, Long: 81°29'50"W), on Ellesmere Island, was named in 1982 after Constable Reginald Andrew Taggart, RCMP #10303, for his patrol in 1929 with Inspector A.H. Joy (O.221).

Taggart served in the Force from May 27, 1927, to December 7, 1957, in "N," "E," "D," "G," Depot, "F," and "A" Divisions, retiring as a sergeant. In 1929 he made an exceptional trip of exploration in the area of Ellesmere Island, covering 2,736 kilometres in 81 days.

He died on April 24, 1994, at Victoria, B.C.

See **Joy River** entry for details on the trip of 1929.

Talbot Creek, B.C. (Lat: 59°59'00"N, Long: 136°52'00"W), at the Yukon border, is named after Constable William Alfred Talbot, NWMP and RNWMP #3816.

We have not been able to determine the reason for a B.C. place named after this member, as no record has been found of any specific incident. He came from Ontario and served in the Force only a short time—October 22, 1901, to October 23, 1905—and then only in the Yukon at Whitehorse, Dalton Trail, and Dawson.

Prior to his service in the Force, Talbot served in the Boer War in 1900 with the Special Services Battalion, Royal Canadian Regiment. No record has been found of his later life.

Tashme, B.C., on Highway #3 about 23 kilometres east of Hope, was a Japanese internment camp, built in 1942 after the Japanese attack on Pearl Harbor, and was named by combining letters from the names of various officers, including an RCMP member.

At war with Japan as well as Germany, the Canadian government feared sabotage or other assistance to the empire of Japan by the considerable Japanese-Canadian population on the West Coast of Canada. By order-in-council, they were removed from their homes and businesses to internment camps in the interior of B.C. The task of supervising their move and security fell to the RCMP, then fulfilling its federal role in the province.

A total of 347 "homes" were built to house the internees. Tashme, although sounding Japanese to our ears, actually comes from the names of the officers of the B.C. Securities Commission that was set up to accomplish the evacuation and to deal with the internees' properties. The commission consisted of Austin T. TAylor, Vancouver businessman; John SHirras of the B.C. Provincial Police, and F.J. MEad of the Royal Canadian Mounted Police. The camp was opened in September 1942 and closed on August 12, 1946.

Frederick John Mead, RNWMP and RCMP #5117, served from July 18, 1910, to March 1, 1947. He was promoted to commissioned ranks on April 1, 1919 (as O.192), and retired as deputy commissioner. In 1914 he was commended for his efforts in the Hillcrest Coal Mine disaster (Alberta) in which 180 miners lost their lives. As the Second World War opened in the Pacific, he was appointed to the B.C. Securities Commission to undertake the removal of the Japanese-Canadians from sensitive areas of the West Coast. He died on September 9, 1961, at West Vancouver, B.C.

Telford Creek, Yukon (Lat: 63°11'00"N, Long: 138°58'00"W), flowing into the Stewart River from the south, was most likely named after Superintendent Edward Miller Telford, NWMP, RNWMP, and RCMP #2691, O.159.

Telford served in the NWMP from June 9, 1891, in Depot Division, the NWMP Band, and the Yukon. In 1895 he was in the first contingent to the Yukon with Superintendent Constantine. He left the Force in 1897, reengaged in 1900, and served again in the Yukon in charge of the Mayo detachment in 1917 (then RNWMP). He was promoted to the commissioned ranks on November 1, 1910, as O.159 and retired as the commanding officer of "E" Division on January 17, 1927 (then RCMP). He died on January 22, 1935, at Victoria, B.C.

His son, Corporal James E. Telford (#14792), also served from 1946 to 1966.

See **Constantine (Mount Constantine)** for details of the early NWMP in the Yukon.

Telford Lake, Alberta (Lat: 53°16'00"N, Long: 113°31'00"W), 1.5 kilometres from Leduc, is named after Constable Robert Taylor Telford, NWMP #1532.

See following entry.

Telfordville, Alberta, is a hamlet named after Constable Robert Taylor Telford, NWMP #1532.

Constable Telford served from July 1885 to July 5, 1889, mainly at Calgary. He then moved to the Leduc area and was the first settler on Telford Lake. In 1905, when Alberta became a province, he was elected a member of the first provincial legislature.

Tidd (Mount Tidd) (1,695 m), Yukon (Lat: 62°04'00"N, Long: 131°19'00"W), about 45 kilometres west of Pelly Lake, was named in September 1971 to commemorate Sergeant Claude Brittiff Tidd, RNWMP and RCMP #6290.

Tidd served in the Force from September 11, 1914, to September 10, 1935. Except for a year in Regina and a year in Vancouver, he served entirely in the Yukon at Dawson, Rampart House, Atlin, Ross River, Whitehorse, Forty Mile, and Mayo. His extensive collection of photographs of his journeys and the members with whom he served has occasionally been on display. The last known exhibition was in 1997 at the Glenbow Archives in Calgary.

Following his retirement, he moved to Burnham, England, where he died June 12, 1949.

Tofield, Alberta, is named after Doctor James H. Tofield, acting assistant surgeon with the NWMP.

See the following entry.

Tofield Street, Fort Saskatchewan, Alberta, recognizes Doctor James H. Tofield, an assistant surgeon with the NWMP. Although never a member of the Force, Doctor Tofield was under contract in 1889 at Fort Saskatchewan, referred to as the "acting" assistant surgeon, which conferred an honorary commissioned rank status.

Tredgold Lake, Nunavut (Lat: 67°34'00"N, Long: 70°52'00"W), on south-central Baffin Island, is named after Constable Thomas Henry Tredgold, RCMP #9295.

Tredgold served from May 1920 to August 1, 1938, in Headquarters, Ottawa, "O," and "G" Divisions.

While stationed at the Pangnirtung detachment during February and March of 1926, he accompanied Sergeant Wight (#6296) on a 2,070-kilometre dog team patrol from Pangnirtung to Lake Harbour and back.

After leaving the Force he remained in the north, and while fishing in the fast water at a hydro project on October 1, 1940, he drowned when his canoe tipped over. His body was never recovered.

See the **Wight Inlet** entry.

Tremaine Avenue, Regina, Saskatchewan, is named after Constable Cecil Edward George Tremaine, NWMP and RNWMP #3345.

Tremaine served in the Force from October 18, 1898, to November 30, 1906, mainly in Depot Division, policing present-day southern Saskatchewan.

On leaving the Force, Tremaine began Regina Cartage—a business of hauling goods—at Regina. He had as many as 100 draught horses in his stables before the advent of motor trucks. During his many years at Regina, he was the director of the Regina Exhibition board and also chairman of the Light Horse Show Committee from 1943 to 1955.

He died on December 10, 1967, at Regina.

Turner (Mount Turner), Yukon (Lat: 65°24'00"N, Long: 136°14'00"W), east of the Hart River, was named in May 1973 to commemorate Constable Frederick Turner, RNWMP #4889.

Turner served from only 1909 to 1910 in the Yukon, but he was still residing there in 1911 when word was spread of the "Lost Patrol." Although he was no longer in the Force, he volunteered to accompany Corporal Dempster in the search for the lost Fitzgerald patrol.

See **Dempster (Mount Dempster)** and **Fitzgerald Settlement** entries for details of the search for the "Lost Patrol."

Unity Peak, (3,153 m), Alberta (Lat: 51°26'45"N, Long: 116°04'25"W), in Banff National Park about eight kilometres from Lake Louise, is named in honour of the men and women of the Canadian Armed Forces and the Royal Canadian Mounted Police who lost their lives in service to Canada.

Students of South Carleton High School, Richmond, Ontario, obtained government approval to name this mountain. Plans were made for the inaugural climb in June 1998, when a plaque was to be dedicated at the summit. The Lake Louise detachment of the RCMP assisted with the organization and necessary support as part of the Force's 125th Anniversary celebrations.

On June 21, 1998, the peak was scaled by a number of students and support staff for the ceremonies. The students took turns carrying the sixteen-kilogram plaque and firmly installed it at the summit.

The plaque reads in English, French, and a local native language as follows:

On June 21, 1998, an expedition of Canadian youth climbed and dedicated this peak to Canada and to the members of the Canadian Armed Forces and the Royal Canadian Mounted Police who gave their lives in defense of the freedoms of all Canadians.

Corporal Gail Secord (#37156) of the Lake Louise detachment gave the dedication on behalf of the Force.

Bellevue Restaurant in Bellevue, Alberta, where Corporal Usher was murdered

Usher Street, Depot Division RCMP, Regina, Saskatchewan, is named in honour of Corporal Ernest Usher, RNWMP #6096, Honour Roll #43.

Corporal Usher served from September 4, 1914, until 1918, when he volunteered for "A" Squadron Cavalry in the First World War. His military number was #2684134. On return from the war he was posted back to "K" Division until his death on August 7, 1920, at Bellevue, Alberta.

On August 2, 1920, three men boarded the Canadian Pacific passenger train at Lethbridge, Alberta, and headed west. En route they pulled pistols and herded the passengers and crew into one coach, where they robbed them of their cash and valuables, including the conductor's watch. When the train stopped at the Sentinel siding, the three men jumped off and disappeared into the bush. By the time the train reached the Crow's Nest telegraph station, word was spread of the robbery.

The Alberta Provincial Police (APP), assisted by the RNWMP, launched a massive manhunt and soon learned that they were looking for three Russians—George Akoff, Alex Auloff, and Tom Basoff—who had arrived in Lethbridge from Montana. Many "Wanted" posters were spread far and wide. On August 6 the trio tried to cash a cheque at Coleman, so it was known they were still in the local area. On August 7 a Justice of the Peace at Bellevue saw two men fitting the police's description enter a café; he promptly informed three policemen.

Constables Frewin and Bailey of the APP and Corporal Usher entered the café and saw the two fugitives sitting in a booth. Frewin drew his gun and told them to put their hands up. Instead, they reached down, and Frewin shot Akoff in the neck. By now Basoff had his pistol drawn, so Usher began to grapple with him. Despite being shot, Akoff was shooting back. Then Basoff broke free and began shooting, hitting both Usher and Bailey. Now all were shooting, and the police retreated to the street, where Usher and Bailey both fell. Basoff shot and killed both at point-blank range, then killed his wounded partner, Akoff. By then the Justice of the Peace had joined in the shooting; however, Basoff still escaped.

A few days later, the Canadian Pacific Railway police quietly arrested Basoff near Pincher Creek. It was determined that Auloff had parted company with the others because of a disagreement soon after the robbery. Basoff was convicted of murder and hanged at Lethbridge, Alberta, on December 22, 1920.

Over three years later, on January 18, 1924, Auloff was located at Butte, Montana, and extradited to Canada for "train robbery." He was sentenced to seven years' imprisonment and died in prison in 1926. The conductor's watch was found in a pawnshop in Portland, Oregon, and returned.

Constables Bailey and Usher were buried side by side in the Protestant Cemetery at Fort Macleod, Alberta.

Uvauk Inlet, Nunavut (Lat: 63°52'00"N, Long: 92°45'00"W), in the western shore of Hudson Bay near Rankin Inlet, was the name accepted by Northern Affairs in 1966, taken from a 1954 RCMP chart prepared by members who had served in that area and referred to the inlet as "Oovauk."

Vernon Lake, Saskatchewan (Lat: 59°45'00"N, Long: 106°37'00"W), southeast of Fond du Lac, is named after Sergeant Fitzpatrick Vernon Vernon, RNWMP and RCMP #6656.

Vernon joined the Force on February 22, 1917, and was posted to Edmonton, Alberta. He soon appeared twice in Orderly Room, charged on both occasions with "absence"; he was fined two dollars on November 2, 1917, and five dollars on February 7, 1918. He then volunteered for the "A" Squadron cavalry draft and went overseas in the First World War as Canadian Expeditionary Force member #2684059.

On return from the war, he left the Force to join the recently formed Alberta Provincial Police until the takeover of that department by the RCMP on April 1, 1932. He was then back in the Force and served until his retirement October 31, 1940.

Following his retirement, he moved to Trepanier, B.C., and later to nearby Summerland, where he died June 5, 1961.

Victoria Creek, Yukon, which flows into Louise Lake—the westernmost of the Kathleen Lakes, was named by Inspector Albert Edward Crosby Macdonell, NWMP O.117. Peter Ehret found the first placer gold in this creek in the summer of 1902, and when he recorded his claim on May 24, the mining recorder, Inspector Macdonell, named the stream for the occasion.

Vowles (Mount Vowles), Yukon (Lat: 61°25'00"N, Long: 136°11'00"W), east of Aishihik Lake, was named by D.D. Cairnes after Constable Stanley Tom Vowles, RNWMP #4206. While mapping the geology of the area with the Canadian Geographical Society in 1910, Cairnes named this landmark on the Dalton Trail.

Vowles served from May 19, 1904, to July 19, 1908. Most of his service was spent in the area of the Yukon where Mr. Cairnes knew him. We have found little of his service, except for the fact that he had disciplinary problems.

Walker Island, Nunavut (Lat: 63°55'00"N, Long: 93°08'30"W), near Cape Jones on the west side of Hudson Bay, was named in 1979 after Constable Robert Henry Walker, NWMP and RNWMP #3829.

Walker served from March 1902 until 1914, then reengaged in early 1919 and was medically invalided soon afterward on October 5, 1919. He had served in Alberta, the Yukon, the Hudson Bay area, and at Depot Division.

In 1908 he accompanied Inspector Ephrem A. Pelletier (O.122) and two other members for the purpose of establishing a link between eastern and western Arctic. They set out from Fort Saskatchewan, Alberta, and travelled to Athabasca Landing; then they went by way of the Hudson Bay boat across the lake and down the Slave River to Fort Smith on the Alberta–Northwest Territories border. They then used canoes to cross the Great Slave Lake, paddle down the Hanbury and Thelon Rivers to Baker Lake, and then to Chesterfield Inlet on the western shore of Hudson Bay. They were met there by a whaleboat. That winter they returned south by dog team to Churchill, Norway House, and finally Gimli, Manitoba. In all, they had travelled over 4,830 kilometres. It was for this feat that the island was named after him.

In 1911 he was chosen to be in the RNWMP contingent to England for the Coronation of King George V.

See also **Pelletier Point**.

Walker (Colonel James Walker Building), Calgary, Alberta, is named after Colonel Superintendent James Walker, NWMP O.18.

See following entries.

Walker (Colonel Walker House), Calgary, Alberta, was the home of Colonel (Superintendent) James Walker, NWMP O.18.

This house became a provincial heritage site in 1977 and remains a useful area station for the Calgary Parks and Recreation Department.

Walker (Colonel Walker School), Calgary, Alberta, is named after Colonel (Superintendent) James Walker, NWMP O.18.

Walker (James Walker Creek), Alberta (Lat: 50°45'00"N, Long: 115°15'00"W), twenty kilometres from Kananaskis village, is named after Colonel Superintendent James Walker, NWMP O.18.

Walker (James Walker Park), Calgary, Alberta, a rooftop mini-park on the Alberta Telephone Building in Calgary, is named after Colonel (Superintendent) James Walker, NWMP O.18.

The Telephone Building became the home of another remembrance: a bust of James Walker in bronze sculpted by Calgary artist Hazel O'Brien. Walker built Fort Calgary's first telephone system in 1882.

Colonel James Walker Building in Calgary, Alberta

Walker (Mount James Walker), Alberta (Lat: 50°48'00"N, Long: 115°13'00"W), located in the Kananaskis Valley, is named after Colonel (Superintendent) James Walker, NWMP O.18.

Walker was previously a captain in the Canadian militia when he was appointed sub-inspector in the NWMP on March 30, 1874. He was an assistant officer in charge of "D" Division in the March West of 1874. He later served at Fort Walsh and established the first police post at Battleford in 1876. He served until February 1, 1881, leaving as superintendent.

He left the Force to work on the Cochrane Ranch and later opened the Bow River mills. When the Canadian Pacific Railway reached Calgary, he supplied timber for the railway ties and bridges. Additionally, as a contractor, he organized the first school in Calgary. On April 17, 1886, he met with 23 other former members and organized the original Veterans' Association of the NWMP and was elected the first president.

In the First World War he was colonel of the Forestry Corps, from which he retained the rank. For his many years as a leading citizen of Calgary he was declared "Calgary's Citizen of the Century" in 1975. He died at Calgary March 31, 1936, and was buried in Burnsland Cemetery.

See also **Walsh (Fort Walsh)** entry.

Wallace Drive, Depot Division RCMP, Regina, Saskatchewan, is named in honour of Sergeant Thomas Sellar Wallace, RCMP #11326, Honour Roll #58.

Wallace served during the First World War with the Gordon Highlanders, then in the Alberta Provincial Police from the war's end until it was absorbed into the RCMP on April 1, 1932. At the time of his death, on October 8, 1935, he was a sergeant at the Banff detachment in Banff National Park.

Wallace was shot and killed near Banff, Alberta, while manning a roadblock for the suspected slayers of two policemen in Manitoba. For full details of this unfolding violence, stretching from Manitoba to Banff, refer to the **Shaw Street** entry.

Walsh, Alberta, a hamlet on Highway #1 at the Saskatchewan border, is named after Superintendent James Morrow Walsh, NWMP O.7 and O.109.

See following entries.

Walsh Drive, Lethbridge, Alberta, is named after Superintendent James Morrow Walsh, NWMP O.7 and O.109.

Walsh (Fort Walsh), Saskatchewan, a post that the NWMP established in 1875 in the Cypress Hills, was named after Major James Morrow Walsh, NWMP O.7 and O.109.

Fort Walsh, Saskatchewan

This fort was abandoned in 1882 when the barracks of "A" Division were moved to the railway at Maple Creek. The buildings of this historic site were reconstructed in the 1950s.

Walsh (Fort Walsh Creek), Saskatchewan (Lat: 49°34'00"N, Long: 109°53'00"W), flowing southwest into Battle Creek, was named in 1918 by the Department of the Interior's Reclamation Service—as suggested by a Mr. Rowley—after Fort Walsh, located near the mouth of the creek.

Walsh (Fort Walsh Historic Park), Saskatchewan, includes the Battle Creek Valley and Farwell's Trading Post.

Walsh Glacier, Yukon (Lat: 60°53'00"N, Long: 140°37'00"W), in the St. Elias Range, is named after Superintendent James Morrow Walsh, NWMP O.7 and O.109.

Walsh (Mount Walsh) (4,505 m), Yukon (Lat: 61°00'00"N, Long: 140°01'00"W), in the south St. Elias Mountains of north-central Kluane National Park, was named in July 1900 by J.J. McArthur of the International Boundary Commission after the administrator of the Yukon, Superintendent James Morrow Walsh, NWMP O.7 and O.109.

Walsh Street, Maple Creek, Saskatchewan, is named after Superintendent James Morrow Walsh, NWMP O.7 and O.109.

Walsh Trail, Battleford subdivision, Swift Current, Saskatchewan, is named after Major (Superintendent) James Morrow Walsh, NWMP O.7 and O.109.

Walsh was born at Prescott, Upper Canada (Ontario), in 1840. He attended the Royal Military College at Kingston, Ontario, and served in the militia. He was appointed to the commissioned ranks in the NWMP on September 25, 1873, as the seventh officer chosen for this new police force. He had been a major[79] in the military and always chose to use this rank. His nephew, William P. Walsh (#50, Original Series), also joined soon afterwards on October 2, 1873.

Superintendent Walsh led the first contingent of one non-commissioned officer and 32 privates west from Ottawa on October 2, 1873. They travelled by train to Collingwood, where they had a two-day delay awaiting the steamer *Chicora*; then they sailed to Arthur's Landing (present-day Thunder Bay, Ontario). The group then took the Dawson Route, with teams and wagons, to Shabandwin. From there they travelled in small boats to Rainy

James Morrow Walsh,
seen here at a
later point in his
NWMP career

Lake. At the Lake of the Woods, a steamer met them in a blizzard. The remainder of the trek to Fort Garry, Manitoba, was on foot, with their baggage hauled in ox carts. On the March West of 1874, Walsh commanded the "D" Division.

Walsh then served at Fort Macleod until May 1875, when he was ordered to take 30 men of "B" Division and build a fort in the Cypress Hills; Fort Walsh was built in a picturesque valley by Battle Creek and was finished in July. Walsh then commanded at this location. His nephew, Sub-Constable Walsh (#50), died at the fort from mountain fever (typhoid) on September 1, 1879, and was buried there.

Walsh's area of responsibility stretched 240 kilometres east to the Wood Mountain area, where Chief Sitting Bull crossed into Canada with 5,000 Sioux following the battle of the Little Big Horn (this event caused the defeat of General Custer's 7th U.S. Cavalry). Although Walsh's headquarters were at Fort Walsh, most of his time was now spent at Wood Mountain, and through his continuing dealings with Sitting Bull, he became well-known for his firmness and fairness in dealing with the Indians.

He shunned the uniform and usually wore a fringed buckskin jacket and wide-brimmed Stetson-style hat; he also sported a beard. Many of his men copied the beard to the extent that his Division was known simply by appearance. After a distinguished career in the west, Walsh resigned his commission on September 1, 1883.

When the Klondike gold frenzy broke out, the Canadian government called upon him to govern the newly formed Yukon Territory. He was appointed administrator of the Yukon, and to give him needed authority he was reappointed as superintendent in the NWMP on August 26, 1897. He promptly journeyed to the Yukon, armed with almost dictatorial powers. As well as being given the post of administrator (or governor), he was handed the sole command of the NWMP in the territory and also appointed supervisor of Customs and mail services.

Walsh only spent a year in the Yukon. Although there were many criticisms of his methods and ethics, there is no denying that under almost intolerable circumstances he skillfully organized order out of chaos. He was ably assisted by some of the great names of the NWMP such as Steele, Jarvis, Constantine, Wood, Belcher, and others. He was hindered by honest but inefficient civil servants, whose inability to cope with the huge number of people flooding into the territory led to unproven charges of governmental graft and corruption.

Walsh died of a stroke on July 25, 1905, at Brockville, Ontario.

Wapella, Saskatchewan, a village on Trans-Canada Highway #1 about 54 kilometres west of the Manitoba border, was named by Major (Superintendent) James Morrow Walsh, NWMP O.07, from a Sioux word meaning "water under ground." Good wells could be brought in at a shallow depth in this area.

Wardenville, Saskatchewan, a hamlet near Cutknife, is named after Staff Sergeant Stephen "Sandy" Warden, NWMP #516 (Original Series), #286 and #507 (New Series).

Warden was first engaged with the NWMP on July 20, 1876. In 1878 he received a new service number (#286). He served until he had completed three years, received Land Warrant #0262, and took his discharge. He reengaged later, received a new number (#507), and served until February 10, 1886. He had served in what is now Alberta and Saskatchewan.

In 1884 Warden was one of the members in the "Craig Incident," a disruption on Poundmaker's Reserve and a step in the unrest among Indians and Métis that led to the North-West Rebellion.

After his service, he operated both a stage line between Battleford and Swift Current and an inn at 25 Mile Creek. He also served for a time as Indian agent on the Poundmaker and Little Pine Reserves. He died on August 13, 1906, and was buried at Battleford, Saskatchewan.

See also **Crozier Lake** entry.

Wascana Centre, Regina, Saskatchewan, a 930-hectare area in the heart of Regina, was established by the Wascana Centre Act of 1960 in the Saskatchewan Legislature.

See next entry.

Wascana Creek, Regina, Saskatchewan, a meandering creek through the city of Regina and adjacent to the original NWMP post of the same name. In 1882 the site became Headquarters. In 1885 it subsequently became Depot Division and continues as such today.

Originally the creek and area were known as "Pile of Bones," so-called by Captain Palliser, who was through this area in 1857. The reference was apparently taken because of buffalo bones being set up along the creek when the Indians were drying meat.

At the arrival of the NWMP, visitors would comment, "It's a pity that the creek should be called Pile of Bones." Sam Steele is purported to have said that "Wascana" in the Sioux language meant the same thing, so it became known instead as "Wascana."

Waters River, Yukon (Lat: 67°23'35"N, Long: 137°01'15"W), which flows into the Bell River at Lapierre House, is believed to be named after Corporal William Cragg Waters, RNWMP and RCMP #6273.

Corporal Waters served from September 15, 1914, to July 15, 1929, mainly in the Yukon. In 1917 he assisted the Geological Survey of Canada when it was mapping the area of the named river. Late in his service he was transferred to Vancouver, from where he was medically invalided.

He died at Vernon, B.C., on August 8, 1958, and was buried at Penticton, B.C.

Wests Bay, Saskatchewan (Lat: 55°34'00"N, Long: 102°38'00"W), eighteen kilometres from Island Falls, is named after Superintendent Christopher Harfield West, NWMP, RNWMP and RCMP #2141, O.118.

Staff Sergeant West (#2141) served as hospital steward in Depot Division and at Battleford from May 10, 1888, until an unknown date. He left the Force to complete medical training, and as a qualified doctor he was appointed to the commissioned ranks on August 1, 1900, as O.118. He then served to August 31, 1922, retiring as superintendent.

He died on January 12, 1935, at North Battleford, Saskatchewan, and was buried there.

Wight Inlet, Nunavut (Lat: 62°15'00"N, Long: 68°13'00"W), on the south coast of Baffin Island on Meta Incognita Peninsula, is named after Sergeant James Edward Freeman Wight, RNWMP, and RCMP #6296.

Wight served in the Force from September 23, 1914, to March 14, 1945, in "K," Depot, "G," "A," and "H" Divisions. He was another from a family of members in the Force: his brother, Corporal Robert Wight (#4961), served from 1909 to 1917, and his son, Constable Alexander Wight (#15526), also served in the north. (In 1953 his son was at the Lake Harbour detachment, Northwest Territories. With radio instructions from a doctor, he performed a successful appendectomy on an Inuit, Mingeeneeak, with the assistance of the local Hudson's Bay Company factor, Mr. Pilgrim. The operation undoubtedly saved Mingeeneeak's life.)

In 1915, with Inspector (later Assistant Commissioner) Charles D. LaNauze (O.180) and Corporal Dennis Withers (#4794), he made a fourteen-month patrol by dog team from Fort Norman to the mouth of the Coppermine River in the Northwest Territories, seeking two Inuit (Sinnisiak and Kormick) who were alleged to have murdered two missionaries.

In the First World War he volunteered for service in the RNWMP "A" Squadron cavalry draft to serve in France with the Canadian Expeditionary Force as #2772629. On his return from the war he was sent back north with the Force.

While in charge of the Pangnirtung detachment during February and March of 1926, he made another long dog team patrol. He completed this 2,070-kilometre trip with Constable Thomas Tredgold (#9295), travelling from Pangnirtung to Lake Harbour and back.

He died on July 5, 1959, at Yarmouth, Nova Scotia.

Wilde, Manitoba (Lat: 55°43'35"N, Long: 96°48'46"W), a Canadian National Railway station at Mile 231 from The Pas (northeast of Pikwitonei) en route to Hudson Bay, was named in 1928 after Sergeant William Brock Wilde, NWMP #857, Honour Roll #21.

See following entries.

Wilde Lane, Depot Division RCMP, Regina, Saskatchewan, is named in honour of Sergeant William Brock Wilde, NWMP #857, Honour Roll #21.

Sergeant Wilde sitting in Pincher Creek, Alberta, 1895

Wilde Road, Calgary, Alberta, is named after Sergeant William Brock Wilde, NWMP #857, Honour Roll #21.

Wilde had served seven years in the Royal Irish Dragoons and two years in the 2nd Life Guards before coming to Canada and joining the NWMP on July 13, 1882. He saw service in the North-

West Rebellion in 1885 before being posted to Fort Macleod. Later, he was put in charge of the Pincher Creek detachment.

On October 11, 1896, a man named Charcoal, also known as "Bad Young Man," from the Blood Reserve—in jealousy over his wife—murdered another Indian, Medicine Pipe Stem. The following night Charcoal shot through the window of a former farm instructor on the Blood Reserve, wounding him. A warrant was issued for his arrest, and both Inspector Arthur Jarvis (O.104) and Superintendent Gilbert Sanders (O.52) directed a wide search throughout the Blood Reserve and Cardston areas.

Numerous sightings were reported, and many threats were heard concerning whom he intended to kill next. When the first snows came in the fall, police and scouts were able to track him. His camp was surrounded, but it was found that he had fled with two wives and a son. Three other people that he left behind were removed.

The next reports were that Charcoal was seen in the Porcupine Hills along Beaver Creek, and because of his reputation, other Indians were afraid of him. On November 5, 1896, he was reported near Pincher Creek, so Sergeant Wilde quickly gathered a patrol group to join the hunt. A few days later a Peigan scout found Charcoal's trail, so Sergeant Wilde's posse joined him there.

Charcoal was spotted in the distance as darkness was falling on November 10. Charcoal then yelled to the other Indians in the posse to stay back. They did, so Wilde rode ahead alone. Near Dry Forks, Sergeant Wilde called on Charcoal to stop, and then he rode to within a metre of him. On horseback, Charcoal whirled, pulled his rifle from under his blanket wrap, and shot Wilde at almost point-blank range. The sergeant fell from his horse, mortally wounded in the chest. Charcoal leapt from his horse and shot him again, and then he took the police horse and rode away.

Unknown to Charcoal, his two brothers, Left Hand and Bear's Back Bone, had earlier promised Superintendent Steele that they would help in his arrest. Two days after Wilde's murder, Charcoal rode up to his brothers' house. He entered, stared at them a moment, and said, "You have betrayed me." He then turned and left. As he was mounting his horse, they overpowered him, tied him up, and called Sergeant William Macleod (#1985), who had been standing by for such word.

Charcoal was tried in court at Fort Macleod, found guilty of murder, and hanged at Fort Macleod on March 16, 1897. Sergeant Wilde was buried in the Protestant Cemetery at Fort Macleod. The citizens of Pincher Creek erected a monument in his memory. It now stands in the Pincher Creek Memorial Park.

See also **Jarvis River** and **Steele Street** entries.

Wilkinson Avenue, Regina, Saskatchewan, is named after Sergeant Martin Blakiston Wilkinson, NWMP and RNWMP #3601.

See next entry.

Wilkinson Street, Regina, Saskatchewan, is named after Sergeant Martin Blakiston Wilkinson, NWMP and RNWMP #3601.

Wilkinson served in the Force from April 7, 1900, to April 6, 1907, and was credited with arresting the first armed "hold-up" robber in the city of Regina. He was an ardent sportsman and was one of the founders of the Regina Boat Club in 1907. On completing his contracted time in the Force, he left to join the Sheriff's Service in Regina, where he remained until the First World War. He then served overseas in the 28th Battalion; in 1918 he was wounded at Arras and spent six months recovering in hospital.

On his return to Canada, he went back to the Sheriff's Service and was sheriff for Regina from 1922 to 1942. He died at Regina on June 15, 1974.

Williams Crescent, Regina, Saskatchewan, is named after Corporal James Williams, NWMP #2217.

See next entry.

Williams Street, Regina, Saskatchewan, is named after Corporal James Williams, NWMP #2217.

Williams served for six years in the 12th Lancers and Royal Irish Regiment before coming to Canada. He then served in the Force from November 1888 to 1892, when he left to become the first town constable for Regina.

He later farmed at Wapella, Saskatchewan, and following that was weighmaster at Regina for seventeen years. He died September 6, 1938, at Regina and was buried in the Force Cemetery at Depot Division.

Willis Coulee, Saskatchewan (Lat: 49°33'00"N, Long: 108°49'00"W), three kilometres from Eastend, is named after Constable Harry Ralph Willis, NWMP and RNWMP #3280.

Willis served from 1898 to March 1909 at Maple Creek, Ten Mile, and at Eastend, Saskatchewan, where he left the Force as the member in charge of the Eastend detachment. He married a daughter of Constable Peter O'Hare, NWMP #198. In turn, his own daughter married Corporal Mervyn Ashby, RCMP #10324.

When he left the Force, Willis filed on a homestead and ranched northwest of Eastend with the Bar 4 brand. He died at Eastend, Saskatchewan, on January 29, 1938.

Willmett Place, Depot Division RCMP, Regina, Saskatchewan, is named in honour of Constable George Ernest Willmett, RNWMP #4584, Honour Roll #32.

Constable Willmett served from May 9, 1907, until his death April 12, 1908, in "K" Division. At the time of his death he was posted at the Frank detachment.

Due to a series of burglaries, Willmett was on night patrol in the town of Frank's business area. In the early morning of April 12, 1908, his body was found in an alley behind the Imperial Hotel. He had been shot by a shotgun at close range. The member in charge, Sergeant William Haslett (#1649), immediately spread the alarm. Inspector Thomas S. Belcher (O.146) was sent in to command the investigation, and he brought in Sergeant Major Charles Raven (#1128), Staff Sergeant John S. Piper (#2349), and Sergeant Peter Egan (#3309). A $200 reward was promptly posted, and every effort was made to identify Willmett's killer, including house-by-house interviews for any hint or suspicion. Nothing of value was learned.

Over three years later, Staff Sergeant Piper, with a reputation in the Force for his detective abilities, received a tip pointing to Mathias Jasbec and Fritz Eberts—recent immigrants—as Willmett's murderers. Jasbec was located in B.C.; he gave a confession implicating Eberts as the murderer. He said, in part, that he and Eberts had been attempting to break into stores, and when Willmett unexpectedly confronted them, Eberts shot him.

Sergeant Herbert F. O'Connell (#4767), following up leads from Jasbec, located Eberts in Montana and had him extradited to Canada. Both Jasbec and Eberts were charged with murder, and at their trial Eberts was found guilty and sentenced to hang on June 1, 1912. The Crown withdrew the murder charge against Jasbec, who had entered a guilty plea to a charge of attempted break, enter, and theft. Since he had already been in jail for one year, he received a suspended sentence.

While he was on death row, Eberts convinced a fellow inmate—who was soon to be hanged—to confess to Willmett's murder, but a deathwatch guard caught them planning. Eberts then went on to appeal his sentence, which was commuted to life imprisonment in Stony Mountain Penitentiary.

Constable Willmett was buried in the Union Cemetery, Fort Macleod, Alberta.

Wilson Falls, Saskatchewan (Lat: 55°19'00"N, Long: 102°03'00"W), near Island Falls, is named after Assistant Commissioner James Osgoode Wilson, NWMP and RNWMP O.64.

For some unknown reason, Wilson was known among his subordinates as "Pie Face Wilson." He joined the NWMP June 9, 1879, as #392, served his contracted three years in what is now Saskatchewan, and left the Force with one of the last Land Warrants issued, #0496. From civilian life, he was reappointed as an inspector on September 15, 1885. He then served in what is now Alberta and then Depot Division.

In 1911 he was in the Force contingent that went to England for the Coronation of King George V. He retired on January 17, 1919, as an assistant commissioner. He then moved to Victoria, B.C., where he died on April 29, 1927.

Wilson Industrial Subdivision, Edmonton, Alberta, is named after Doctor Herbert Charles Wilson, an acting assistant surgeon with the NWMP.

Dr. Wilson was born in Ontario in 1859. He arrived in Edmonton in 1882 and opened up a drugstore. In 1885 he held the position of acting assistant surgeon on contract to the NWMP in Edmonton and at Fort Saskatchewan. While never actually a member of the Force, the title was given to provide him with officer status.

Dr. Wilson sat on the Northwest Territories council and was the first speaker in 1888. He served as mayor of Edmonton in 1895–1896 and died in 1909.

Wilson (Mount Wilson) (3,240 m), Alberta (Lat: 52°01'00"N, Long: 116°47'00"W), five kilometres from the Saskatchewan River Crossing in Banff National Park, was named in 1898 after Constable Thomas Edmund Wilson, NWMP #506.

See next entry.

Wilson Road, Calgary, Alberta, may have also been named after Constable Thomas Edmund Wilson, NWMP #506.

Constable Wilson served in the Force from September 22, 1880, until May 16, 1881. He then joined Major A.B. Rogers[80] to explore and survey possible routes for the Canadian Pacific Railway through the Rocky and Selkirk Mountains into B.C. On August 24, 1882, he stood on the shore of Lake Louise[81] and is credited with being the first white person to do so. Soon afterward he discovered the equally beautiful Emerald Lake and Takakkaw Falls (now in Yoho National Park). While Rogers was surveying what is now

Rogers Pass, Wilson explored the Bow River, Howse Pass, and Blaeberry River. These explorations came to an end when the "Rogers" route was chosen.

In 1884 Wilson began a packing and guiding business at Banff. He later operated a trading post on the North Saskatchewan River since—by then—there were many exploration parties in these areas. With the outbreak of the North-West Rebellion in 1885, he joined Steele's Scouts[82] and was involved in some of their skirmishes.

On November 7, 1885, the driving of the "last spike" on the Canadian Pacific Railway at Craigellachie, B.C., was an affair for posterity. There is a widely distributed photograph of that moment when the railway's architect, William Cornelius Van Horne, watched the spike being driven. Passing unnoticed in the very back row in a light-coloured Stetson hat is Wilson.

During the 1920s, Wilson lived for a time at Enderby, B.C., before moving back to his beloved Banff, where he died on September 22, 1933. He was buried in the Banff Cemetery.

Winder Ranch, in southwest Alberta, takes its name from the original owner: Superintendent William Winder, NWMP O.5.

William Winder

Winder was appointed as the fifth officer in the fledgling NWMP on September 25, 1873. On the March West of 1874 he commanded "C" Division. He served until April 1, 1881, and then established the Winder Ranch Company in southwest Alberta, just north of Fort Macleod.

He died in Fort Macleod on November 6, 1885.

See also the **Dead Horse Coulee** entry.

Wood Mountain, Saskatchewan, got its name from a low range of hills that runs along the south-central boundary of the province, as did the old NWMP post nearly 6.5 kilometres south of the town.

In the fall of 1874 the North West Mounted Police purchased the International Boundary Commission's supply depot at Wood Mountain. That winter, a number of sick horses were left there in the care of two constables, while the remaining members returned to Fort Livingstone. When Fort Walsh was established in 1875, the detachment was removed and the crude log structures were used as an occasional stopping place for the police.

When Sitting Bull and his followers crossed into Canada following the Battle of the Little Big Horn, the NWMP established an important detachment at Wood Mountain. From 1876 until 1881 the post was the centre of much activity. From 1882 until the closing of the post in 1918, the Wood Mountain detachment was tasked with many duties, including border patrol, stock inspection, and assisting new settlers.

In 1928 the Canadian Pacific Railway ran a branch line west from Maxstone to Mankota, and it passed north of the old post. A town grew up by the railway, taking its name from the old NWMP post, Wood Mountain.

Wood Mountain, Saskatchewan

Wood (Mount Wood) (4,842 m), Yukon (Lat: 61°14'00"N, Long: 140°30'00"W), in the St. Elias Range on the northwest border of Kluane National Park, was named in July 1900 by J.J. McArthur—while surveying the International Boundary—after Superintendent Zachary Taylor Wood, NWMP O.54.

See following entry.

Wood Street, Whitehorse, Yukon, is named after Assistant Commissioner Zachary Taylor Wood, NWMP O.54.

Assistant Commissioner Zachary Taylor Wood was the first of another dynasty in the Force. He was the great-grandson of Zachary Taylor, the twelfth U.S. president. His son, Stuart Taylor Wood, attended the Royal Military College at Kingston, Ontario, and in 1912 was commissioned in the RNWMP as Inspector O.171. He went on to serve as commissioner from 1938 to 1951. He died in 1966 and was buried at Depot Division.

In turn, Commissioner Stuart Taylor Wood had three sons. The eldest was Donald Zachary Taylor Wood, who served in the Royal Canadian Air Force in the Second World War and died in an air crash on October 14, 1944. The second son, Herschel Taylor Wood, joined the RCMP as #14757 in 1946 and served in "K" Division until he was killed in a motor vehicle accident on July 16, 1950. He was buried at Depot Division. The third son, John Taylor Wood, joined the RCMP in 1951 as #16821. He was promoted to the commissioned ranks as O.628 and retired as superintendent in 1988. He died in 1991 at Ottawa, Ontario.

Zachary Wood attended the Royal Military College at Kingston, Ontario, and then served in the North-West Rebellion in the 90th Battalion, Canadian Militia. Immediately afterward, he was appointed an inspector in the NWMP on August 1, 1885. He served in what are now "F," "K," "E," and "M" Divisions and was the officer in charge of a portion of the Yukon as assistant commissioner when he was granted sick leave in late 1914. On January 15, 1915, while still on sick leave at Asheville, North Carolina, he died.

In 1998 a six-member team climbed Mount Wood as part of the Force's 125th Anniversary celebrations, completing the tenth successful ascent of the mountain. The following Force members were involved in the climb: Constable J. L. Chris Pratte (#38177) of "M" Division, Constable Dave P. Olson (#36694) of "E" Division, Corporal Pat J. Egan (#36729) of "M" Division, and Constable J. Blake Leminski (#37289) of "A" Division. Paul Randall, an Alaska State trooper, and Andrew Lawrence, a Kluane Park warden, also took part.

Yates River, Alberta (Lat: 60°00'00"N, Long: 116°05'00"W), flowing from Alberta into Buffalo Lake within the Northwest Territories, is named after Corporal Richard Norris Yates, RCMP #11234.

Corporal Yates served from December 1, 1931, until December 23, 1955. He served in "D," "G," and "K" Divisions and retired from the Olds detachment. Corporal Yates died on August 14, 1994, at Calgary, Alberta.

Yorkville School District #1537, Alberta, south of Fort Saskatchewan, is named after Sub-Constable James G. Yorke, NWMP #51 (Original Series), #1738 (New Series).

Yorke served in the first contingent of the NWMP as Sub-Constable #51, from September 25, 1873, to an unknown date. He was in the 1874 March West, and he served for at least three years because he received Land Warrant #0137. He rejoined the Force on January 15, 1886, as #1738 and served until 1889, mainly at Fort Saskatchewan. Most of his duties with the Force were as a veterinarian.

From 1890 to 1907 Yorke farmed in the "Yorkville" area. This area, which takes his name, is about five kilometres south of Fort Saskatchewan. Yorke supposedly died on May 17, 1917, at Duncan, B.C., but his name does not appear in the B.C. Vital Statistics death records.

Appendix 1

Divisions of the Force, 1873–2000

The formation of the NWMP started with an order-in-council on August 30, 1873. Prime Minister Sir John A. Macdonald ordered, "The Force should consist of 300 men, exclusive of officers, and should be divided into six divisions of 50 men each, such Divisions to be lettered from 'A' to 'F' consecutively."

From that time forward, Divisions of the Force have had letter designations, although their placement and headquarters have moved as necessary over the years. The original six divisions made the March West in 1874, and with rare exception they have been separated ever since.

For the reader's benefit, the letters used in the entries for Division postings are current (2002) designations and not as they may have been at the time of the individual's earlier service.

"A" Division
1874 March West
1874 Fort Edmonton
1875 Fort Walsh
1883 Maple Creek
1920 Western Ontario with HQ
      Ottawa

"B" Division
1874 March West
1874 Fort Macleod
1877 Fort Walsh
1880 Qu'Appelle
1882 Regina
1888 Wood Mountain
1891 Regina
1895 not in use
1898 Dawson
1938 not in use
1949 Newfoundland with HQ
      St. John's

"C" Division
1874 March West
1874 Fort Macleod
1886 Battleford
1920 Brandon
1924 not in use
1932 Quebec with HQ Montreal

"D" Division
1874 March West
1874 Fort Dufferin
1876 Fort Macleod
1878 Shoal Lake
1880 Battleford
1886 Fort Macleod
1887 Fort Steele
1889 Fort Macleod
1919 Manitoba with HQ
      Winnipeg

"E" Division
1874 March West
1874 Swan River
1878 Battleford
1880 Fort Walsh
1882 Calgary
1919 B.C. with HQ Vancouver
1950 B.C. with HQ Victoria
1982 B.C. with HQ Vancouver

"F" Division
1874 March West
1874 Fort Macleod
1876 Calgary
1878 Fort Walsh
1881 not in use
1885 Prince Albert
1932 Saskatchewan with HQ
      Regina

"G" Division
1885 Edmonton
1886 Fort Saskatchewan
1910 Northwest Territories and
      Yukon with HQ Edmonton
1933 Northwest Territories and
      Yukon with HQ Ottawa
1974 Northwest Territories
      with HQ Yellowknife

"H" Division
1885 Fort Macleod
1895 not in use
1898 Tagish
1900 Whitehorse
1910 not in use
1920 Vancouver
1924 not in use
1932 Nova Scotia with HQ
      Halifax

"J" Division
1932 New Brunswick with HQ Fredericton

"K" Division
1885 Battleford
1887 Lethbridge
1932 Alberta with HQ Edmonton

"L" Division
1932 Prince Edward Island with HQ Charlottetown

"M" Division
1904 Fullerton
1908 Churchill
1915 Fort Nelson
1919 not in use
1924 Fort Macleod
1931 not in use
1974 Yukon with HQ Whitehorse

"N" Division
1905 Lesser Slave Lake
1908 Athabasca
1916 Peace River
1919 not in use
1920 Rockcliffe
1987 discontinued and became the Canadian Police College

"O" Division
1920 Southern Ontario with HQ Toronto
1992 HQ moved to London

"P" Division
1966 Penhold
1969 discontinued

"V" Division
1999 Nunavut with HQ Iqaluit

Depot Division
1885 Regina
1988 designation discontinued
1995 reinstated

The name was clearly taken from the Royal Irish Constabulary "Depot" in Dublin. Established in 1885 as a training centre, Depot was also the headquarters for all of southern Saskatchewan for many years. Since then, most of over 45,000 recruits have experienced their basic training in this centre that has now grown to being its own self-contained "town."

Reserve Division
1915 Regina
1916 discontinued

Appendix 2

Honour Roll Of The Force

The Force has maintained a "Roll of Honour" that lists those members who have lost their lives in the performance of their duty. They are listed here sequentially. Those who have been remembered with a place name in Canada are marked with two asterisks (**).

In 1936 a Roll of Honour Memorial was purchased, through subscription by the 2,500 members serving at that time, and installed at the Parade Square at Depot Division. It was unveiled and dedicated by Reverend A.E.G. Handy, Force chaplain, at the invitation of Assistant Commissioner S.T. Wood. At the time of dedication, 48 members were listed; as of 2000, 147 more have been added.

RCMP Honour Roll Monument, Training Academy, Regina, Saskatchewan

	Reg.#	Rank	Name	Cause of death/year/place	Place name (**)
1	135	Sub-Constable	Nash, J.D.	Accident 1876; near Fort Macleod, NWT	**
2	409	Sub-Constable	Mahoney, G.	Drowned 1877; near Battleford, NWT	
3	335	Constable	Graburn, M.	Shot 187; near Fort Walsh, NWT	**
4	181	Constable	Hooley, C.S.	Drowned 1880; Belly River near Slideout, NWT	
5	N/A	Sub-Constable	Wahl, A.	Drowned 1882; Missouri River, Montana	
6	1003	Constable	Gibson, T.J.	Shot 1885; Duck Lake, NWT	
7	852	Constable	Garrett, G,K,	Shot 1885; Duck Lake, NWT	
8	1065	Constable	Arnold, G.P.	Shot 1885; Duck Lake, NWT	
9	635	Constable	Cowan, D.L.	Shot 1885; near Fort Pitt, NWT	
10	565	Corporal	Sleigh, R.B.	Shot 1885; Cut Knife Hill, NWT	**
11	402	Constable	Burke, P.	Shot 1885; Cut Knife Hill, NWT	**
12	907	Corporal	Lowry, W.H.T.	Shot 1885; Cut Knife Hill, NWT	**
13	973	Constable	Elliott, F.O.	Shot 1885; Battleford, NWT	
14	487	Sergeant	Montgomery, A.E.G.	Thrown by horse 1890; Prince Albert, NWT	
15	2439	Constable	DeBeaujeu, G.Q.R.S.	Drowned 1890; Lake Winnipeg, MB	**
16	2162	Corporal	Morphy, H.O.	Drowned 1890; Lake Winnipeg, MB	
17	2086	Constable	Reading, W.T.	Horse fell 1890; Calgary, NWT	
18	913	Constable	Herron, J.	Blizzard 1891; St. Mary's River, NWT	
19	605	Sergeant	Colebrook, C.C.	Shot 1895; Kinistino, NWT	**
20	3100	Constable	Kern, O.A.	Drowned 1896; near Estevan, NWT	
21	857	Sergeant	Wilde, W.B.	Shot 1896; Dry Fork, NWT	**
22	3040	Constable	Kerr, J.R.	Shot 1897; Minnichinas Hills, NWT	**
23	3106	Corporal	Hockin, C.H.S.	Shot 1897; Minnichinas Hills, NWT	**
24	2972	Constable	Campbell, N.M.	Drowned 1901; Stikine River, Alaska	
25	3463	Constable	Heathcote, S.G.	Drowned 1901; Stikine River, Alaska	

26		Sp/Constable	Sam, S.	Drowned 1903; Kaskawulsh River, Yukon	**
27	1102	Staff Sergeant	Brooke, A.F.M.	Drowned 1903; near Gleichen, NWT	
28	4152	Constable	Russell, J.	Drowned 1905; Cape Fullerton, NWT	
29	4119	Constable	Jackson, T.R.	Drowned 1906; Battleford, SK	
30	2836	Corporal	Haddock, A.G.	Drowned 1906; Ogilvie, Yukon	
31	O.148	Acting Surgeon	Flood, W.S.	Froze in blizzard 1906; Churchill, MB	
32	4584	Constable	Willmett, G.E.	Shot 1908; Frank, AB	**
33	3566	Sergeant	Donaldson, R.M.	Drowned 1908; Marble Island, Hudson Bay	
34	2127	Sp/Constable	Carter, Samuel	Froze 1911; Wind River, Yukon	**
35	O.156	Inspector	Fitzgerald, F.J.	Froze 1911; Wind River, Yukon	**
36	4582	Constable	Kinney, G.F.	Froze 1911; Wind River, Yukon	**
37	4346	Constable	Taylor, R.O.	Starving/suicide 1911; Wind River, Yukon	
38	4837	Constable	Davies, F.W.	Shot 1912; Brooks, AB	
39	4968	Constable	Bailey, M.G.	Shot 1913; Tofield, AB	**
40	3617	Constable	Fitzgerald, M.J.	Accidental skull fracture 1913; White River, Yukon	
41	5548	Constable	Lamont, A.	Typhoid / caring for sick 1918; Herschel Island, Yukon	
42	979	Staff Sergeant	Bossange, G.H.L.	Lightning 1919; Spirit River, AB	
43	6096	Corporal	Usher, E.	Shot 1920; Bellevue, AB	**
44	4995	Sergeant	Searle, A.G.	Drowned 1921; Creston, BC	
45	4396	Corporal	Doak, W.A.	Shot 1922; Tree River, NWT	**
46	9791	Constable	MacDonald, I.M.	Lost at sea 1924; near Herschel Island, Yukon	
47	9818	Constable	Cox, L.F.	Drowned 1925; LaSarre, PQ	
48	9951	Constable	Rhodes, F.	Burns 1926: Rae, NWT	
49	5611	Sergeant	Nicholson, R.H.	Shot 1928; Molson, MB	**
50	10399	Constable	Macdonell, D.R.	Exposure 1931; Fourteen River, MB	**

51	9669	Constable	Millen, E.	Shot 1932; Rat River, Yukon	**
52	6177	Corporal	Ralls, L.V.	Shot 1932; Foam Lake, SK	**
53	7688	Corporal	Halliday, J.L.	Accidentally shot 1932; Fort Simpson, NWT	
54	O.281	Inspector	Sampson, L.J.	Riot/horse mishap 1933; Saskatoon, SK	
55	6352	Corporal	Moriarity, M.	Shot 1935; near Drumheller, AB	**
56	11582	Constable	Shaw, J.G.	Shot 1935; near Benito, MB	**
57	10946	Constable	Harrison, G.C.	Shot 1935; near Banff, AB	
58	11326	Sergeant	Wallace, T.S.	Shot 1935; near Banff, AB	**
59	11150	Constable	Miller, D.	Car accident 1935; Newcastle, NB	
60	11818	Constable	Horan, G.E.	Car accident 1937; Belleville, ON	
61	12093	Constable	Boorman, W.G.	Accidentally shot 1937; Port Harrison, PQ	
62	12690	Constable	Rhodeniser, W.E.	Shot 1939; Carlyle, SK	**
63	11046	Constable	Gleadow, N.A.	Struck and shot 1939; Esterhazy, SK	**
64	7606	Sergeant	Barker, A.J.	Shot 1940; Shaunavon, SK	**
65	11298	Constable	Counsell, F.G.	Shot 1940; Parkland, AB	**
66	10655	Constable	Rapeer, H.G.	Runaway horses 1940; Regina, SK	
67	12223	Engineer	Gillis, D.E.	Exposure, ship-sinking 1941; near Halifax, NS	
68	10063	Constable	Johnstone, C.J.	Lost at sea 1941; North Atlantic Ocean	
69	10982	Sergeant	Dubuc, L.R.	Air crash 1941; Dundalk, Eire	**
70	11003	Constable	Patterson, C.F.	Carbon monoxide 1941; England	
71	12168	1st Officer	Mithorp, P.R.F.	Torpedoed ship 1942; North Atlantic Ocean	
72	12572	Constable	Oliver, P.S.	Killed in Action 1942; Dieppe, France	
73	12130	Master	Bonner, J.W.	Torpedoed ship 1942; Gulf of St. Lawrence	**
74	13205	Constable	Bedlington, J.H.D.	Army motorcycle accident 1943; England	**
75	O.298	Surgeon	Powers, M.	Air crash 1943; near North Battleford, SK	
76	13064	Constable	Watts, T.G.N.	Killed in Action 1943; Italy	

77	12856	Constable	Cameron, E.A.	Killed in Action 1943; Italy	**
78	13157	Constable	Moon, D.C.G.	Killed in Action 1943; Italy	**
79	12965	Constable	Bondurant, G.E.	Killed in Action 1944; Italy	*
80	13678	Constable	d'Albenas, K.L.	Killed in Action 1944; Italy	**
81	20307	Constable	Hoey, J.T.	Shot 1958; Botwood, NF	
82	12398	Constable	Nelson, J.F.J.	Killed in Action 1944; Italy	
83	12108	Constable	Stackhouse, D.G.	Killed in Action 1944; Italy	
84	12983	Constable	Cobble, W.J.	Struck by truck 1946; Vegreville, AB	
85	11645	Constable	Wilson, C.F.	Struck by vehicle 1948; Portapique, NS	
86	5816	Constable	Gamman, A.	Shot 1950; Montreal, PQ	
87	14819	Constable	Sander, J.K.	Drowned 1954; Barrows, MB	
88	16141	Constable	Bloomfield, R.C.	Drowned 1954; Barrows, MB	
89	18050	Constable	Melsom, W.L.	Police car accident 1956; Port Alberni, BC	
90	O.385	Inspector	McCombe, D.J.	Exposure 1955; Cut Knife, SK	
91	17298	Constable	Cobley, J.R.	Struck by car 1957; near Salmon Arm, BC	
92	14588	Corporal	Smart, H.M.	Drowned 1958; Lake Simcoe, ON	
93	19469	Constable	Melnychuk, M.	Drowned 1958; Lake Simcoe, ON	
94	19478	Constable	Farough, G.F.	Drowned 1958; Lake Simcoe, ON	
95	19879	Constable	Perry, D.M.	Drowned 1958; Lake Simcoe, ON	
96	19915	Constable	Ransom, G.H.E.	Drowned 1958; Lake Simcoe, ON	
97	10880	Staff Sergeant	Rothwell, S.S.	Air crash 1958; near Penticton, BC	*
98	14740	Constable	Green, R.W.	Air crash 1958; near Penticton, BC	
99	10410	Sp/Constable	Cormier, J.E.R.	Air crash 1958; near Penticton, BC	**
100	19731	Constable	Lelliott, C.E.	Shot 1960; Cambridge Bay, NWT	
101	20366	Constable	Ekstrom, R.A.	Police car accident 1961; Lytton, BC	

196

102	S4218	Sp/Constable	Jarvis, H.C.	Drowned 1941; Iroquois, ON	
103	S3185	Sp/Constable	Joseph, H.	Struck by car 1941; St. Catharines, ON	
104	10155	Constable	Chartrand, A. J.	Died on *St. Roch* 1942; Pasley Bay, NWT	**
105	11371	Corporal	Ryder, L.P.	Assault, hemorrhage 1943; Woodstock, NB	
106	14890	Constable	Henderson, J.B.	Drowned 1948; St. Lawrence River, ON	
107	14757	Constable	Wood, H.T.	Car accident 1950; Glacier Park, MT	
108	16810	Constable	Kasper, S.	Air crash 1953; Prince Rupert, BC	
109	15802	Constable	Ferguson, D.E.	Carbon monoxide 1954; Bathurst Inlet, NWT	**
110	14694	Constable	Laird, R.E.	Police car accident 1955; Medicine Hat, AB	
111	15303	Constable	Reay, C.W.	Drowned 1955; Island Falls, SK	**
112	18656	Constable	Chandler, H.C.A.	Motorcycle accident 1956; Halifax, NS	
113	18165	Constable	Sundell, C.L.	Accidentally shot 1958; Herschel Island, Yukon	
114	20958	Constable	Sinclair, W.	Motorcycle accident 1961; near Regina, SK	
115	18200	Constable	Thompson, J.T.	Car hit by aircraft 1961; Lethbridge, AB	
116	19233	Constable	Keck, E.J.	Shot 1962; Kamloops, BC	
117	20215	Constable	Weisgerber, D.G.	Shot 1962; Kamloops, BC	
118	20865	Constable	Pedersen, G.E.	Shot 1962; Kamloops, BC	
119	21512	Constable	Lepine, A.O.	Motorcycle accident 1962; Surrey, BC	
120	17334	Constable	Foreman, J.W.	Struck by car 1963; Sangudo, AB	
121	17368	Sergeant	Laughland, K.M.	Air crash 1963; Saskatoon, SK	
122	19626	Corporal	Asbil, R.W.	Air crash 1963; Carmacks, Yukon	
123	18570	Constable	Malcolm, P.L.A.	Air crash 1963; Carmacks, Yukon	
124	19206	Constable	Annand, W.J.D.	Air crash 1963; Carmacks, Yukon	
125	22055	Constable	Dubois, J.P.F.	Car accident 1964; Fauvel, PQ	
126	17644	Corporal	Giesbrecht, E.J.	Drowned 1964; Hybord, MB	
127	22240	Constable	Amey, R.W.	Shot 1964; Whitbourne, NF	

128	23499	Constable	Williams, R.W.	Drowned 1964; Sooke, BC	
129	20598	Constable	Robinson, D.B.	Accidentally shot 1965; Saskatoon, SK	
130	20824	Constable	Bruce, N.M.	Shot 1965; Westbank, BC	**
131	20388	Constable	Carroll, T.P.	Air crash 1966; Cyril Lake, MB	
132	24014	Constable	Tidman, P.J.	Car accident 1966; Wakaw, SK	
133	23018	Constable	Pearson, G.D.	Shot 1966; Winterburn, AB	
134	25214	Constable	Tomfohr, T.E.	Fell from cliff 1967; Burnaby, BC	
135	17129	Corporal	Harvey, D.A.	Shot 1967; Grande Prairie, AB	
136	2181	Constable	Perry, A.	Drowned 1889; near Lethbridge, NWT	
137	25094	Constable	Varney, R.W.	Police car accident 1967; Raymond, AB	
138	26042	Constable	Kerr, J.A.	Struck by car 1968; St. Anne, NB	
139	19508	Constable	Williams, T.G.	Drowned 1968; Sheet Harbour Passage, NS	
140	26402	Constable	Green, W.J.	Police car accident 1970; Invermere, BC	
141	15445	Sergeant	Schrader, R.J.	Shot 1970; Macdowall, SK	**
142	21129	Constable	Anson, D.B.	Shot 1970; Macdowall, SK	**
143	15190	Sergeant	O'Malley, J.A.	Drowned 1970; Gillam, MB	
144	25165	Constable	Ivany, D.T.	Police car accident 1971; St. Arthur, NB	**
145	22976	Constable	Seigel, H.S.	Shot 1971; Ile Des Chenes, MB	
146	22830	Constable	Mason, M.R.	Air crash/drowned 1971; Courtenay River, BC	**
147	29984	Constable	Pierlet, R.E.	Shot 1974; Cloverdale, BC	
148	28371	Constable	Letourneau, J.M.	Police car accident 1974; St. Etienne des Gras, PQ	
149	29978	Constable	Tremblay, J.H.C.	Police car accident 1974; St. Etienne des Gras, PQ	
150	27160	Constable	Draginda, J.T.	Police car accident 1974; Surrey, BC	
151	25163	Constable	Baldwinson, J.B.	Police car accident 1975; Surrey, BC	
152	25308	Constable	Shwaykowski, D.M.N.	Thrown from truck 1977; Red Deer, AB	**
153	24526	Corporal	Lidstone, B.W.	Shot 1978; Hoyt, NB	

*
*

154	33554	Constable	Brophy, J.P.	Shot 1978; Hoyt, NB
155	32104	Constable	Onofrey, D.A.	Shot 1978; Virden, MB
156	31915	Constable	King, T.B.	Shot 1978; Saskatoon, SK
157	S1692	Sp/Constable	Foster, G.D.	Air crash 1977; Saltspring Island, BC
158	30791	Constable	Davis, L.B.	Train/car crash 1979; Portage La Prairie, MB
159	31962	Constable	McLachlan, M.P.	Car accident 1979; Carmacks, Yukon
160	31641	Constable	Seward, W.I.	Car accident 1978; Toronto, ON
161	32217	Constable	Doucet, J.L.M.	Air crash 1979; St. Antoine, NB
162	30749	Constable	Brooks, G.A.	Drowned 1979; Cape Dorset, NWT
163	S623	Sp/Constable	Etidloi, N.	Drowned 1979; Cape Dorset, NWT
164	26522	Constable	Karwaski, R.J.W.	Police car accident 1980; Prince Albert, SK
165	29833	Constable	Sedgwick, R.J.	Police car accident 1980; Airdrie, AB
166	33580	Constable	Agar, T.J.	Shot 1980; Richmond, BC
167	25876	Corporal	Larsen, O.R.	Shot 1981; Climax, SK
168	29685	Constable	Thomas, J.F.	Police car accident 1981; Christina Lake, BC
169	31787	Constable	McKinnon, B.F.	Car accident 1981; Brantford, ON
170	36327	Constable	Butler, D.A.	Police car accident 1982; Oxbow, SK
171	S2706	Sp/Constable	Myers, W.G.	Helicopter crash 1983; near Toquart Lake, BC
172	25289	Corporal	Jones, F.E.	Helicopter crash 1983; near Toquart Lake, BC
173	28754	Constable	Keough, D.L.	Police car accident 1983; Anglin Lake, SK
174	26574	Constable	Anderson, R.C.	Police car accident 1984; Kamloops, BC
175	28498	Constable	Bourgoin, R.A.	Heart attack in chase 1983; Piapot, SK
176	30318	Constable	Giesbrecht, A.G.	Shot 1985; Vegreville, AB
177	33631	Constable	Buday, M.J.	Shot 1985; Teslin Lake, BC
178	S2427	Sp/Constable	Boskill, W.P.	Air crash 1986; Wollaston Lake, SK
179	S3015	Sp/Constable	Wilson, J.F.	Air crash 1986; Wollaston Lake, SK

180	S2886	Sp/Constable	Thomas, R.W.C.	Shot 1986; Powerview, MB
181	21066	Corporal	Johanson, B.M.	Police car accident 1986; Lethbridge, AB
182	A3512	Aux/Constable	Abel, F.A.	Police car accident 1986; Lethbridge, AB
183	37412	Constable	Tessier, J.E.M.	Shot 1985; Gatineau, PQ
184	36152	Constable	Berry, S.G.	Electrocuted 1986; Clandonald, AB
185	S1550	Sp/Constable	Kowalczyk, G.Z.	Shot 1987; Calgary, AB
186	31162	Corporal	Flanagan, D.J.	Fell from moving truck 1989; Change Mia, Thailand
187	40153	Constable	Beyak, D.S.	Police car accident 1989; near Assiniboia, SK **
188	33607	Constable	Riglar, C.C.	Hit by car 1991; Colwood, BC
189	30967	Constable	Breese, G.V.M.	Motorcycle accident 1990; Penticton, BC
190	25032	Sergeant	Burkholder, D.C.	Shot 1996; Martin's Brook, NS
191	44134	Constable	Gagne, J.E.A.	Police car accident 1995; Deep Brook, NS
192	36330	Constable	Hutchinson, B.J.	Blow to head 1990; Oka Reserve, ON
193	41129	Constable	Carriere, J.L.F.	Drowned during scuba search 1997; Cole Harbour, NS
194	37348	Corporal	Cumming, G.C.	Fire as police car struck 1998; near Lethbridge, AB
195	35689	Constable	Bourdon, J.E.J.G.	Struck by semi-trailer 1999; near Saskatoon, SK

Appendix 3

The March West

When this great trek west began from Dufferin, Manitoba, on July 8, 1874, it must have been an impressive sight. There were 21 officers (including two surgeons), 254 constables,[83] 20 employed civilians, 310 horses, 142 oxen pulling 187 wagons or carts, 93 head of cattle, two nine-pounder field guns, two mortars, mowing machines, portable forges, and field kitchens. "A" Division led on dark bay horses, followed by "B" on dark brown horses, and "C" rode on chestnut-coloured horses with the field guns. Then came "D" on grey horses, "E" on black ones, and "F" on light bay horses. The wagons and ox carts followed. The procession stretched 2.5 kilometres in close file, but was usually spread over 8 kilometres because of breakdowns and the uneven pace between the horses and oxen.

This map shows the main route west, Jarvis's side trip to Fort Edmonton, and his return east.

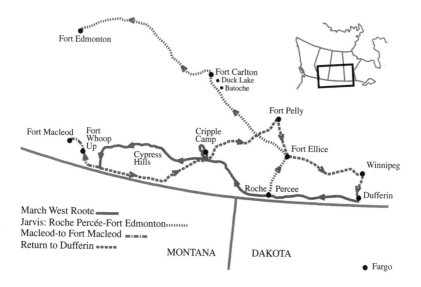

March West Roote ▬▬
Jarvis: Roche Percée-Fort Edmonton ....
Macleod-to Fort Macleod ▬■▬■▬
Return to Dufferin ▬▬▬▬

MONTANA | DAKOTA

Paraphrased From Diary of
John Henry McIllree, NWMP O.6

July 8: (2 miles from Dufferin, Manitoba) Left camp 6 p.m., marched about 2 miles and made camp near small lake. Scarcity of provisions. Young suspended [referring to Inspector Charles Young (O.3), suspended for being intoxicated and accosting the commissioner].

July 9: Left camp 4 p.m. Richer left us today. [He's referring to Inspector Richer (O.15), arrested and charged for insubordination.] Complaints among men about rations. Dust bad.

July 10: Left Morais River early, travelled all day. Camped near boundary line, made about 20 miles.

July 11: At noon reached a post run by Grant, laid in wood here, went onto dusk about 6 miles from Pembina Mountain.

July 12: Sunday, went about 7 miles. Violent thunderstorm. Grasshoppers like clouds of smoke.

July 13: Started out at 6 a.m., made about 25 miles, cut hay for horses.

July 14: Reached Pembina River Valley 11 a.m., crossed river after lunch up steep hill and 7 miles more. 20 miles today. Sent party ahead with gifts and to explain to Indians why we were passing through.

July 15: 2 p.m. crossed Long River, only had two biscuits in 24 hours, driving bullock to 1:30 a.m. very slow, camped at Badger Creek. Horses tiring.

July 16: About 25 miles today, only hard tack and tea. Bad feeling for horses.

July 17: 6 a.m. started, shot few plover, went onto 9 p.m., 23 miles to Turtle Creek.

July 18: Made 19 miles, undulating country, horses tiring badly. Ox train long way behind. Men short tempered—lack of food. First crossing of Souris River.

July 19: Stayed over, bathed, shot ducks.

July 20: Still in camp, two horses died. Two oxen killed, so we will have meat.

July 21: Up 3:30 a.m., started out 5:30, dreary country. Rested after 14 miles, then on to 10:30 p.m.

July 22: Left South Antler Creek 5:30 a.m., hot, noon by swamp, water too bad for tea. 5 p.m. glad to see Souris River and crossed for second time. About 20 miles made.

July 23: Started 5 a.m., reported Indians near. Barren country, made 12 miles and stopped at a river, slept remainder of day.

July 24: Started at 5 a.m. All morning no wood or water, at noon at St. Peters Spring, but little sign of water and after digging it out, enough water for horses. Travelled until dark, camped near place called Roche Perce, made 24 miles.

July 25: Stayed in camp, good grass and wood, many ducks shot by men.

July 26: Sunday, still in camp. Near stampede from someone carelessly shooting and hitting a horse.

July 27: Still in camp, preparing wagons.

July 28: Still in camp, loafed all day.

July 29: Busy getting ready, started 6 p.m. and arrived Wood End 8:30 p.m. Left a troop and part of stores and sick horses with Colonel Jarvis. They will go to Fort Ellice and meet us at Bow River.

July 30: Stayed at Wood End, had to cut road up one side valley and down other for teams.

July 31: Up 4:30 a.m., very cold, made 27 miles by 6:30 p.m., camped at second crossing of the Long Creek. Shot two ducks.

Aug 1: Made 14 miles in a.m. and crossed Long Creek third time. Saw grave here of man who had drowned in creek in April. Made 28 miles.

Aug 2: Remain in camp all day, horses getting rest. Slaughter of ducks by men with sticks.

Aug 3: Left camp 5 a.m. 14 miles by noon. Grass better, made 27 miles by dusk. Wakened by wind, dust blowing, tent blew away. Nearly every tent down and men rushing around in classical costume. Rained and hailed. Saw two buffalo.

Aug 4: Started 7:30 a.m. made 7 miles in a.m. Saw many antelope, camped at Spring Coulee, Plateau of Missouri on our right and Sand Hills on our left. Two men lost, did not turn up till morning, 21½ miles.

Aug 5: Started 5:30 a.m., heavy road, many coulees to cross.

Aug 6: Started 5 a.m., many berries, had 4 miles of winding ascent with tired horses. Finally to top of Dirt Hill and camp.

Aug 7: Remained here all day waiting for guns and some ox carts to catch up.

Aug 8: Left 5 a.m.

Aug 11: Started 6 a.m. 14 miles in a.m., hilly. Horses playing out, 13 miles in p.m., good wild fruit. Camped at Old Womans Creek.

Aug 12: Started 9 a.m. Sioux Indian into camp, gave him tobacco. Four horses died. Two or three Sioux lodges camped nearby.

Aug 13: Indians to camp and smoked, then shook hands all round, then begged for flour—gave them some and calico, and they left.

Aug 14: Cutting hay and shooting ducks. Colonel Macleod left in evening with twelve ox carts for Woody Mountain to get oats.

Aug 15: Still in camp. Walked about 6 miles down Old Womans Creek, shot eight ducks. Prairie on fire west of creek. Lots of Indians loafing about camp and begging.

Aug 16: In camp.

Aug 17: In camp, man to camp said engaged as Scout, suspicious of him. Train of pony carts passed; they were searched, but not carrying whiskey. They took mail with them. Commissioner bought seven ponies and carts from them loaded with pemmican. Fired two rockets in evening to let Major Macleod know we were moving on if he could see them.

Aug 18: Left at 3 p.m. and moved 5 miles. Major Macleod arrived with 60,000 pounds of oats.

Aug 19: Left 10 a.m. Formed Cripple Camp near pools of water, left ten men and 20 or 25 horses that were not well, also some cattle and wagons. The men are to cut hay and get dry wood for our return trip. Made another 14 miles. Annoyed by swarms flying ants.

Aug 20: Left at 6 a.m. Better grass, camped near dusk and went on guard. Horses stampeded, all collected. Made 23 miles.

Aug 21: Left at 5 a.m. Advance guard. 15 miles and met party of Métis with priest. Then made another 10 miles.

Aug 22: Up at 6 a.m., raining hard. Macleod left to meet Boundary Commission and get more oats. Left camp 3 p.m. and made 9 miles. Met train of traders, no contraband.

Aug 23: In camp all day, found petrified tree trunk in creek. Broke off some, makes good flint.

Aug 24: Left at 6 a.m. Made 10 miles to Lac Outard for dinner. Another 6 miles in p.m. and stopped at Goose Lake. Another 7 or 8 miles after supper and camped at foot of Cypress Hills. Orders for precautions as now entering Blackfoot territory.

Aug 25: Left 7:30 a.m., making road across creek. West 14 miles and camped by pond.

Aug 26: In camp. One man shot an antelope.

Aug 27: In camp.

Aug 28: Same place, took horses to better grass. Thunderstorm at night.

Aug 30: All up at daylight as horses stampeded. Drove them back. First buffalo shot today. Report that Major Macleod about 20 miles away and would be in tomorrow.

Aug 31: Started at 2 p.m. and made 14 miles. Camped by nice lake, raining and blowing.

Sept 1: Nights cold now. Started 7 a.m. Made about 8 miles in a.m., camped in evening by clear brook. Night clear and wolves howling.

Sept 2: Left at 7 a.m. Very dull country, grass eaten by buffalo, men rounded up five and drove them toward wagons. Lots of shooting and they got the five. We cut them up and into ox carts. Made 15 miles, camped by spring. Meat tough.

Sept 3: Left 7 a.m., skirting Cypress Hills, camped on high ground. Artist who came with us shot a buffalo. Made 18 miles.

Sept 4: Left 5 a.m. 9 miles by dinner, another 5 miles and very steep hill down. Some ox carts upset. Lots of wild cherries and Grizzly bear seen. Party of Sioux came in and slept in camp.

Sept 5: Left 5 a.m. Rough and hilly. A good deal of road making. I shot an antelope, very good meat. Made 15 miles.

Sept 6: Divine Service and left 2 p.m. Ox carts breaking down, late into camp on banks of South Saskatchewan River.

Sept 7: Made 4 miles by noon then had grand buffalo hunt. We killed eight. Cold night.

Sept 8: Left 5 a.m. Camped at dusk, country barren, blowing hard and cold. Made 20 miles.

Sept 9: Raining heavy, horses chilled and weak. Left two men behind with sick horses. Left 9 a.m. At dusk camped 3 miles from river, raining all day, more horses dying. We all gave up a blanket to cover horses. Nothing to eat.

Sept 10: Left 8 a.m., tea and hardtack only.

Sept 12: Walsh sent off to look for good grass and to try and find Whoop-Up Trail. Denny sent to find grass and Bow River. At 1 a.m. it began to rain and by daylight snow.

Sept 13: Walsh came in—found no grass, trail, or Indians. Left at 11 a.m., went 2 miles and camped near river. We break up here and go no further this year. B goes to Edmonton, C and F go to Sweet Grass Hills and build huts for winter, getting supplies from Benton 60 miles off. D and E (mine) make our way back to Garry.

Sept 14: B under Major Walsh crossed river and rest left at 3 p.m. to Sweet Grass Hills. I had to wait for Major Macleod, then Denny returned and reported on Bow River. Some oxen played out and had to leave them.

Sept 15: Left at 8 a.m. Horses and men very weak, except those driving teams; they have no boots. Stopped at a lake 3 miles long, not on map, named Commissioner's Lake. At dusk camped at a mud hole.

Sept 16: Left at 7 a.m. Watered horses 3 miles from camp. Went 14 miles and found enough water for tea, but none for horses.

Sept 17: Left at 5 a.m., rain and snow. Very cold. Camped near fair grass. C's horses are dying.

Sept 18: Left 8 a.m., tumbled from horse chasing buffalo. Camped in coulee, which is supposed to be dry bed of Milk River, found coal and rock with Indian drawings on it.

Sept 19: In camp. 23 horses have died past 3 weeks. Men badly off for boots, one walking in old slippers.

Sept 20: In camp. B Troop have lost a man for five days.

Sept 21: Missing man got into camp to great relief. Leave 2 p.m., D and E to return east, the rest to winter out. C and F to winter near western butte. We made 12 miles with about 685 to go.

Sept 22: Colonel French, Major Macleod, and others left for Benton to get supplies, to meet us in five or six days at Wild Horse Lake. Made about 9 miles and camped in coulee.

Sept 23: Left 8:30 a.m. made 9 miles and had dinner where Yankee Cavalry had camped. Very hilly, enough buffalo and antelope shot to keep us in provisions.

Sept 24: Left 9 a.m. Camped on open prairie, made 22 miles.

Sept 25: Left 4:30 a.m., came to Milk River, made 22 miles and have about 8 left to get to Wild Horse Lake, where we wait for Commissioner.

Sept 26/29: In camp. I am laid up. Swamp full of ducks, plenty of fresh meat. Wolves plentiful. 29th Commissioner arrived with 20 new horses, lots of oats and corn, moccasins, mitts, tobacco, potatoes. Reports Benton as small place with two stores and rest of houses mainly whiskey shops. Found out where Whoop-Up is—B, C, and F Troops are to go there for winter.

Sept 30: Left at noon, 14 miles and camped.

Oct 1: Left 7 a.m., made 23 miles and camped at East Forks of Milk River.

Oct 2: Left 6 a.m. Went to sundown with no water. I am still unwell, unable to ride, 28 miles today.

Oct 3: Left 7 a.m. Still hilly, made 24 miles.

Oct 4: Left 7 a.m. Made 15 miles before dinner. Walker went out and met Sergeant Sutherland [#229 (Original Series)] on his way from Cripple Camp to bring us supply of oats. He gave news, lost sixteen horses and found only three. Made another 9 miles in p.m. [James Sutherland served in 1874 and 1875 on March West and was left at Cripple Camp. He reengaged as #297 in 1876 and served to 1882. He died in 1936 at New Westminster, B.C.]

Oct 5: Made another march of 22 miles and found missing horses. Crossed White Mud River mid-afternoon and had pow-wow with a lot of Sioux.

Oct 6: Left 7 a.m. The Colonel left us with wagon to go to Wood Mountain and to meet us at Cripple Camp. Made 22 miles, stopped in open prairie with no water.

Oct 7: Left 7 a.m. Found water, stopped for night by swamp full of ducks, made 23 miles.

Oct 8: Left 7 a.m. Made 19 miles and camped on Old Wives Creek. Met small party of Métis starting out on their winter hunt. Windy.

Oct 9: Left 8 a.m. 4 miles to Cripple Camp. Sick men left behind had made snug camp, two men lost, went back and found them. Loaded up Cripple Camp and made 6 miles.

Oct 10: Made 26 miles today, horses doing good.

Oct 12: Left 7 a.m. Crossed Souris River, made 22 miles and stopped by Moose Jaw Creek.

Oct 13: Left 7 a.m. Made 26 miles and camped by Souris. Oxen playing out.

Oct 14: Left 7 a.m. Dinner by Boggy Creek. Made 21 miles, prairie burnt and burning to the south. Very hot day. Met party of Métis on their way to Cypress Hills to hunt. They said we were about 35 miles from Qu'Appelle.

Oct 15: Made it to Qu'Appelle and met Mr. McLean of Hudson's Bay Post.

This ends the entries of McIllree's diary until March of 1876, when he was stationed at Swan River near present-day Pelly, Saskatchewan. McIllree had travelled from Dufferin, Manitoba, to very near present-day Fort Macleod and then returned two-thirds of the way back.

With their troops, Macleod had been left to winter in the west, Walsh was at Fort Edmonton, and the commissioner's body of men returned safely to Dufferin in early November 1874.

Appendix 4

North-West Rebellion 1885

In the North-West Rebellion, Canada had to respond to the uprising of Métis and Indians with a scant militia and the North West Mounted Police, who were already in the west. From their meagre numbers—in total 880 members—all who were available responded. This appendix is only intended to relate the deaths and wounded in the principal battles.

Principal Battles involving the NWMP

Duck Lake, March 26, 1885

#1065	Constable	Arnold, George Pearce	killed
#852	Constable	Garrett, George Knox	killed
#1003	Constable	Gibson, Thomas James	killed
O.10	Superintendent	Crozier, Lief Newry Fitzroy	wounded
O.48	Inspector	Howe, Joseph	wounded
#1045	Corporal	Manners-Smith, Alfred	wounded
#532	Sergeant	Gilchrist, Thomas Haddon	wounded
#1117	Sergeant	Gordon, Sidney Francis	wounded
#935	Constable	Miller, August	wounded
#425	Constable	Murray, Arthur Thomas	wounded
#1048	Constable	Wood, John James	wounded

Fort Pitt, April, 1885

#635	Constable	Cowan, David Latimer	killed
#925	Constable	Loasby, Clarence McLean	wounded

Cut Knife Hill, May 2, 1885

#907	Corporal	Lowry, William Hay Talbot	killed
#565	Corporal	Sleigh, Ralph Bateman	killed
#402	Constable	Burke, Patrick	killed
#36	Sergeant	Ward, John Henry	wounded

Batoche, May 12, 1885

#1312   Constable   Stafford, James Palmer   wounded

Battleford, Scouting Patrol, May 14, 1885

#973   Constable   Elliott, Frank Orlando   killed
#983   Constable   Spencer, William Isaac   wounded

Frenchman's Butte, May 28, 1885

#716   Sergeant   McRae, Donald   wounded

Loon Lake, June 3, 1885

#333   Sergeant   Fury, William   wounded

Endnotes

1. "Force" is the common term for members of the NWMP, RNWMP, or RCMP.
2. Newfoundland was not a part of Canada until joining Confederation in 1949.
3. Under Royal Assent, May 23, 1873, the North West Mounted Police became a living, sentient organism (36 Vic, ch 35).
4. As an inducement for recruiting in the first few years of the NWMP, land warrants were granted to members who had completed three years of good service. These warrants could be exchanged for a quarter section of farmland.
5. The "O" before the number stands for "Officer." Members (or others) who became part of the commissioned ranks were assigned these numbers.
6. The Honour Roll lists all members of the Force who died in the line of duty (see Appendix 2). The streets of the training facility at Depot Division are named after members who were drawn by lot from a long list of members to be honoured.
7. Originally the ranks were Sub-Constable, Constable, and Staff Constable, which were later changed to Constable, Corporal, and Sergeant.
8. Regimental numbers were issued sequentially from #1 in 1873, but with handwritten records and widely scattered recruiting, numerous errors crept in. In 1878 the system was stopped and numbering of those then serving began anew—again from #1. This first series is now referred to as the "Original Series." The new system that commenced in 1878 has continued to the present day and is referred to as the "New Series."
9. See **Macleod (Fort Macleod)** entry.
10. The *St. Roch* was the RCMP supply vessel for northern detachments. It was also the first vessel to successfully traverse the Northwest Passage in both directions and to circumnavigate North America.
11. Those members who did not complete their contracted term of service could purchase their discharge at a set fee for each unexpired month left in their term.
12. See **Crozier Lake** entry.
13. Belcher's regimental number was changed with the renumbering in 1878.
14. See **Kennedy Point** entry.

15. See **Herronton** entry.
16. A "Sam Browne" consists of waist belt, shoulder strap, side-arm holster, and ammunition pouch.
17. Retired Staff Sergeant Jack Hest, RCMP #21265, was a driving force behind the projects of the park and school. He had been a personal friend of Constable Bruce and faced the traumatic problems of being the first member on the scene following the shooting.
18. When Force members were levied a fine in Orderly Room for some disciplinary offence, such monies went into a fund known as the Fine Fund. Then, when a member accomplished some very noteworthy feat beyond the normal duty, he might be awarded a token amount from that fund. This system was discontinued about 1960.
19. Dutch Henry was a rustler who fled north after problems in Dodge City, Kansas. With his partner, Tom Owens, he quickly organized a gang of rustlers and a steady traffic of stolen horses back and forth across the border between Montana and Canada. They had a main hideout in the Wood Mountain-Big Muddy area of Saskatchewan. By 1903 he had joined forces with the Nelson-Jones gang known as the "Wild Bunch," and they terrorized ranches throughout this area. The end came in 1906 when Dutch Henry was shot in a gunfight in the U.S. A henchman, "Bloody Knife," was killed in a brawl while two others—"Pigeon-Toed Kid" and Jones—were also shot in the U.S. Nelson, of the Nelson-Jones gang, is said to have died of old age at Battleford, Saskatchewan.
20. See **Steele Street** entry for details of Steele's Scouts.
21. See the **Walsh (Fort Walsh)** entry.
22. The southeast quarter of 24-10-25 on Piapot Creek.
23. From a geographical survey of 1950 and approved in 1966.
24. See **Strickland Lake** entry.
25. See **Crozier Lake** entry.
26. Commissioned officers had the powers of a Justice of the Peace and could therefore try criminal cases in the absence of a civil court.
27. See Appendix 4, listing the dead and wounded of the rebellion.
28. See **Tidd (Mount Tidd)** entry.
29. See **Fitzgerald Settlement** entry.
30. See **Macleod (Fort Macleod)** entry.
31. See **Crozier Lake** entry.
32. After the rebellion, Mongrain was charged with and convicted of Cowan's murder. He was sentenced to hang, but had his sentence commuted to life imprisonment.

33. Dickson's two brothers were Constable Adam Dickson (#2102), who served from 1888 to 1889, and Constable Andrew Dickson (#3164), who served from 1896 to 1900.
34. For details see the **Phillips Channel** entry.
35. See the **Larsen Sound** and **St. Roch Island** entries.
36. "Forest" is spelled incorrectly.
37. "Surgeon" and "Assistant Surgeon" were early-day ranks of the Force that applied to doctors and provided commissioned officer status.
38. Officers were not assigned numbers until about 1900, and then the decision was taken to assign them to personnel files going back to the beginning in 1873. Although the tenth officer appointed, as the first commissioner French was arbitrarily given #1. Colonel W. Osborne Smith had been appointed a temporary commissioner and served in that capacity for about two weeks in September and October of 1872.
39. See **Steele Street** entry.
40. See **Beyts Cove** entry.
41. See Appendix 2, Honour Roll #100.
42. See **Saskatchewan (Fort Saskatchewan)** entry.
43. In 1908, five independent local militia units were amalgamated into the 102nd Rocky Mountain Rangers. They served in both World Wars; today they remain as a reserve unit headquartered at Kamloops, B.C.
44. See **Saskatchewan (Fort Saskatchewan)** entry.
45. It was a common practice in the early days of the Force for a member to be given a term of imprisonment with hard labour for a disciplinary infraction. This time might be served with common criminals. When the term was up, the disciplined member returned to duty.
46. See **Walsh (Fort Walsh)** entry.
47. See **Macleod (Fort Macleod)** entry.
48. Although Canadian ships were permitted to trade east of Herschel Island, Klengenberg insisted on supplying his family. Constable Ian MacDonald (#9791) was assigned to accompany the vessel to ensure no wrongful trading was carried out. He recorded a list of what was unloaded, but he mysteriously disappeared on the return passage. His notebook was later found, floating on his parka, and was recovered. Captain Klengenberg had been charged in 1905 for the murder of one of his crew in San Francisco, a charge that leaves the disappearance of Constable MacDonald open to conjecture.
49. A voluntary payment made for damages to innocent parties during official duties.

50. See **Steele (Steele Street)** entry.
51. See **Crozier Lake** entry for details regarding his troop's actions in the North-West Rebellion.
52. See Appendix 3, which contains his account of the March West of 1874.
53. The last official horse patrol was made in 1937 by Constable Douglas H. Minor (#11788), who had for some time patrolled on horseback the Saskatchewan–U.S. border in the Big Muddy area. Minor served from 1932 to 1958 and died in 1966.
54. A non-commissioned officer (NCO) is a corporal, sergeant, staff sergeant, or sergeant-major.
55. See **Crozier Lake** entry for details.
56. Stories of the "Mad Trapper" case that have made their way to print are about equally divided on assigning nicknames to Constable Millen. Some suggest that he was called "Spike," and some suggest "Newt." We favour "Newt," for when his last surviving close friend, McDowell, was asked if Millen had a nickname, he answered without hesitation, "He was Newt."
57. McDowell is believed to be the last surviving member involved with this incident. As of publication in 2002, he lives quietly in healthy retirement.
58. King recovered and went on to serve until 1953. He died in 1978 at Petrolia, Ontario.
59. Staff constable was made equivalent to the rank of sergeant when rank designations changed.
60. Since the museum is not publicly owned and funded by government, the Force must raise its own funds outside of the normal budget for police operations to support it.
61. This car was a 1915 Model 55 McLaughlin convertible with a fold-down canvas roof. One of the early chauffeurs told the story that a particular senior officer insisted the top always be down, rain or shine, because "horses didn't have roofs and neither should cars."
62. Although the Manitoba Provincial Police then policed Manitoba, the RCMP still held the federal responsibilities for the Indian Act, Customs and Excise Acts, and so on.
63. Officer numbers were not assigned until about 1900, when they retroactively began with the start of the Force in 1873. In doing so, Nicolle (then many years out of the Force) was overlooked. He would have been O.24 sequentially. To place his number in the proper order, he was squeezed into the list as a half number. Commissioner Smith was assigned between O.2 and O.3 for the same reason.
64. See **Millen Street** entry for details.

65. In 1880 ex-Constables James Bruneau (#216), Isaac May (#234), and Alfred Lynch-Staunton (#241) took up land for the first ranch at Pincher Creek.

66. See **Constantine (Mount Constantine)** entry for details of this trail-building project.

67. Novakowski later changed his name to Nolan.

68. At that time, members joined as third class constables if under the age of 21, or second class if over 21. Promotion to first class constable came after a stipulated period of good service.

69. The Victoria Cross (VC) is Great Britain's highest award for bravery under fire.

70. Upon engagement with the Force, a member contracted for a specified term of service. If he wished to leave before the contract's expiry date, he would have to "purchase" or pay a fee for each month of unexpired time left in it. In the early days of the Force a member would be allowed a free discharge if he could provide a substitute member.

71. Many early-day officers preferred to be known by an equivalent military rank, apparently feeling that the general public would not recognize the significance of the lesser-known police ranks. A few had served in the military with commissioned rank.

72. See **Wallace Drive** entry.

73. See **Belcher (Colonel Belcher Hospital)**.

74. See **Constantine (Mount Constantine)** for details of the "Peace–Yukon Trail" project.

75. From the description of their camp, we believe that Lake was buried close to the centre of the present-day downtown core of Golden, B.C.

76. See **Constantine (Mount Constantine)** entry.

77. See **Wood (Mount Wood)** entry.

78. See **Perry River** entry for details of Perry's service.

79. Initially, members were referred to by military ranks. Police ranks patterned after Irish and English police departments would come later.

80. Rogers Pass is named after Major A.B. Rogers. Located in Glacier National Park, midway between Golden and Revelstoke, B.C., it was the chosen route for the Canadian Pacific Railway and later—in the 1960s—for the Trans-Canada Highway #1.

81. The world-renowned Lake Louise is one of the most popular tourist spots in Banff National Park.

82. See **Steele Street** entry for details on Steele's Scouts.

83. The term "constable" then included sub-constables, constables, and staff constables, the equivalent of today's constable, corporal, and sergeant.

Notes on Reading the Text

Possible Change of Place Names

In 1999 Nunavut was proclaimed as a separate territory from the
Northwest Territories, generally encompassing the eastern portion
previously known as the "District of Keewatin" and north through
the islands east of Victoria Island.

The self-governing Inuit are changing many of the previously
anglicized names—with which we are familiar—to traditional Inuit
names, so many of the place names in this book that are within
Nunavut will not appear on future maps.

Many place names are spelled differently than the surnames
of the officers for whom they were named.

Regimental and Officer Numbers

Regimental and officer numbers are shown throughout the text in
different formats. The regimental numbers follow the Force
designation with a number symbol (#) preceding them; for example,
in the first entry for Sergeant-Major William Richard Abbott, his
membership in the NWMP is shown, followed by the number
symbol and his regimental number (#314). In the entry for Aklavik
Channel, Superintendent George Leslie Jennings' name is followed
by the designation of RNWMP and RCMP, and then his officer
number O.147 (which replaced his regimental number) without a
number symbol preceding it.

Abbreviations of Decorations and Medals

CB	Companion Most Honourable Order of the Bath
CdeG	Croix de Guerre
CMG	Companion Most Distinguished Order of St. Michael and St. George
DSO	Distinguished Service Order
FRGS	Fellow of Royal Geographical Society of Canada
GCStJ	Grand Cross of the most Venerable Order of the Hospital of St. John of Jerusalem
ISO	Imperial Service Order
KCB	Knight Commander Most Honourable Order of the Bath
KCMG	Knight Commander Most Distinguished Order of St. Michael and St. George
LLD	Honorary Doctor of Laws
MC	Military Cross
MM	Military Medal
MVO	Member Royal Victorian Order (Class IV)
OBE	Order of the British Empire
OC	Order of Canada
Pm	Polar Medal
PmB	Polar Medal with Bar

Bibliography

Akrigg, G.P.V. and H.B. *1001 B.C. Place Names.* Discovery Press, 1970.

Anderson, Ian. *Sitting Bull's Boss: Above the Medicine Line with James Morrow Walsh.* Surrey, BC: Heritage House Publishing Company Ltd., 2000.

Anderson, Frank W. *Outlaws of Saskatchewan. Gopher Book #25.* Saskatoon, SK: Frank Anderson Publishing, (year unknown).

Aubrey, Merrily K. *Place Names of Alberta Volume IV: Northern Alberta.* Calgary, AB: University of Calgary Press, 1966.

Canadian Automobile Association. *Canadian Book of the Road.* Montreal, PQ: Reader's Digest Association (Canada) Ltd., 1979.

Coutts, R. *Yukon Places and Names.* Sidney, BC: Gray's Publishing, 1980.

Denny, Sir Cecil E. *March of the Mounties.* Surrey, BC: Heritage House Publishing Company Ltd., 1939.

Glenn, John (RCMP #7118). *"A Tale of the RNWMP."* Unpublished manuscript.

Harrison, Tracey. *Place Names of Alberta Volume III: Central Alberta.* Calgary, AB: University of Calgary Press, 1994.

Haydon, A.L. *The Riders of the Plains.* Edmonton, AB: Hurtig Publishers, 1971.

Ham, P. *Place Names of Manitoba.* Saskatoon, SK: Western Producer Prairie Books, 1980.

Holmgren, E.J. and P.M. *2000 Place Names of Alberta.* Edmonton, AB: self-published, 1972.

Horrall, S.W. *The Pictorial History of the RCMP.* Toronto, ON: McGraw-Hill Ryerson Ltd., 1973.

Humber, Donna Mae. *What's In a Name...Calgary?* Calgary, AB: City of Calgary, 1995.

Karamitsanis, Aphrodite. *Place Names of Alberta Volume II: Southern Alberta.* Calgary, AB: University of Calgary Press, 1992.

Klancher, D.J. *The NWMP and the NW Rebellion.* Kamloops, BC: Goss Publishing, 1999.

Knuckle, Robert. *In The Line of Duty.* Burnstown, ON: General Store Publishing House, 1994.

Long, Philip S. *Jerry Potts: Scout, Frontiersman and Hero.* Calgary, AB: Bonanza Books, 1974.

Meadowcroft, Shena. *Keeping the Peace.* Calgary, AB: Word Spinner Publishing, 1998.

Mein, Lillian and Stewart (editors). *Regina: The Street Where You Live: Origins of Regina Street Names.* Regina, SK: Regina Public Library, 1992.

North, Dick. *Trackdown: The Search for the Mad Trapper.* Toronto, ON: Macmillan of Canada, 1989.

Outlaws & Lawmen of Western Canada: Volume One. Surrey, BC: Heritage House Publishing Company Ltd., 1983.

Outlaws & Lawmen of Western Canada: Volume Two. Surrey, BC: Heritage House Publishing Company Ltd., 1983.

Outlaws & Lawmen of Western Canada: Volume Three. Surrey, BC: Heritage House Publishing Company Ltd., 1987.

Paquet, Maggie. *The B.C. Parks Explorer.* Vancouver, BC: Whitecap Books, 1986.

Parker, P. *Dead Right – Dead Wrong.* Calgary, AB: Benjamin Books, 1991.

Ream, Peter T. *The Fort on the Saskatchewan.* Self-published, 1974.

Russell, E.T. *What's in a Name?* Calgary, AB: Fifth House, 1997.

Smallwood, Joey (editor). *Book of Newfoundland.* St. John's, NF: Newfoundland Book Publishers, 1968 (reprinted England: Hazell Watson and Viney Ltd., 1979).

Steele, Samuel B. *Forty Years in Canada.* New York, NY: Dodd, Mead, 1915.

Turner, John Peter. *The North-West Mounted Police, Volumes 1 and 2.* Ottawa, ON: Edmond Cloutier, King's Printer, 1950.

Yukon Historical and Museums Association. *Exploring Old Whitehorse.* Whitehorse, YK: 1996.

Periodicals and Other Sources

Cemetery records – Canada-wide

Friends of the Mounted Police Museum. *Friendly Notes.* Regina, SK: 1988 through 2001.

MacLeod Gazette newspaper. McLeod, AB: 1885 to 1910.

McIllree, John H. (Assistant Commissioner O.13). *Personal diaries of 1874 March West.*

North West Mounted Police Annual Reports. Ottawa, ON.

North West Mounted Police General Orders. Ottawa: ON, intermittent 1879 through 1904.

Orders-in-council – 1873 through 1952.

Public Archives, Ottawa. *Geographical Features of Canada.* GH-1520-14.

RCMP Veterans' Association. *Keeping In Touch.* Ottawa: ON: various issues.

RCMP Veterans' Association. *Scarlet and Gold.* Vancouver, BC: 1919 through 1996.

Royal Canadian Mounted Police Annual Reports. Ottawa, ON.

Royal Canadian Mounted Police General Orders. Ottawa, ON: 1920 through 1928.

Royal Canadian Mounted Police. *Pony Express.* Regina, SK: 1987 through 2001.

Royal Canadian Mounted Police. *Quarterly.* Ottawa, ON: 1933 through 2001.

Royal North West Mounted Police Annual Reports. Ottawa, ON.

Royal North West Mounted Police General Orders. Ottawa, ON: intermittent 1904 through 1919.

Photo Credits

If you know of any Canadian place names that honour a member of the Force, the authors and publisher would like to hear from you! Please send your information to: Editor, Heritage House Publishing Co. Ltd., #108 – 17665 66A Avenue, Surrey BC, V3S 2A7 or publisher@heritagehouse.ca

Police Stories from Heritage House

Robert Teather Trilogy

Mountie Makers	*Scarlet Tunic*	*Scarlet Tunic*
Putting the	*Inside our Cars...*	*On Patrol with the*
Canadian in RCMP	*Inside our Hearts*	*RCMP Vol. 2*
ISBN 1-895811-41-4	ISBN 1-895811-52-X	ISBN 1-895811-01-5
$14.95	$11.95	$11.95

B.C. Provincial Police Stories
Cecil Clark

Vol. 1 • ISBN 1-895811-77-5 • $9.95
Vol. 2 • ISBN 1-894384-29-6 • $12.95
Vol. 3 • ISBN 1-895811-75-9 • $12.95

Heritage House Canadian History

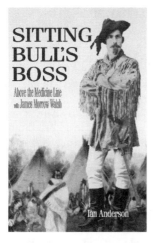

Sitting Bull's Boss
Above the Medicine Line
with James Morrow Walsh
Ian Anderson
ISBN 1-895811-63-5 •
$17.95

Steele's Scouts
Samuel Benefield Steele
and the North-West Rebellion
Wayne E. Brown
ISBN 1-894384-14-8 •
$16.95

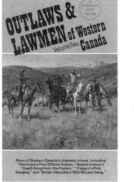

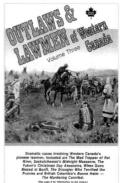

Outlaws & Lawmen of Western Canada
***Vol.1* •** ISBN 1-895811-79-1 • $10.95
***Vol. 2* •** ISBN 1-895811-85-6 • $10.95
***Vol. 3* •** ISBN 1-895811-87-2 • $12.95

About the Authors

Staff Sergeant William J. Hulgaard, retired, served in the RCMP from 1952 to 1989. He was first posted on the 1953 Musical Ride, performing in eastern Canadian cities and in New York City. In his early career he was a motorcycle instructor. He escorted numerous dignitaries and was personally presented to Her Royal Highness Queen Elizabeth and Prince Phillip, Duke of Edinburgh. Following a career on highway patrol, he was Traffic Supervisor for the Province of British Columbia during his last year of service. He was awarded the Royal Canadian Mounted Police Long Service and Good Conduct Medal with Gold Clasp. Following his retirement, he travelled thousands of kilometres visiting the old Mounted Police historic sites in the western provinces, Yukon, and the Northwest Territories. He located and photographed most of the sites listed in this book.

Chief Superintendent John W. White, also retired, served in the RCMP from 1950 to 1985 in "E" Division (British Columbia) and "B" Division (Newfoundland), in General Investigation, Section NCO, drug enforcement, Officer Commanding Sub-Divisions, and Contract Policing Officer for British Columbia. In 1962, he was one of many to respond to the murder of three Force members at Kamloops, B.C. (see Appendix 2, 116, 117, and 118), resulting in a shootout with the assailant and a Commissioner's Commendation for White. He was also awarded the Canada Centennial Medal in1967, a second Commendation for a murder investigation in 1968, the Queen's Jubilee Medal in 1977, and the Long Service and Good Conduct Medal with Gold Clasp. After he retired, he began compiling service histories of all Force members who have served since 1873. The research and subsequent record is a valuable resource to historians and serving Force members, and also provided the research base for his share of this book.